Activist Educators

"*Activist Educators* provides guidance for those of us who at different points in our careers have not known how to combine our commitment to social justice with our day-to-day work in schools. For too long teachers and school leaders have been silent witnesses to injustice in schools. This book helps us find our voices and reclaims teaching and leading as highly moral and political enterprises."
—**Gary L. Anderson, Professor of Educational Leadership, Steinhardt School of Education, New York University**

"This amazing book can be read as a research report, a methods text, or an inspirational demonstration of collaborative inquiry. It is full of fascinating insights into the identities, commitments, risks, and strategies of teacher-activists who take up a variety of causes. Readers will value not only the individual case-studies, but Marshall's brilliant cross-case analysis and the story of how the research was conducted."
—**Sandra Acker, Professor of Sociology and Equity Studies in Education, Ontario Institute for Studies in Education, University of Toronto**

Taking an active stand in today's conservative educational climate can be a risky business. Given both the expectations of the profession and the challenge of participation in social justice activism, how do educator activists manage the often competing demands of professional and activist commitments? *Activist Educators* offers a view into the big picture of assertive, idealistic professionals' lives by presenting rich qualitative data on the impetus behind educators' activism and the strategies they used to push limits in fighting for a cause. Chapters follow the stories of educator activists as they take on problems in schools, including sexual harassment, sexism, racism, reproductive rights, and GLBT rights. The research in *Activist Educators* contributes to an understanding of professional and personal motivations for educators' activism, ultimately offering a significant contribution to aspiring teachers who need to know that education careers and social justice activist causes need not be mutually exclusive pursuits.

Catherine Marshall is Professor of Educational Leadership and Policy at the University of North Carolina at Chapel Hill.

Amy L. Anderson is an Evaluation Specialist with Evaluation, Assessment, and Policy Connections in the School of Education at the University of North Carolina at Chapel Hill.

The Teaching/Learning Social Justice Series

Edited by Lee Anne Bell, Barnard College, Columbia University

Activist Educators:
Breaking Past Limits

Edited by
Catherine Marshall
and
Amy L. Anderson

Routledge
Taylor & Francis Group

NEW YORK AND LONDON

First published 2009
by Routledge
270 Madison Ave, New York, NY 10016

Simultaneously published in the UK
by Routledge
2 Park Square, Milton Park, Abingdon, Oxon OX14 4RN

Routledge is an imprint of the Taylor & Francis Group, an information business

Typeset in Minion Pro by EvS Communication Networx, Inc.
Printed and bound in the United States of America on acid-free paper by Walsworth Publishing Company, Marceline, MO.

Library of Congress Cataloging in Publication Data
Activist educators: breaking past limits / edited by Catherine Marshall and Amy L. Anderson.
p. cm.—(Teaching/learning social justice series)
Includes bibliographical references and index.
ISBN 978-0-415-95666-6 (hb : alk. paper)—ISBN 978-0-415-95667-3 (pb : alk. paper)—ISBN 978-0-203-89258-9 (ebk : alk. paper) 1. Education—Political aspects—United States. 2. Social justice—United States. I. Marshall, Catherine, 1946- II. Anderson, Amy L. III. Series.
LC89.A5417 2008
370.11'5—dc22
2008006828

ISBN 10: 0-415-95666-8 (hbk)
ISBN 10: 0-415-95667-6 (pbk)
ISBN 10: 0-203-89258-5 (ebk)

ISBN 13: 978-0-415-95666-6 (hbk)
ISBN 13: 978-0-415-95667-3 (pbk)
ISBN 13: 978-0-203-89258-9 (ebk)

Contents

Series Editor Introduction

The Teaching/Learning Social Justice Series explores issues of social justice in classrooms and communities—diversity, equality, democracy, and justice. "Teaching/learning" connotes the essential connections between theory and practice that books in this series seek to illuminate. Central are the stories and lived experiences of people who strive both to critically analyze and challenge oppressive relationships and institutions, and to imagine and create more just and inclusive alternatives. My hope is that the series will balance critical analysis with images of hope and possibility in ways that are accessible and inspiring to a broad range of educators and activists who believe in the potential for social change through education and who seek stories and examples of practice, as well as honest discussion of the ever-present obstacles to dismantling oppressive ideas and institutions.

Through the stories of a broad group of educators around the country who have taken up issues of social justice in their roles as teachers and administrators the editors and authors of *Activist Educators* flesh out the dilemmas, opportunities, fears, and risks involved for those who choose activism, going against the grain of historical and contemporary assumptions about their appropriate roles. The book illuminates how professional culture and socialization, tacit rules and norms, and bureaucratic constraints proscribe and tamp out educator activism while also drawing on historical and contemporary examples of educator activists who have resisted these constraints to act on principles of justice. The book is framed by a thoughtful exploration of the social movements that derive from and support ongoing practice—Civil Rights, feminist, and queer movements—and theoretical frameworks that developed out of and extend the lessons of these movements—critical race theory, feminist theory, queer theory. What causes people to choose activism while others quietly go along with business as usual? What price do they pay for these choices? What impact does their courage have for the lives of students and colleagues in their schools and communities? These are some of the critical questions taken up in this volume.

At a time when the term *social justice* runs the risk of appropriation and dilution, the stories in *Activist Educators* reveal on the ground examples that can inspire others whose principles and ethics compel them to act but who feel isolated by the lack of a broader community of peers and models to sustain their resistance and perseverance. The Educator Activist Research Project itself demonstrates a creative model that might be replicated to amass an anthology of stories authorizing educators as rightful agents of the ideals of educational equality and justice. The lessons and stories in *Activist Educators* show us how educators can overcome fear and inertia and cultivate themselves and others as activists and allies to inspire action in the face of injustice and carry forward a vision of public education as a crucible for cultivating participants for a just and democratic society.

Lee Anne Bell
Series Editor for Teaching/Learning Social Justice
Barnard College, Columbia University

Is it Possible to be an Activist Educator?

CATHERINE MARSHALL AND AMY L. ANDERSON

What happens when professional educators[1] are involved in political activism for social justice causes? Given the expectations of the education profession and the challenge of participation in social activism, how do educator activists manage the often competing demands? How do they protect their career status when they are involved in political activism that challenges the status quo? What dilemmas and choices do they face, what are their fears, and how do they manage the challenges? This book explores these questions using research on 52 educators who have espoused social justice causes, heroically, subtly, sometimes painfully, but more often with pride.

The Context: Educators' Professional Cultures

Education is often imagined as an apolitical enterprise. Both education and educators are assumed to maintain a respectful distance from hot-button issues and significant political and social movements. Venturing too close, in fact, carries risks. The professional risks associated with standing too firmly at any space along the political continuum can lead educators to avoid political activism. Teachers and administrators create boundaries, separating their private lives and their beliefs about social and political events from their educator work lives. Are educators in effect neutered politically? Must they check their interests at the schoolhouse door? Must they become less-than-full citizens to be educators? What do they do with their strongly held beliefs about political and social issues? The case studies presented in this book explore these questions head on.

This book is based on interviews with 52 teachers and administrators identified because of their reputations for taking some action, some stand, to address social justice issues. Such activism is often understood as an arena for making the personal political (Epstein, 1990), and as requiring advocates who are willing to take a vocal stand in support of projects often seen as controversial. Our research focused on several strands of social justice activism—for African Americans, the rights of gays and lesbians, women's reproductive freedom, advancing girls' and women's opportunities, and for protections against sexual harassment. Certainly these are progressive liberal causes, and they are only a few among the range of progressive issues. Certainly other educators' passions, beliefs, and activism can entail conservative agendas, but these are not our focus. As explored below, our understanding of social justice led us to study educators active in the service of those long-marginalized or silenced: people of color, girls and women, gays and lesbians. Our book opens the questions and agendas on educators' activism, and with these five causes and 52 cases we have uncovered fascinating patterns and a wide range of educators' dilemmas, choices, and coping strategies as they asserted their beliefs *and* kept their jobs.

This chapter begins by situating educators' activism in the context of their professional and socio-cultural socialization, and describes the theories we found important for framing our study of educators' choices and actions. It then introduces the subsequent chapters of the book that tell stories of educators' efforts to reconcile their interests in social justice issues with their work as school teachers and administrators.

Educators' Professional Socialization and the Limits on Activism

Teachers and administrators are socialized to steer clear of overtly political positions that might interfere with their roles as school and community leaders. Those who seek leadership positions in education learn that taking a clear values stance or political action may mean losing sponsorship and career opportunities, because certain actions may alienate educators from students or their parents (Marshall, 1993b; Marshall & Mitchell, 1991; Ortiz, 1982). Anderson (2001) notes that "administration programmes increasingly are in the business of providing future administrators with 'safe' discourses that will not offend pluralist interest groups" (p. 211). The appearance of neutrality, so the argument goes, increases the likelihood of one's acceptance among various constituencies. Teachers are also socialized to neutrality and passivity vis-à-vis political issues.

Leaping back in time, we see the historical origins of these safe positions: The overarching goals for schools in the Massachusetts Bay Colony were to control religious and moral development, and these are the roots of schooling in the United States. Town ministers expected teachers to adhere to the same religious and moral codes as the clergy; this applied not only to their professional conduct, but contractual expectations guided their personal lives as well. One contract stated that female teachers were "[not to] dress in bright colors, not to dye her hair, to wear at least two petticoats, and not to wear dresses more than two inches above the ankles" (Harbeck, 1997, p. 107). Female teachers had to promise to "take vital interest in all phases of Sunday school work, donating of my time, service, and money without stint for the uplift and benefit of the community."

They complied with contracts prohibiting "immodest dressing," they pledged, "I promise not to fall in love, to become engaged or secretly married," and "I promise to sleep at least eight hours a night, to eat carefully, and take every precaution to keep in the best of health and spirits, in order that I may be better able to render efficient service to my pupils." In addition, they pledged to remain circumspect: "I promise to remember that I owe a duty to the townspeople who are paying my wages, that I owe respect to the school board and the superintendent that hired me, and that I shall consider myself at all times the willing servant of the school board and the townspeople" (pp. 107, 108). With teachers "boarding around" (p. 105) in various homes, townspeople had more opportunities to scrutinize the personality, beliefs, and behaviors of their teachers.

Limitations have persisted to more modern times. Prior to 1960, the courts considered teaching to be a privilege subject to whatever conditions the government wished to impose (Harbeck, 1997). And today, conservative controls on educators are part of growing public sentiments against progressive activism, diversity, and curriculum innovation all of which are presumed to interfere in public schooling. Jerry Falwell (1979), representing the religious right in contemporary politics, was quoted as saying, "I hope to see the day when, as in the early days of our country, we won't have any public schools. The churches will have taken them over and Christians will be running them. What a happy day that will be" (pp. 52–53). Thus, more progressive politics may be suspect or unsafe in schools, as the movement back to the days of educators reinforcing and modeling a particular morality may be on the horizon. The "Abstinence Only" movement in education is but one example of government efforts to control curriculum and support a conservative political agenda. Managerial controls have tightened monitoring and accountability in educators' work lives in the early 21st century.

Despite the hopes of more conservative critics, however, contractual requirements for teachers are not quite as extreme as they were in the past. Teacher unions that emerged in the mid-20th century from workers' rights and also the women's rights movements have upended the most egregious limitations on teachers' personal freedoms.

A review of the position statements of educators' professional associations provides a telling context for educators' activist work. Not surprisingly, the National Education Association (NEA) and American Federation of Teachers (AFT) have the strongest statements in regards to the issues detailed in this text. For example, a review of AFT Resolutions reveals well-developed position statements addressing all of the progressive issues in this text, including a 2002 resolution of support for the Ratification of the Equal Rights Amendment; a 2004 *Brown v. Board of Education* 50th Anniversary resolution to "help our nation realize the promise of *Brown*"; a 2006 resolution of Support for Reproductive Rights "to preserve reproductive rights, … call for medically accurate sex education programs in public schools," and the approval of over-the-counter emergency contraception along with a requirement that pharmacists fill birth control prescriptions; and a 2004 resolution in opposition to the Federal Marriage Amendment. The NEA also has an extensive list of resolutions that support equity for students and educators in regards to issues of race, gender, and sexual orientation. The NEA also takes positions against sexual harassment and in favor of comprehensive sex education.

On the other hand, teachers' and administrators' professional associations take more distanced and much safer positions in regards to progressive issues. Websites of the American Association of School Administrators (AASA), the National Association of Secondary School Principals (NASSP), the Association for Supervision and Curriculum Development (ASCD), the Middle Schools Association, and the National Association of Elementary School Principals (NAESP) were reviewed to determine the scope and strength of the organizations' position statements. Position statements and platforms for AASA, NASSP, NAESP, and ASCD were easily found, but in all cases their content focused on broad educational aspirations and leadership concerns, such as achievement, leadership, security, teacher quality, accountability, and "recognizing and valuing diversity." Although not embedded in organizational principles, most websites also posted articles that provided members with content about issues including harassment and tolerance for gay and lesbian students.

School boards and townspeople are no longer able to contractually proscribe the private behaviors of educators, but professional norms are still at work. Professional associations may espouse broad goals with slight nods to equity, but these goals are nonspecific and stay clear of controversial topics. So what are the hurdles and inhibitions felt by educators who would participate in activism for social justice?

Educators' Avoidance of Political Activism

Wouldn't the specter of injustice, inequities, and silencing of the oppressed lead educators into assertive fights to end the oppression? Wouldn't educators want to join in, becoming vocal and active in social movements? Wouldn't educators, whose passion and caring for those who are treated unfairly and losing out, feel activism to be an extension of identifying with and caring for them? If they do not, isn't this puzzling? Maddening? Missed and wasted opportunity for progressive energies?

Educators do see needs: Schoolteachers, teacher's aides, school administrators and counselors recognize situations where "something must be done." To offer just one example, the need for gay and lesbian students to have advocates and activists is illustrated in "Choices, Not Closets: Heterosexism and Homophobia in Schools" (Friend, 1993). In this text, Friend provides a few student voices and reveals their need. For example, Brenda age 18, says,

There are kids in high school who are scared and don't know where to turn. There needs to be something in the educational system so they have a place to go. Also, the teachers need to mention positive information in sexuality education classes.… it is important to include lesbian and gay teens, we're always left out…we are there. Also, when you try to educate teachers, let them know to include us! (p. 233)

Similarly, in the conservative domain of schooling, social justice activism is needed for women leaders, for prevention of sexual harassment, for Black children, for poor families, for the rights of girls and women, for language and religious minorities, for disabled students, and so on.

In fact, some educators are activists. But they are working in a context characterized by managerial and political controls and a conservative professional culture. Clearly there are tipping points that lead to an educator being overidentified with a particular movement, losing professional status in the face of increasing activist status. What, then, are the conditions that inhibit educators' activism for progressive movements and social justice in schooling?

Informal Professional Rules As educators are socialized, both in universities and on the job, they come to understand often unstated and context-driven constraints. According to Fullan (1993) the conservative nature of education has various manifestations:

> The way that teachers are trained, the way that schools are organized, the way that the educational hierarchy operates, and the way that education is treated by political decision-makers results in a system that is more likely to retain the status quo than to change. (p. 3, emphasis in original)

In *Women Teaching for Change*, Weiler (1988) elaborated the hierarchical and patriarchal nature of schools and school decision making, describing the negative consequences of maintaining the status quo:

> Their hierarchical structure, the content of the formal curriculum, the nature of the hidden curriculum of rules and social relationships all tend to reproduce the status quo. Those who are in control, who dominate and benefit from this structure, attempt in both conscious and unconscious ways to shape the schools so as to maintain their own privilege. In this way, school organization and practices tend to reproduce classism, racism, and sexism.… (pp. 150–151)

Teachers' activism and challenging creates trouble. Paul and Smith (2000) stated, "Teachers who do not toe the line, who question policy, and creatively maladjust to school cultures that do not value all children, are often dubbed as 'troublemakers'" (p.137).

Marshall and Mitchell (1991) studied the careers of school administrators and described "school-site administrators' understandings about the ways to

gain and maintain power, control, and predictability in their environments"
(p. 396). They delineated the unstated rules of the profession referred to as the
"assumptive worlds." These assumptive rules serve to govern behavior within
the context of work:

1. Limit risk taking to small and finite projects.
2. Make displays of commitment to the profession and sponsors.
3. Do not display divergent or challenging values.
4. Remake policy quietly as a street-level bureaucrat.
5. Keep disputes private.
6. Avoid moral dilemmas.
7. Avoid getting a troublemaker label.
8. Cover and guard all areas in your job description.
9. Build trust among the administrative team. (p. 15)

Assumptive worlds' rules are insider information about "exhibiting loyalty,
avoidance of trouble, keeping conflicts private, and avoiding unvalued work,…
behaviors that will help them feel more comfortable in administration" (p. 412).
For administrator aspirants to gain entry into the profession, they must learn
political strategies and get insider information. Coupled with legal constraints,
the professional culture of assumptive worlds serves as a driver and a restrainer.
These understandings help facilitate collegiality among administrators while
simultaneously serving to limit their drive to challenge the status quo.

The assumptive worlds' rules especially come into play when educators seek
to engage in social change. They learn, for example, to quietly fix a problem
when "going though channels" of authority would just cause more problems,
and to "fudge" on strict compliance with laws that get in the way of dealing with
an issue in front of them, functioning as street level bureaucrats (Weatherley &
Lipsky, 1977).

Hartzell, Williams, and Nelson (1995) interviewed 90 first year assistant
principals to frame their work lives in the context of school administration
and found that "the attitudes they develop and the repertoire of responses they
build have substantial influence on later behavior patterns and leadership capabilities" (p. 23). They further suggested, "The first-year socialization will likely
influence whether they become keepers of the status quo, rebels against the
system, or real leaders with a sense of role innovation" (p. 24). A study of female
principals regarding the degree to which women in principalships were equity
advocates—based on research about the inequitable treatment most women
received in administration positions—left the researchers "disappointed, frustrated, alarmed, and angry" (Schmuck & Schubert, 1995). They found that the
female principals studied showed little support or action to encourage equitable
practices in schools. It appeared that, even with evidence of a need for change,
these educators were still limited in what they would do.

Educators must tread carefully as they engage in behavior that illuminates problems of the profession. Marshall and Kasten (1994) warned, "Those who respond by bringing attention to the problems are viewed as disloyal, trouble-makers, or poor team players" (pp. 14–15). Activist work that is noncompliant with the governance of the assumptive worlds could impact career patterns, job promotion, and possibly lead to ostracism from colleagues and even the profession.

Evasion and the Social Construction of Non-Events Facing dilemmas, but finding few quick solutions and receiving almost no training or political support, educators concentrate their energies on the more manageable daily work. Taking attendance and creating workable lesson plans are manageable; reporting attendance and creating School Improvement Plans are within the administrator's control. Educators learn to comply with the social agreements which indicate that their jobs do not include tackling sensitive issues stemming from historical and institutional racism, sexism, and sexual hierarchies and dominance. Demanding that policies against bullying and sexual harassment be enforced, questioning why so few girls take advanced math, why so few Black children are in gifted programs, and why so few women can find enough support to advance to the superintendency are provocative questions over which educators feel little control. They learn to accept that professionals like themselves keep quiet, and learn to classify the array of emotions, observations, and insights that might be seen as disruptive to the status quo as private and personal. Further, they learn that there are limits on the kinds of personal lifestyles, hobbies, and social causes that they as professionals can publicly embrace, much less pursue.

Events and circumstances that otherwise compromise a child's education are transformed into nonevents. Policies and programs are devised in ways that treat educators as banks in which to deposit useful knowledge that will enable them to signify that the problem has been treated. In their working lives, educators are not exposed to deeply upsetting theories or insights that would take time and distract from daily work; succumbing to calls to redress these ills is seen as distracting, pulling educators from their required tasks. Reforms, professional literatures, training, and staff development offer packages and rhetoric, labeled as diversity training, color blindness, or equal opportunity. These serve to drive issues underground, silencing those who sense that the needs are deeper, and are tightly connected to societal ills that have included discrimination and unequal opportunity in housing and employment, domestic violence, homelessness, intergenerational poverty, hate speech, hate crimes, and physical assault, and women and girls faced with unplanned pregnancies.

In the context of this work, evasion is a consequence of rhetorical strategies designed to convince particular publics (including educators, perhaps especially educators) that policies are in place while at the same time discouraging activism to address ongoing inequities.

Educators' Sociocultural and Regional Socialization and the Limits on Activism

Conditions for educators' political and social activism vary because educators are affected by regional, political, and sociocultural contexts. Over 70% of our participants' career experiences were primarily in Southern states, so conservative professional expectations were often exacerbated by expectations of the conservative South (Billington, 1969; Keith, 2002), often as part of their own background and as a constraining force in their on-the-job-socialization. For example, in the South, religion can provide motivation both for and against social change (Nesbitt, 2001; Stott, 1999). The story of the civil rights movement in the South includes the roles of the Christian faithful in stimulating social action through "moral energy and social discipline" (Marsh, 2005, p. 7).

Yet the South is more often associated with conservative traditions. McFadden and Smith (2004) argued that Southerners see themselves as more traditional and conventional, more religious and mannerly.[2] Southern traditions include not challenging authority, and not regulating those with power—in government, in corporations, or class hierarchies. At the same time, traditions supported formulation and enforcement of antiliquor, anti-ERA, antisex education, and antipornography policies (Reed, 1993, p. 22). Southern states were slow to enact women's suffrage and most never ratified the ERA. Guiding beliefs included assumptions that labor unions, civil rights, gay rights, and feminisms were disruptive.[3]

Progressive incursions on gender and sexuality met resistance in the South. The traditional stereotype of the middle-class Southern White woman is that she is raised to project a genteel and fragile façade, trained to flatter her male protectors, and is educated for romance and marriage (Reed, 1993, p. 48); family and neighbors enforced rules of decorum—sit with legs together, no white after Labor Day, appear scatterbrained, but also be the caring saint (p. 49). Although categories of "Southern lady" and "belle" weakened in the late 20th century as women worked for prosperity and opportunity, traditional gender roles prevailed nonetheless. Wolfe (1995) argued that Southern women never renounced their femininity, so lesbians and feminists are often seen as antiservice, unladylike, and antimakeup and fashion. De Hart (2006) argued that feminism did come to the South, just later and to a narrower demographic than elsewhere (liberal, middle class, educated, less religious) (McFadden & Smith, 2004). In keeping with the feminist movement's initial whitewashing of issues, however, Black women were conflicted with the arrival of the rights' movements, often pressured to choose between being an activist for Black causes or feminist causes. In the 2002 report of the Institute for Women's Policy Research, Southern women were least likely to participate in political life, in the bottom third of the nation (except for North Carolina for reproductive rights) (McFadden & Smith, 2004).

Traditions of Southern Appalachia included glass ceilings for females and the segregation of African Americans; "national norms about race and gender... [were] not successfully challenged until recently" (McFadden & Smith, 2004, p.

75). White "worthwhile," local men became school superintendents; they were Protestant, conservative, likely to reflect racial biases grounded in segregation, skillful at getting along with other men, and in rural and Appalachian areas, solicitous of mountain dignity. Southern and Rocky Mountain states have the lowest percentages of women superintendents (Glass et al., 2000, p. 82, cited in McFadden & Smith, 2004, p. 21). "Regional attitudes about the proper place of Southern ladies and racial minorities had long been and linger as shapers of access and performance…yet regions are complex, varied, in flux, and populated by different people with different aspirations" (McFadden & Smith, 2004, pp. 22–23).

Still, "the new Southerner" may move from a more local orientation to a more cosmopolitan orientation (Reed, 1993, p. 53). According to Luebke (1990), "modernizers" in the South put faith in public education and accommodate African Americans; some acknowledge affirmative action, the ERA, and women's needs when pushed, but are still hostile to labor unions and other upsets of the economic order (pp. 25–27; see also Fleer, 1994). Modernizing and urbanizing influences in the late 20th century brought confounding influences, including outsiders with multinational firms that offer same-sex partner benefits in the same region where county commissioners voted down arts funding which was viewed as excessively homosexual. At the same time, the Southern Education Foundation (2007) found "For the first time in more than 40 years, the South is the only region in the nation where low income children constitute a majority of public school students—54 percent" (p. 2).

Thus, Southern traditions, especially those concerning women's roles and sexuality, affect many teachers and influence their sense of propriety. Also affected are beliefs about the appropriateness of activism for progressive causes, as will be seen in chapters 3 through 6.

Avoidance of Activism: A Summary Educators, thus, sense the informal rules, the hierarchies and patriarchies embedded in education professions, the tacit agreements about avoiding uncomfortable issues, and the constraints presented by cultural traditions that define proper behavior and guard against upsetting influences introduced by "outsiders." What are the supports, then, for educators who wish to change the world through their activism?

Breaking Past the Limits

Teaching is fundamentally a political activity in which every teacher plays a part by design or by default. (Cochran-Smith, 1991)

Ginsburg, Kamat, Raghu, and Weaver (1995) remind us:

Educators are political actors regardless of whether they are active or passive; autonomous or heteronomous vis-à-vis other groups; conservative or change-oriented; seeking individual, occupational group, or larger collectivities' goals; and/or serving dominant group, subordinate group, or human interests. (p. 34)

In other words, there is no escaping the political impact and import of education and thus, educators' actions.

In spite of the presumed neutrality and apolitical nature of education, our research assumes that we are all political actors, agreeing with Ginsburg (1995) and others that political work is not distinct from the professional and intellectual work we do as educators, nor is it only public activity divorced from personal and private interests (Grumet, 1988). As Ginsburg (1995) argued,

Educators do not operate in a political vacuum and educators are not neutral. What educators do occurs in a context of power relations and distribution of symbolic and material resources, and what action (or inaction) educators engage in has political implications for themselves and others. (pp. 7–8)

When educators break past their political neutrality, what does it look like?

Macropolitics

One potential form of educator activism for social justice is in formal groups. For example, the National Coalition of Education Activists is a network of parents, teachers, and other school staff, community activists, and teacher educators, who work for equitable and excellent schools and hold a yearly conference to share ideas and strategies. The Education for Liberation Network is a collaborative of educators and community activists encouraging education that encompasses critical thinking, social involvement, positive racial identity, and a sense of personal efficacy. Rethinking Schools, similarly, develops and shares social justice curriculum through national networking and publications. Since the passage of No Child Left Behind legislation, educators and community groups have formed coalitions to point out ways this national legislation can, in fact, have harmful effects on minority and poor children and undermine educators' best efforts with the children often left behind.

In spite of the advances they have achieved, teacher unions are not necessarily hotbeds of social justice activism. Teachers associations were formed with combined goals: an array of unionlike goals to improve educators' working conditions, and the goal of amassing enough power to influence education policy in the directions matching teachers' values and professional knowledge (Selden, 1985; Urban, 1982, 2000; West, 1980). When enough interest in social, political, or workers' rights emerges from association members, task forces are formed in state and national levels. Thus, women's leadership and health, retirement, the rights of gay, lesbian, bisexual, transgender, and queer educators (GLBTQ), African American educators, diversity, and the like, became task forces (Marshall, 2002). This tradition of grassroots constituency/majority rule subdues the more radical demands of subgroups. When groups of educators want the teacher unions to promote major social or political change, representatives from a large number of states must agree. For example, it was not possible to get strong support in the 1990s for taking a strong stand which asserted that birth control and abortion were part and parcel of teachers' health care rights.

Micropolitics

At a more micropolitical level, educators' activism may consist of getting personally involved with an issue or movement; promoting social justice through personal intervention, program creation, or by extending the curriculum; or simply taking up cases to get just and equitable treatment for individual students. Weiler (1988) shares examples of women educators who work in quiet ways, and this practice is seen in chapters 2 and 3 of this text, as African American and women educators find ways to use their jobs as platforms for pursuing social change. Activism, then, makes the personal political (Epstein, 1990). It is subtle, almost sneaky activism, as Hood-Williams found, what one participant described as acting "on the down-low" (Hood, 2005, p. 90) to try to stay out of trouble. It sometimes requires that advocates are willing to take a vocal stand in support of projects often seen as controversial in the conservative corridors of education. Even when learning the assumptive worlds' rules (e.g., limit risk taking, make change quietly as street level bureaucrats), educators find ways to use and expand their jobs that promote social justice.

Educator Activists

Although theirs may be limited risk taking and only subtle displays of divergent values, educators do identify with social movements. Given their professional socialization, which shapes apolitical neutrality and thus places limitations on their sense of being civically engaged, educators frequently are underestimated or marginalized as agents of change in the academic literature, often presented as pawns of the dominant culture and reproducers of the status quo. Connell (1995) critiqued the notion of teachers as pawns in the social reproduction game or as mere producers of future members of the workforce, suggesting instead that teachers are formers and transformers of *capacities* for practice. Ginsburg et al. (1995) argued that decision making regarding curriculum, pedagogy, assessment, and research, as well as collegial and familial relations, are imbued with politics. Educators' actions, therefore, never fall outside politics.

There is a rich history of individual educator activists, those who chose to make the personal political (Casey, 1993; Crocco, Munro, & Weiler, 1999; Dove, 1995; Epstein, 1990; Freire, 1990; hooks, 1994; Urban, 1989). As described in the literatures on the lives of educator activists, these individuals are often motivated by resistance to status quo or a desire to change status quo. Clifford (1987) expli-cated the traditions of women teacher activists that emerged between 1850 and 1930, naming the concurrent development of women's increasing independence and financial security after becoming teachers, alongside their development of speaking, organizational, and networking skills as critical events that facilitated their increasing activism. Munro (1995) detailed the lives five education activ-ists in Chicago at the turn of the 20th century who recognized that activism for women's emancipation was important not only for individual women, but for teachers and as part of "a larger vision of social change" (p. 274). These women drew on and enhanced traditions of women as educator activists.

In addition, there is generally a clear moral dimension to activism; the focus is on improving education for all students through changes in practices, policies, or curriculum. More recently, teacher personal narratives reveal, for example, layers of thinking and educators' working through "White America's repression of the voices of people of color" (Hankins, 2003, p. 23) and teachers' fine-tuned awareness of the "subtextual dynamics of classroom life" (Gallas, 1998, p. 22) that influence children's identities. Other examples of spaces for teachers to take exception to the conservative nature of education include organizations such as Rethinking Schools[4] and Teach for America.[5] However, as much as these orga-nizations create locations for teachers to draw on curricula that challenge the Eurocentric bias of mainstream curriculum as with Rethinking Schools, or spaces to tap into pressing educational needs for more teachers, it is worth noting that these two organizations exist outside organized structures of education. Teach-ers that go to either must move beyond the normative practices of educational practice and preparation.

In this text, there are stories of educators acting at the micropolitical level, from Black women's community work as described in chapter 2, "The Fight of the Their Lives: African American Activist Educators," to the underground feminist educators at work as described in chapter 3. These narratives on teach-ers embracing social justice break the stereotype of the sociopolitically neutral teach-to-the-test employee in public schools (see especially Allen, 1999; Michie, 2005; Perry, 2000).

The Activism Choice

The decision to be involved in a social movement is a choice that can have varied and unanticipated effects on the lives of the participants. Such outcomes may be positive or benign, but also have the potential to result in negative or extreme consequences, depending upon the political and social significance of a movement. Such effects can occur within the private sphere of an individual's existence; however, particular causes or activities could also affect the work life of such an activist. The educator's identities and values, along with their social-ization as professionals affect (and are affected by) their choosing to intervene micropolitically, and choosing to join a movement.

The educators whose work is presented in this book delve into their own lives, using their own words, and this book is thus an exploration and interpretation of their lived experiences. It shows the interweaving of both personal and professional resources and factors that frame how educators identify with social justice issues and how that identity drives their activism choices, their interventions, and the impact of their activism on the educators involved.

Theory and Methodology for Studying Activists for Social Justice

This book presents research that identifies struggles faced by educators affiliated with particular movements. The research progressed framed by common overarching theories, with the addition for each project of specific theories and literatures pertaining to each particular movement, and an elaborate and labor-intensive research design. The individual investigations looked at the implications of educational and extra-educational activism on the careers of educators and thus challenged the idea that educators avoid political activism in spite of the risks involved in taking public stands about social issues.

As citizens, it is reasonable that educators have personal investments in many social issues of our time. Yet as will be elaborated in chapters 2 through 6, the educators we spoke with did not necessarily endow their actions with the politics of activism and social movements. This is due, perhaps, to their profession's avoidance of political issues (Anderson, 1990). It is also important to repeat that while there are activists for various issues along the political spectrum, and while it seems to many of us that those on one end of the spectrum have dominated the rhetorical ground of late, *we* chose to focus on educators active for progressive politics as part of our study. Casey's (1993) findings about the lives of educator activists were significant to our planning:

> As the progressive teacher increases her participation and collaboration in the development of the political project, her pedagogic intentions become increasingly incongruent with the prevailing objectives of the educational institution, and she must continually (re)position herself inside (or outside) of the established (public or parochial school system. (p. x)

Our study, then, sought to reveal the extent to which educators experienced their activism as congruent or competing with their professional lives as educators. Must activists with progressive agendas experience discontinuity with their roles as educators?

The Educator Activist Research Project sought to answer that question. In a seven-year collaborative effort, six scholars examined the role dilemmas educators faced as they engaged in educational, social, or political activist projects. The original conceptualization of the project sought to capture the lived experiences of activist educators, which required a qualitative approach. Following the recommendations of Miles and Huberman (1994) on group research, we developed a common interview protocol and procedures that guided our individual research. Common interview protocols were based on extensive research in the literatures of social movement theory, activism, and educator identity development, literatures that shaped our original thinking in this research. The qualitative design of the protocol questions was chosen to solicit participants' responses about definitions, background, experiences, meanings, and dilemmas related to activism in the context of their professional and personal lives.[6]

To capture a breadth of experiences, currently or formerly employed teachers and educational administrators in K-12 public education also involved in activist work were interviewed to look for patterns across a variety of activist projects. Each researcher conducted approximately 10 interviews with educators. Participants were chosen through a combination of snowball, convenience, and opportunistic sampling measures in order to locate cases that could provide meaningful data. Respondents were also sought from varied regions of the United States to create demographic diversity among responses. Interview transcripts and field notes were used to name and describe the themes that emerged within each researcher's area of inquiry. Each researcher used NVivo software to analyze data with group themes and to generate themes unique to each area of activism.

This research needed the freedom to evoke reflections, perspectives, and knowledge driving educators; choices to engage in activism, and the barriers, constraints, and dilemmas they face in their activist work. Interviews with teachers and educational administrators involved in activist projects that include sexual harassment in schools; feminist educators in leadership positions; race-oriented issues; gay, lesbian, bisexual, and transgendered rights; and reproductive rights led researchers in this project to a better understanding of the experiences of educator activists as well as the identification of patterns across the variety of activist projects. Findings show that different reasons for and different ways of enacting change emerged among participants. Participants' activism was at times hidden, at times overt; reasons for acting included role expectations, a spiritual calling, personal experiences, and deeply embedded identity issues. While we began by treating these areas of activism as discrete, dividing feminists in educational administration from educators involved in race-related activism, our cross-case analysis identified the shared motivations and challenges as educators engage in activist work.

Using Theory to Frame the Explorations of Educator Activists' Choices

It helps to have a mental picture to conceptualize a question, and to design a way to explore for answers. Theories provide such pictures. The early meetings of our Educator Activist research group focused on identifying the primary research literatures we believed important to our study of educator activists. We chose social movement theory, identity theory (particularly educator identity), and existing literatures on educator activists as points of departure for our collective research. As each researcher began her individual work, it was necessary to study additional literatures customized to the investigation of activists in particular areas (e.g., the civil rights movement, the women's movement; the emergence of sexual harassment legislation, LGBT rights movement, and prochoice activism). This section provides a brief overview of our collective research in the areas of social movements, identity, and educator activism. During the course of our research, it became clear that introducing additional literatures would help us more fully understand and contextualize the work of these educator activists, so this section also includes literatures examining how critical race theory, feminist theories, and literatures on the special contexts of Southern culture helped us explore and explain the patterns emerging from the research. Several of the authors in this text (see chapters 2 through 6) developed a conceptual model that enabled the researcher to apply theories to her particular focus in the research.

Social Movement Theory   Social movements are large scale events or organizations that attempt to effect change or resist changes that affect large numbers of people (Oberschall, 1993). Social movements (e.g. proenvironment, peace, civil rights, etc.) have an identity, adversaries, and a vision or goal. The movement's identity is its goals, values, actions, leaders, slogans. Collective actions of a social movement result from collective identity, the development of which is an "ongoing process in all social movements struggling to overturn existing systems of domination (Taylor & Whittier, 1992, p. 510). A movement's vision or goal is the "kind of social order or organization it hopes to achieve through collective action" (Castells, 1997). Movements are also characterized by identification of a clear opponent or opponents and are motivated by social breakdown or social solidarity (e.g., "big oil"; the Pentagon; patriarchy). In fact, Buechler (2000) argued that these collective actions are a reaction to societal stress or strain by individuals "who are experiencing various forms of discontent or anxiety" (p. 20). The advent of new social movement theory in the 1960s suggested that new social movements are increasingly noninstitutional (Darnovsky, Epstein, & Flacks, 1995; Epstein, 1990).

Social movements may be socially conservative or revolutionary or both. According to Castells (1997), there are no good or bad social movements: "They are all symptoms of our societies, and all impact social structures with variable intensities and outcomes" (p. 71). Larger numbers of social movements began to appear in the 18th century and are traditionally organized around three different features. One feature is *formal hierarchical organization* whereby goals are identified and attempts are made to accomplish these goals. Another feature of a social movement is its *organization at the "point of contact with opponents"* (Tarrow, 1998). Variations on this structure range from temporary gatherings of challengers, to informal social networks, to formal branches, and clubs and can be controlled by formal organizations, or by no specific person. *Connective structures* are the final feature of social movements. These structures connect leaders and followers and other aspects of the movement allowing the movement to continue despite the absence of formal organization. Keeping in mind these features, we developed a working definition of social movements as *collective political action aimed at challenging and changing social routines or institutions*.

It is not the isolated, alienated individual who joins a social movement; it is the socially connected individual who exchanges ideas with other individuals to produce cognitive frameworks that question existing dominant frames. These submerged networks, according to Melucci (1989), are not always recognized by social scientists as playing a crucial role in movement recruitment, development, and maintenance. An important feature, however, is that submerged networks or social-movement communities support members and act as abeyance structures during periods of time when the political climate is not receptive to the movement's agenda (Buechler, 1990; Taylor & Whittier, 1992). As our data will show, it is important to consider the abeyance functions of movements in the lives of the educators described in this work.

Participation in a social movement can occur along a spectrum of activity—from active and public activity (perhaps a demonstration or public awareness campaign) to more passive, symbolic displays of support. The level of participation a social movement receives varies according to the individuals who offer support, and as noted above, support depends on individuals' identification with the movement. Oberschall (1993, pp. 22–23) offers a continuum of activist levels that is useful to consider. Participation in a social movement is typically not an all-consuming activity for individuals, although at the core of any movement are *leaders and activists* who work more or less full time for the movement (*core activists*). These leaders are the public face of the movement that the media and others associate with the movement's activity, at times spokespeople, at times subjects of criticism. Supporting the leaders are *part-time participants*, or *transitory teams*. These individuals attend rallies, help with mailings, and gather names on petitions, supporting activities planned by the core activists. Costs in terms of time and money are minimal at this level, though feelings of solidarity are high. *Sponsors* are another level of participant, individuals who make small financial contributions, sign petitions, and generally nurture a positive climate for the movement's goals among friends, neighbors, and coworkers. This "*consciousness-constituency*" is attracted to the movement because it appeals to their sense of justice or fairness. Little is asked of them; their reward is the feeling of doing the right thing. Finally, at the edge of the movement are sympathizers, sympathetic but passive bystanders. Rational-choice theories of social movement participation (Friedman & McAdams, 1992), according to which individuals make deliberate rational decisions to join a movement "only when they expect the private benefits to exceed the costs" (p. 159), also note *free riders* as those who reap the benefits of a movement without participating or bearing any of the costs. Oberschall (1993), however, argued that this designation underestimates individuals' needs for social and psychological affiliation with a social movement.

Social movement literatures, especially those that consider participants' identity issues, emphasize that an individual's identities significantly influence that person's activist choices. In this research, social movement theory points our attention to the social networks an educator claims or mentions; her sense of shared purpose or solidarity with a movement; forms and levels of involvement; experiences of collective action; and belief in clear or powerful opponents. Participation in a social movement occurs along a spectrum of activity—from active and public activity (perhaps a demonstration or public awareness campaign) to more passive, symbolic displays of support. Educator activism can fall anywhere along this continuum.

Identity Theory Gilroy (1993) stated, "We live in a world where identity matters. It matters both as a concept, theoretically, and as a contested fact of contemporary political life" (p. 301). Identity theory was an initial focus of our collective research because it required us to consider how an individual's attitudes, commitments, beliefs, and behaviors influenced her or his activist decisions. Though identity theories have emerged from diverse disciplines (including the social sciences and political sciences), ours was a deliberately sociocultural focus on identity—or rather identities—recognizing that "persons [take] form in the flow of historically, socially, culturally, and materially shaped lives" (Holland, Lachicotte, Skinner, & Cain, 1998, p.5). Identities are thus fluid and adaptable, not fixed and unchanging (Calhoun, 1994).

When studying educator activists, issues of identity impact the decision to participate in activism, the kind of activism (individual or collective) one might choose to get involved with, the level and extent of participation, and the selection of social networks within a movement. As a group, we chose a working definition of identity that shaped our research, framing it as *a person's self-concept at a particular time, within a given context, and subject to ongoing construction and modification through various processes and experiences.* Potential themes related to identity significant for our study included understanding a person's educational and family background as well as other named social networks (hooks, 1994); evidence of critical events or "a-ha" moments that provoked decisions to participate in activism; professional and personal identity correspondence or competition related to activism (Stryker, 2000); identity politics related to issues including race, class, gender, or sexual orientation (Darnovksy et al., 1995); and perceptions of personal risk associated with participation in activist networks.

Our previous discussions of the impact of Southern culture and the conservative nature of educators' professional cultures demonstrate how salient identity theories are for understanding educators' choices, particularly the majority of activists in this study who were raised or work in the South. Some identities are of our choosing (e.g., educator, outdoor enthusiast), but others influence our lives and choices in ways we may not even recognize without the lens of theory. Many may fail to recognize the influence of Southern culture on their life choices, for example, so embedded are they in the fishbowl that is the South. Theories of identity provide lenses for studying the beliefs and structures that belie and underlie "the way things are." Thus theories of identity are explored with more depth in individual chapters of this book as they relate to choices made by educator activists. Chapter 4, "Approaching Activism in the Bible Belt," for example, introduces the impact of being a victim of harassment as an impetus in activist decision making, and queer theories of identity development emerge in chapter 5, "Surprising Ways to Be an Activist."

Educator Activism Our collective research into activism serves as the basis of this chapter's section on "breaking past the limits" (see above). As indicated, we initially focused on literatures that took educator activism as their focus, and developed a working definition of an activist as *an individual who is known for taking stands and engaging in action aimed at producing social change, possibly in conflict with institutional opponents.* In keeping with more recent developments in literature, we also focused on the language of social justice, framing it as *activism aimed at increasing inclusivity, fairness, empowerment, and equity and fairness, especially for heretofore oppressed and silenced groups.*

These were the literatures that shaped our initial research before interviews began. As the work progressed, as dissertations were written, and as this text came together, it became clear that additional literatures were necessary to fill out our images of educator activists and to more fully explore the interview data we gathered. As data were analyzed, social movement theory, though useful, did not emerge as the most salient when considering the lives of these educator activists. To explore their experiences, it was necessary for us to tease apart identity and critical theories to examine their significance for the stories we collected. Accordingly, we went back to the literature armed with the practices of the educator activists in this study in order to expand our framework. The next section explores critical race, queer, and feminist theories and their significance for this work.

Empowering, Reframing and Disruptive Knowledges

Decades of theory and research have provided perspectives that enable educators to view their work and themselves as citizens with special insights and missions for reframing the work of education. Many educators see incidents that beg for such reframing, but exposure to critical perspectives that would facilitate pursuit of action for social justice are increasingly limited in educators' professional socialization. In this section, we introduce aspects of critical race, queer, and feminist theories that inform the research presented in this book.

It is important to note that the movements that frame the work of the educator activists in this text emerged from the civil rights movement, a critical social movement and political moment in U.S. history. Civil rights activists in the late

1950s and early 1960s fomented the energy that begat the women's liberation movement, which in turn begat second wave feminism, the abortion rights movement, and activism against sexual harassment. The civil rights movement was also a model for the gay rights movement that followed the Stonewall Riots

Table 1.1 Timeline of Key Civil Rights Events

1950s

1954	*Brown v. Board of Education* makes segregation in schools illegal
1955	December 1: Rosa Parks refuses to give up her seat in Montgomery, AL bus
1957	Little Rock schools desegregated
1958	National Defense of Education Act provided public and private aid to education

1960s

1960	Women represent 4% of elementary school principals
	1st Sit-In, Greensboro, NC
1963	President John F. Kennedy assassinated
	March on Washington for Jobs and Freedom; Dr. Martin Luther King's "I Have a Dream" speech
	President's Commission on the Status of Women Report documenting gender discrimination
	Equal Pay Act abolishing wage differentials based on sex
	Emergence of 2nd Wave Feminism
1964	Title VII of the Civil Rights Act establishes the Equal Employment Opportunity Commission
	Freedom Summer attempts to register African Americans in Mississippi, a state noted for excluding Black voters
1965	Voting Rights Act made literacy tests, as a requirement for voting, illegal
1966	National Organization for Women (NOW) formed
1967	Thurgood Marshall named 1st African-American Supreme Court Justice
1968	Dr. Martin Luther King, Jr. assassinated
1969	Stonewall Riots launched the Gay Rights Movement

1970s

1970	Women earn .59 to men's $1
	3.5% school superintendents are women
1972	Title IX of the Education Amendments bars gender discrimination in school programs
	Ms. Magazine founded
1973	*Roe v. Wade* legalizes abortion in the United States
1975	US ends involvement in Vietnam War

1980s

1981	Sandra Day O'Connor named first female Supreme Court Justice
1982	Equal Rights Amendment defeated

1990s

1996	Defense of Marriage Act – federal law forbidding recognition of same-sex marriages
1998	Matthew Shepherd murdered

2000s

2000	Civil unions sanctioned in Vermont
2005	Same-sex marriage recognized in Massachusetts
2007	Supreme Court ruling outlaws a late-term abortion procedure

of 1969. The timeline above identifies critical social, political, and educational dates in the history of the movements that frame this research.

As noted above, this text takes up progressive social causes, from race-related activism to abortion rights. It is interesting to note that the precipitating events for the activism described in this work occurred 30 to 50 years ago; as the timeline demonstrates, these rights movements date to the 1950s in the United States. The academic and theoretical literatures that followed the movements studied them in relation to existing theories (e.g., Marxism), and also developed new theories in response to the movements. It will be interesting to consider whether a sense of public, political, theoretical, educational, or discursive energy is required to support and extend the life of a social movement. For example, if there is no longer a common sense of urgency or injustice in relation to a movement, to what extent does the public recognize the issue as problematic? Consider, for example, the suggestion of some postfeminist theories that gender discrimination is "solved" and is no longer at issue. It will also be interesting to note the extent to which activists in this text identify with the actions that gave rise to the movements of consequence in this text. Do ready points of entry for these movements still exist?

The critical theories that follow in this section are also legacies of the energy that drove civil rights activism in the United States. Critical theorists examine the roots of oppressive and unequal practices to uncover the ways they have become historically embedded in institutions, including schools, legal precedents, political arenas, and community life. Critical perspectives help us see beyond explanations such as "that's just the way things are," and "we don't know what to do about it." Critical race, queer, and feminist theories start with this examination but concentrate on the insights that come from focusing on race, gender, and sexuality, and their intersections. Such theories could help educators move far beyond "that's the way things are" explanations for much of what they observe and feel in schools and society. An additional strength of this line of research is the recovery or reframing of theories and theorists long marginalized, perspectives essential for more complex understandings in contemporary times.

Critical Race Theory

Critical race theory (CRT) centers race as the domain of analysis, directing attention to the ways in which White power and privilege are protected and reified. CRT critiques "traditional claims of neutrality, objectivity, color-blindness, and meritocracy as camouflages for the self-interest of dominant groups in American society" (Solórzano, 1998 p. 6). Many societal institutions and interactions silence or minimize realities of racism and its effects. Critical race theory, emerging in the 1970s from legal theory, initially examined how laws reproduce, reify, and normalize racism in society. "By unmasking the hidden faces of racism, critical race theory aims to expose and unveil White privilege...and reveal a social order that is highly stratified and segmented along racial lines" (Lopez, 2003, p. 84).

While laws address blatant racism and categorize those committing conspicuous racist acts as bad people, Lopez (2003) points out that this perspective protects White privilege by focusing on the blatant but downplaying the hidden and structural facets of racism. As a consequence, most individuals see the "race problem" as something for others to solve since Whites are not challenged to confront racist beliefs (indeed, believe they have none), and because the topic is not part of their daily lives. CRT aims to present counterstories that depict how society has set up a system that actively subordinates, marginalizes, and silences people of color and their perspectives in indirect and often subtle ways (Lopez, 2003). According to Jay (2006), CRT has been embraced in the past 15 years in education by those "interested in the various forms racism takes in education and how schools assist in the maintenance of a subordinate status for students of color" (p. 9).

Critical race theory is significant in the present work as a lens for considering the actions of educators who are working to decenter or speak back to dominant culture ideologies that normalize master narratives that presume neutrality, objectivity, meritocracy, and color-blindness, for example, as guiding principles in educational practice (Jay, 2006).

Queer Theory

Queer theory is another significant lens for considering the work of educator activists. The term *queer* describes behaviors and activities at odds with traditional norms, not only about sexuality but also other facets of society (Hall, 1996). Queer theory, used to encompass the range of possible identities of gay, lesbian, bisexual, and transgendered students (GLBT),[7] is also useful for highlighting the limiting labels individuals put on others and themselves (Turcotte, 1996). Stimulated by the nonresponsiveness of governments to the AIDS crisis and hate crimes in the 1990s, queer theory seeks to break down dominant notions of what is considered normal so as to stop stigmatizing actions, beliefs, or behaviors (Pinar, 1998). Highlighting the damage of homophobia, queer theory begins by demonstrating how compulsory heterosexuality messages in institutions (e.g., schools, families, churches) cause harm.

Educators' silence around sexual orientation, however, affects students in various negative ways. In the early stages of developing nonheterosexual identities, students can experience feelings of confusion, depression, and alienation under the best of circumstances (Cass, 1979), and children feel alone if they do not see gay/lesbian role models while they are developing same-sex affectional and sexual orientations. When schools are unsafe for gay and lesbian students, they may drop out of school, abuse drugs and alcohol, or commit suicide:

> In 1989 the leading cause of death for gay, lesbian, bisexual, and transgendered youth was suicide. Lesbian and gay youth are two to three times more likely to attempt suicide than their heterosexual peers, and they

account for up to 30% of all completed suicides among youths. (Besner & Spungin, 1995, p. 46)

Too often, educators remain silent on heterosexism and homophobia, despite pleas from students, because they are afraid of what talking about sexual orientation will lead to—that breaking the silence around sexual orientation will lead to significant public scrutiny and backlash from conservative publics (Friend, 1993). Ideological groups and parent groups that try to restrict school settings from fostering a greater understanding of genders and sexualities, provide evidence of the kinds of pressures a young person or group of young people could similarly experience (Leck, 2000). Queer theory is another significant lens in this work when considering the motivations of educators working to make schools safer places for all students.

Feminist Theories

The feminist movement is often described in terms of waves. First wave feminism encompasses women's activism in the 19th and early 20th centuries, and its focus was on basic rights for women, beginning with women's suffrage. Feminism's second wave emerged in the early 1960s as a successor movement to the civil rights movement in the United States. The third wave of feminism emerged in the 1990s in response to the perceived shortcomings and omissions of second wave feminism, including the experiences of nonmajority (i.e., non-White, nonheterosexual, non-Western) women worldwide.

Feminist theories developed as feminism—its principles and practices—began its slow movement into the academy. Feminism writ large begins with a critique of patriarchy and the recognition that many societal practices and institutions are structured to value and favor the progress of men. What came to be known as *liberal feminism* is widely recognized as the first iteration of feminist theory and practice. Liberal feminism focuses on providing equal access to the benefits of societal institutions, like school programs and employment. Socialist and maternal feminist theories demonstrate ways in which women are devalued, excluded, or silenced, and, then work to reframe structures and practices through the incorporation of women's needs, voices, and preferences. On the heels of these first feminist critiques of patriarchy, however, came various other feminisms that questioned the overwhelmingly White, Western, and heterosexual biases of the dominant culture (as well as their traces in feminism). Critical feminist theories identify the political and power moves that marginalize women's agendas. Feminist poststructuralist theories focus on the positive possibility of recognizing multiplicity in language as a means of understanding the contingent, in-process nature of people and actions, thereby allowing us to form a different conception of events, people, and change. The 1980s also saw the advent of postfeminists who questioned the relevance and focus of contemporary feminisms, with some postfeminist arguments suggesting that the feminist movement was no longer necessary. Researchers operating out of feminist and critical frameworks, such as Britzman (2000), Connell (1987), Knight (2000), Laible (1997), Lather (2000), Marshall (1997), Stromquist (1997), and Young (2003), though diverse in their orientations, share a critique of patriarchal structures in education and often develop research agendas aimed at empowerment from repressive and oppressive structures.

Feminist theory highlights not only gender stereotyping and thwarted opportunities but also a range of issues about relationships, emotion, and issues often relegated to the private sphere. In recent reexaminations of the feminist movement, several themes emerge. The first is that as part of the movement's mantra the "personal is political," the personal must acknowledge and indeed embrace women's commitments to children and family. For example, Willett (2002) asserts that the women's liberation movement of the 1960s did not take into account the power of cultural desire for children, the protections mythically afforded women by patriarchal institutions, and the power of family life. *Who's Afraid of Feminism?* (Oakley & Mitchell, 1997) also raises a range of issues about children, parenting, and family. It points to women's vulnerability since "the term *feminist* is the name now given to the disliked or despised woman, much as *man-hater, castrating bitch, harridan,* or *witch* were used before the advent of second wave feminism" (Oakley & Mitchell, 1997, p. xix). Women increasingly want to or are expected to be in the workplace, but women report that men still do not share major burdens in housework, child, and aging-parent care. Meanwhile mothers are blamed for crime, and breakdowns in families and community support (taking place in the midst of governmental retreat from provision of safety nets and social services). In addition, it has become clear that hegemonic patriarchal forces orchestrate this backlash with rhetoric that increases feelings of vulnerability. The hidden curriculum, reinforced by hyperreal media and other social forces, continues to influence hypermasculinity for boys as well as adolescent girls' perceptions of educational and career opportunities. Girls' sense of choice is also undermined by pressures for unprotected sex although at the same time, the Christian right clamors against sex education in schools, and against women's right to choose. Sexuality, sex education, and sexual harassment policies, schooling for pregnant and parenting girls, and professionals' lack of training for dealing with gender issues, then, are often evaded in discourses about schooling. It becomes clear that class and race issues that intertwine with gender are often untouched—despite laws eliminating sex stereotyping in coursework and career counseling—as the life patterns of males and females continued to be channeled along class, race, and gender lines. The liberal feminist agenda, while bringing small gains for mostly White and middle-class women, was not able to address the needs of many poor women and women of color. What Collins (1991) has called "matrices of domination" had not been challenged.

Sex, gender, and sexual orientation rear up in human resource and hiring practices, as in the awkward groping to find out women applicants' family planning methods and intentions while avoiding illegal direct questions. They appear by avoidance, when men in power may avoid unspoken discomforts with being sponsors and mentors to aspiring women, and, conversely, when women victims of sexual harassment simply keep quiet rather than being labeled as troublemakers. However, clearly sexual dynamics in education was untouched; sexual harassment of students was not covered; and educators' training and the male-dominated hierarchy of schools were unchanged in most educational institutions.

Critical race, feminist, and queer theories frame new issues for education politics, move such taboo issues from the margins of the private spheres to education politics, questions of curriculum, educator recruitment and retention, counseling, and employee and student rights. Their very visibility makes them subject to inquiry, and backlash.

Backlash and Historical Selectivity

Critical race, queer, and feminist theories are movements of the late 20th century that continue to exercise influence in academic literatures as well as the popular imagination. Given the persistent visibility of activism for civil rights for all citizens, backlash from the dominant majority remains a likely consequence. For example, backlash against the women's movement is interwoven with the ways in which right-wing Christians are challenging multiculturalism and attempting to reassert church-based, Christian values through legislation and political influence (Cooper, 1997).

Backlash against the feminist movement meant that in gender equity debates, opponents easily invoke antifamily, antifemininity, antimarriage, antichildren claims and challenge the appeals of the feminist movement. Women and girls who are exploring the offerings of the women's movement, while lured by promises of equal pay, personal freedoms, and changed perspectives, may also fear the (media-inflamed) specter of feminism. The perception exists that to embrace the movement may result in limited chances for a husband and children, and for being seen as normal and proper.

Conflicts arise in schools over curricular decisions about studying, or even acknowledging, sexual orientation; recognizing the sexual orientation of historical figures or literary personae may be seen as too inflammatory in some schools. GLBTQ students and their allies politick for space and budgets for student activities in schools. By force of Title IX[8] or because incidents no longer are swept under the rug, school boards are searching for remedies and formulating policies against peer bullying and sexual harassment, and thus having to recognize the sometimes brutal and sometimes more subtle realities of sexual domination.

In spite of the growth of women's studies, queer studies, and academic disciplines focusing on studies of ethnic and racial minorities (e.g., African American studies, Asian studies), many education scholars and practitioners, as well as the general populace, do not consciously ponder the consequences of the historical and continuing disadvantage of females, people of color, and LGBT citizens. It is as if, with Nancy Pelosi and Hillary Clinton "making it" and Title

IX on paper, for example, the gender problem, if it ever existed, has been taken care of. For example, Elliott (1997) notes the "selective reality" of students in a gender class—their choosing to believe that there is gender equity while at the same time giving personal examples of unequal treatment. Titus (2000) found that some preservice teachers "deny, dismiss, or discount women's oppression, distance themselves from feminism, or express dismay or despair in the absence of any definitive solutions to the inequalities they acknowledge" (p. 26).

Pressing Ahead

The power and vibrancy of critical, critical race, queer, and feminist theories are multiplied when they are interwoven. When a 23-year-old teacher or a principal in her 40s is exploring and negotiating her sense of self she is doing so in the school- and society-generated contexts of her neighborhood, her skin, her sexuality, and her gender, as well as the expectations of her profession and her regional culture. The intersectionality of race, class, gender, and sexuality in these theories allow exploration of the career lives and identities of activist educators.

The insight-laden discourses of critical, critical race, queer, and feminist theories and research empowered and deepened the analyses in our research endeavor. We wonder (and doubt) that these empowering discourses are part and parcel of professional pre- and in-service training or the teacher lounge talk of educators: and that's too bad. Because while these critical discourses are challenging, they also could help educators feel comfortable with their instincts toward expanded identities, liberatory practices, and social movement participation. The discourses could help educators become fuller citizens themselves as well as provide educators with better ways to view their work as liberatory.

At the same time, conversations with practitioners challenged our theories. As stated, we began with one set (social movement theory, activist theory, identity theory), but necessarily revisited those and expanded our focus to account for the complex lives and practices of the educators with whom we spoke. What follows is an introduction to the next five chapters that in turn detail the experiences of educator activists in these times.

Introduction to the Individual Research Projects

In chapter 2, "The Fight of Their Lives: African American Activist Educators," Annice Hood Williams[9] looks at the impact of race-related activism on the careers of African American educators, reflected in her primary research question: What are the influences that motivate some African American educators to participate in race-based activism and how does this participation impact their lives and careers? Interviewing 10 educators, Williams's research explored the elements that prompted Black educators to get involved in race-oriented activism, also seeking to describe and analyze possible impacts of this involvement on their careers.

Susan Walters examined "Activist Women in Educational Leadership—How Likely?" in chapter 3. Recognizing that the acceptance of women in leadership positions in educational administration has been slow, and that the field continues to be dominated by White males in the highest levels of power and influence, Walters interviewed 13 women to examine the impact of the women's movement on their lives. In addition, she explored the women's level of commitment to the ideals of the women's movement as articulated in the field of educational administration, as well as how women educational leaders carry out their activism for women's issues.

Chapter 4 presents Gloria Jones's research, "Approaching Activism in the Bible Belt," in which she studied the significant impact of student-to-student sexual harassment in the K-12 setting. Jones began with two primary research questions:

- How and why do educators emerge as activists to stand against student-to-student sexual harassment in the public K-12 setting; and
- When educators choose to engage in activism to alleviate student-to-student sexual harassment, what professional and personal dilemmas confront them?

She interviewed 11 educators to investigate their motivations and experiences intervening in student-to-student sexual harassment.

Wanda Legrand chose to study the impact of involvement in activism for lesbian, gay, bisexual, and transgendered (LGBT) people in chapter 5, "Surprising Ways to Be an Activist." For this work, she interviewed 10 educators to describe and analyze the impact of political activism for LGBT rights on the personal and professional lives of K-12 educators. This study explored the actions of LGBT activists in the context of the limitations or risks educators face when advocating for rights deemed too controversial for public education. Legrand's primary research questions included:

- What dilemmas and choices do LGBT educator activists face and how do they manage them?
- How safe is it for educator activists to work for LGBT rights within the educational system?
- What tensions, contradictions, and problems occur because of participation in activism related to issues of sexual orientation?

In chapter 6, "Is There Choice in Educator Activism?" Amy L. Anderson focuses on the lives of educators active for issues of reproductive choice. Her work is driven by the following questions: How public can educators be when they work as activists regarding reproductive choice? How do educators reconcile their prochoice activist politics and identities with their identities as teachers? What is the relationship of sanctioned health/abstinence curriculum to educators' prochoice activism? And, given that reproductive choice falls far outside the domain of sanctioned curriculum in the schools, how do activists for reproductive choice compare to activists in other areas? Anderson interviewed eight educators to gain better understanding of their experiences as activists for reproductive freedom.

Chapters 2 through 6 provide the stories of activists for social justice. The inspirations, the choices, the career and personal identity issues and dilemmas, the modes of activist work, and the collaborations and supports in social movements, will be displayed, drawing from these stories. The last two chapters serve two purposes: for those who are interested in using this model of collaborative cross-case comparative inquiry, chapter 8 provides detail and anecdotes to flesh out our procedures. Chapter 7 expounds on the bigger picture for those who are interested in seeing how we took advantage of the possibilities in comparing the five studies; how we used theory to expand and deepen the cross-case comparisons; and, finally, our assertions of the significance of the findings, for educators, for social justice, and for educational practice and policy.

To the Reader

Remember times when you want to scream, make a scene, jump up and immediately right some wrong or stop some stupid practice? Remember how it felt when some internal voice, some advisor, some practical caution prevented you? Ever had the comfort of joining with others who had the same values, the same urge to scream? Have you found ways to "do the right thing" without jeopardizing your career or your marriage or your mortgage? Research that delves into such dilemmas, and then finds that people construct identities and strategies for coping, can give evidence of allies in the work.

Exit, Voice, Loyalty?

When workers perceive their organizational practices to be wrong or ill advised, according to Hirschman (1970) they exercise exit, voice, or loyalty—either they quit, make a loud protest, or suppress their feelings and quietly comply with the practices. Public sector workers like educators work for an ambiguous and often unstated, but nevertheless understood public good, be it middle-class morality, compliance with federal policy to retain district funds, or sorting children into bluebirds and cardinals. Teachers and administrators learn they must help their districts avoid lawsuits, community outcry, and headlines reporting bad practices. Their professional preparation and their school district norms often support their loyalty. Part of the training for fledgling administrators includes learning to make their superiors look good, avoid moral dilemmas, and act as street level bureaucrats, keeping problems quiet, altering policies and programs quietly to suit the particular needs they see. Educators, then, make choices when faced with ethical dilemmas. So, educators face dilemmas upon seeing a pattern of assigning African American boys to special education labels, seeing girls shy away from after-school events, and gay teens commit suicide when harassment goes unpunished, watching women being culled from their school leadership aspirations, observing the effects of state policies preventing sex education as pregnant girls suffer and drop out. More nuanced than exit, voice, or loyalty choices, their behaviors may include conducting a "moral triage" (Sjorberg, 1999), simulation (appearing to do what is required), "secret business, the metaphorical closing of the classroom and office door, complying with things with which they agree and presenting the appearance of compliance with the others) and resistance (overt disobedience)" (Thomson, 2001, p. 7). As Thomson says, "many still carry on the kinds of moral equity work that they hold dear while working within current frames…by tactically taking up submerged and lesser discourses, and mobilizing other aspects of their non-unitary self" (p. 7).

This book explores the behaviors, choices, feelings, hesitations, secrets, as educators carry on moral equity work.

The Promise from Releasing Activist Energies for Education

If educators who identify themselves as activists continue to believe they are working against the mores of their field, their piled-on frustrations are wasted energies. Their psychological, physical, and capital resources are expended not on liberating students through education (hooks, 1994), but on resisting internal conflict, limiting activist effectiveness, and slowing the pace of change. Recognizing the political nature of education professions then will require subsequent reevaluation and modification of educator preparation programs and socialization processes. Opportunities must be put in place for aspiring and practicing educators to reflect on and question political assumptions, then develop their own ways of articulating their political/professional stances.

Finally, educators' sense of professionalism necessitates their taking ethical stands. Their responsibilities to promote and protect students' needs mean that they will, at times, enter political frays when political arrangements and policies (or lack thereof) hurt students. Simply speaking out is a political act. Forming a group of educators and collaborating to create a program or assert a demand is a political act. Activist professionalism then is exhibited in such assertions and actions as helping students and their families when the current programming is not enough or is misguided. It is educators "reclaiming moral and intellectual leadership over educational debates" (Sachs, 2000, p. 81).

Education Professionals' Moral and Intellectual Leadership?

Ever hear complaints from educators about those politicians who stop them from doing what's best for kids? Ever wonder what schools would be like if educators' professional preparation and work lives supported their taking strong stands to promote equity and democracy? Remember being impressed by an educator who seemed so very brave, smart, idealistic, intellectual, and determined to make the world a better place?

Characteristics of professionalism include having training for expert knowledge, having an ethical code, having autonomy for making decisions in one's sphere of expertise, and having control over who gains entrance into the profession. Educators, then, are often viewed as semiprofessionals, since they are in constant professionalism struggles. Recognizing that teachers' professionalism entails not just expertise and a desire for autonomy but also that their ethical concerns center on a desire to look out for students' needs, Sachs (2000, 2001) demonstrated the desirability of activist professionalism and reclaiming moral and intellectual leadership. Such activist professionalism would contribute to democratic practices and emancipatory goals, as activist identities incorporate what Beane and Apple (1995) describe as "the open flow of ideas, regardless of their popularity, that enables people to be as fully informed as possible, … concern for the welfare of others and 'the common good,' … concern … [for] the dignity and rights of individuals and minorities" (pp. 6–7). Assuming that educators feel their primary obligations as being to their constituencies of students and parents, they would work to eliminate any exploitation, inequality, or oppression.

Our research and our book provide an invigorating look at the possibilities of reopening discussion of educators' identities, or their ideals, aims, and purposes. The book reopens conversations about the preparation, the professional status, and the political status of educators. As the following chapters show, educators have an opportunity to flex their political muscle through curriculum decisions, pedagogical actions, student evaluation, and research (Ginsburg, 1995). Readers, take a look at what could be!

Notes

1. We use *educator* as an inclusive term to include education professionals at all levels, including teachers, counselors, administrators, social workers, school nurses, etc. If talking about a specific group, we try to name that group (e.g., teachers).
2. McFadden and Smith (2004) stated that White Baptist traditionalists, for example, require hierarchical and deferential relationships with wives, Blacks, and working-class employees (p. 21). They go on to argue that Southerners are polite, and are more likely to attend church regularly, believe that religious faith is important, be Protestant, and identify as fundamentalist or Pentecostals. Southerners are less likely to drink alcohol, to live in a metropolitan area, or, if they are White, to identify as a Democrat, and to believe that relationships between men and women have grown worse over recent years. They are more likely to maintain clear gender roles for household responsibilities, and to value a sense of home and kin. They see small talk as crucial, communicate indirectly, and avoid open conflict (McFadden & Smith, 2004, pp. 41–42). In Appalachia, outsiders are those "from off" (p. 184), and range from do-gooders, exploiters, tourists and those born elsewhere; for women administrators, outsider status comes with being female, minority, or of a faith other than Protestant.
3. Jesse Helms' successful 1984 Senate campaign in North Carolina was famously against "the homosexuals, labor unions, those militant feminists, all of them…" (Reed, 1993, p 169). And since then the Democratic Party's core supports include conservationists, feminists, public school teachers, and those promoting social programs (Reed, 1993, p. 208).
4. "Rethinking Schools began as a local effort to address problems such as basal readers, standardized testing, and textbook-dominated curriculum. Since its founding in 1986, it has grown into a nationally prominent publisher of educational materials…. Most importantly, it remains

firmly committed to equity and to the vision that public education is central to the creation of a humane, caring, multiracial democracy" (http://www.rethinkingschools.org/index.shtml).

5. "Teach For America is the national corps of outstanding recent college graduates of all academic majors who commit two years to teach in urban and rural public schools and become leaders in the effort to expand educational opportunity" (http://www.teachforamerica.org/).

6. Details of the study's methodology are shared in chapter 8.

7. Although GLBT (or LGBT) is most commonly used as a descriptor, MacGillivray and Kozik-Rosabal (2000) argue that "GLBTQ is currently the most inclusive term used to refer to non-heterosexual people in all of the various identities," with Q requiring the inclusion of queer. They continue: "The term *homosexual* is not a preferred term for GLBTQ people because many consider it to be exclusionary and too clinical. The term *gay* was once considered to apply to all nonheterosexual people but is now used mainly to refer to gay men. The term *lesbian* refers to women who are affectionately (emotionally) and sexually attracted to other women. *Bisexual* people identify as being attracted to both sexes.... *Transgendered* is a broad term that has little to do with sexual orientation and more to do with gender identity. It refers to people whose gender identity as a man, woman, or somewhere in between does not correspond with their genetic sex (female or male). *Queer* and *questioning* are lumped together under Q for simplicity's sake but entail very different identifications. *Questioning* refers to those individuals who are not comfortable claiming a sexual orientation identity, be they gay, straight, or somewhere in between.... The term *queer* is being reclaimed by the younger generation of GLBTQ people and is considered to be more inclusive in that it includes all nonheterosexual people, and is also considered to be empowering" (pp. 288–289).

8. "No person in the United States shall, on the basis of sex, be excluded from participation in, be denied the benefits of, or be subjected to discrimination under any education program or activity receiving Federal financial assistance" (http://www.usdoj.gov/crt/cor/coord/titleixstat. htm).

9. Chapters 2 through 6 are developed from the broader Activist Educators research project from which Hood, Jones, Legrand, and Walters completed research in completion of requirements for the doctorate in Educational Administration. For more information about the studies that produced these chapters, see the following dissertations: Hood (2005), Walters (2004), Jones (2005), and Legrand, (2005). Please note that during the course of the activist educator project Annice Hood became Annice Williams. Her chapter 2 in this text is listed as Annice H. Williams; however, citations in that chapter as well as chapter 7 also reference her dissertation research (Hood, 2005).

2

The Fight of Their Lives

African American Activist Educators

ANNICE H. WILLIAMS

I thought, in my ignorance, that I understood Black children, that I knew what they needed, and how to teach them, and I just really thought I was for all children and that I could make a difference.... I felt so overwhelmed by all the needs, I almost felt like, "I cannot do this. This is impossible." But then I had to realize that if was going to be, it was up to me and if I truly believe that all kids can learn, then I was going to have to do the work and help my teachers buy into it or I needed to leave. So I decided I would give it the best fight of my life. (Hood, 2004, p. 78)

This quotation mirrors my life. All my life, I have been taught by elders in my family, community, and church that I have an obligation to others of my race to be a success and use the advantages gained to help other African Americans. In my professional career as first a teacher, and later, a building level administrator, I have encountered many others who seem to embrace that expectation. The statement of the elementary school principal quoted above is an example of the shared level of passion for the fate of African American schoolchildren. The present climate of accountability focused on students of all demographic descriptions reaching equal academic standards provides a potentially supportive context for African American educators who are committed to seeing children of their race achieve. Gaining greater insight into the lived experiences of activist educators may build awareness of the potential aids and dilemmas they encountered, which could, in turn, build support and reduce perceptions of isolation for these educators.

Framing Their Stories

My study was conceptualized from the literature of Black activism, as well as the literatures mentioned in chapter 1 on identity theory, social movements, and educator careers. Identity influences include being African American or being an educator, and one's identity affects decisions about action and degree of involvement in community work or professional roles. These actions have direct results on achievement of goals for professional success, for changing society, and also on the personal life of an activist educator.

I found limited information about my specific question regarding the impact of activist participation on the careers of African American educators in my search of the literature. Our overall project and the literatures summarized in chapter 1 in the areas of identity and social movement participation widened my exploration. My study focused first on Black activism, and then narrowed specifically to the activism of African American educators. I did find literature on factors impacting the development of educators' careers and on Black educators' lives potentially impacted by activist participation.

African American Identity, Culture, and Class

I ventured to explore how the African American activist educators at the center of this study identified themselves and how their identities impacted their activist lives. Did it affect how they grew within or developed activism? Perhaps they even hid or avoided it. Theories and literature informed my endeavor.

Racial identity can be conceptualized psychologically or culturally (Hall, 1996; Helms, 1990). Helms (1990) described racial identity as "a sense of a group or collective identity based on one's perception that he or she shares a common racial heritage with a particular racial group" (p. 3). Hall (1996) pointed out that identity is socially and culturally constructed by defining the self through difference from others. Much of the research around the racial identity of African Americans has focused on individuals' feelings about membership in that race (Broman, Neighbors, & Jackson, 1988; Demo & Hughes, 1990; Gurin, Miller, & Gurin, 1980). According to Tatum (1997), the development of a racial identity is "the process of defining for oneself the personal significance and social meaning of belonging to a particular racial group" (p. 16).

One characteristic associated with African American racial identity is a cultural standard of unity and group survival against a backdrop of class difference. From slavery, to the time when W.E.B. Dubois and Booker T. Washington debated the best way to elevate "the race," up through the present, there has been and continues to be a clear social expectation amongst Blacks that they will stick together to elevate the social, economic, and political position of African Americans as a collective (Dawson, 1994; Gilkes, 1980: Ginwright, 2002; Higginbotham & Weber, 1992; Lawson, 1992; Peterson, 1992). The imperative to work for the common good consistently appears within the narratives and life histories of African American educators and community workers (Gilkes, 1983; Higginbotham & Weber, 1992; McDonald, 1997; Peterson, 1992). Higginbotham and Weber (1992) found that upwardly mobile Black women felt a much more significant responsibility to give back to their families and communities than their White counterparts.

This long-standing norm presents an interesting contrast to the more recent development of a substantial Black middle class and growing economic polarization between middle-class and poor Blacks (Dawson, 1994; Lawson, 1992). Researchers have begun to ask whether race continues to be the primary group identification for Blacks, particularly in terms of political behavior, or if class has emerged as the most salient factor in social and political decision making (Dawson, 1994; Landry, 1987; Wilson, 1980). As the class stratifications in the Black community increase, paradigms for political action also diverge. In a longitudinal study of previously low-income Black student activists who later became middle class, Tripp (as cited in Ginwright, 2002) noted an ideological shift to more conservative models of community action: "Volunteering in after school programs, mentoring youth, or joining Black civic organizations were social change strategies that did not call into question fundamental beliefs about economic inequality and poverty" (p. 549). The tendency toward less risky action to support the race highlights the ongoing question of the significance of race versus class for middle-class African Americans.

What about class? Scholarship that emphasizes activities and interests of African American teachers refers frequently to the responsibility to others within the race, but reflects little of the race versus class identity conflict, a possible indicator that race still dominates as the primary identification, at least amongst Black educators. Some of the African American teachers interviewed by Casey (1993) described their choice to become teachers as a function of this obligation to the community and race. I expected that a similar emphasis on racial identity for the educators in my sample would be reflected in their statements regarding their reasons for participating in race-related causes. My research focused on African American educators apart from their class status because the nature of their work makes them political actors by default (which may or may not be the case for those in other professions).

Black Activism

The history of Black activism is often conceptualized as if it began with the Montgomery, Alabama, bus boycotts in the mid-1950s. However, collective action in a variety of forms amongst African Americans to improve the socio-political status of the race can be traced as far back as the late 1700s. In 1787, the Free African Society of Philadelphia, the first Black protest organization of record, was established to challenge the social injustices suffered by Blacks, such as discriminatory poll taxes, denial of educational opportunities, and brutality (Brisbane, 1974). Over time, strategies for protest became more organized and extensive, with a continued focus on gaining political power, civil rights, and economic opportunities. In the early 1900s, Black nationalist groups such as the National Association for the Advancement of Colored People (NAACP) emerged with mixed levels of effectiveness and longevity.

The time period from 1954 to 1970 is widely recognized as the most dynamic era of Black activism in the United States as the civil rights movement changed American society (Brisbane, 1974; Williams, 1987). The groups seeking equality for Black citizens during the time of the civil rights movement varied in structure, style, and priorities. The NAACP was highly organized and mobilized significant support as it used institutional means to effect social change. Other organizations, including the Southern Christian Leadership Conference (SCLC) and the Student Nonviolent Coordinating Committee (SNCC), had less emphasis on organizational structure and used extrainstitutional methods such as protests, boycotts, freedom rides, and sit-ins to pursue their goals (Williams, 1987). As the struggle for equality for African Americans grew longer, opponents of these goals became more violent, which catalyzed the emergence of a more radical form of Black activism.

During the late 1960s, existing groups transformed and new organizations developed as many African American activists focused on the ideology of militant Black nationalism, believing that force was the only type of action that would be recognized and responded to by institutional opponents. Many of the events that grew out of this belief system were simply events of parallel, rather than collective action, however; as this philosophy spread, subgroups of previously nonviolent social movement organizations such SNCC and the Congress of Racial Equality (CORE) adopted strategies of armed self-defense (Brisbane, 1974; Umoja, 1999). The revolutionary phase of Black activism was volatile, and received national attention, but its momentum was not sustained over time. In the 1970s, pursuit of political involvement and academic change became more noted forms of activism. As the numbers of Blacks elected to office increased, these officials established movement organizations to pursue political goals in the interest of African Americans. While politicians were pressing for greater representation in local, state, and federal offices, students were pressing for greater representation in the curriculum. The proliferation of Black studies courses in colleges and universities during this time was the direct result of demonstrations, strikes, and other activities by Black student organizations on many campuses. Political participation, academic involvement, and community work have continued to be popular forms of activism into the present time (Ginwright, 2002). So, I wondered, how did this history affect Black educators' activism?

Black Women's Community Work

One present form of Black activism detailed in the literature is community work. It is often described as an outcome of the obligation of middle-class Blacks to uplift the race (Dillard, 1995; Ginwright, 2002; Higginbotham & Weber, 1992).

Although the historical expectation to take care of the race is generalized frequently as pertaining to all Blacks, research describing the present manifestation of this belief frequently focuses on the activities of females (Cannon, 1988; Davis, 1989; Gilkes, 1980; Higginbotham & Weber, 1992; Naples, 1992; Peterson, 1992). Cheryl Townsend Gilkes (1983) used the phrase "going up for the oppressed," a biblical reference, to label occupational and professional mobility for the community. Her research highlighted Black women's "creative use of professional mobility" as they perform the political actions of trying to change the systems within which they work. The African American educators within the current study are similar to such human services professionals in that they impact the quality of life of the students they serve and are likely to be acting politically to change the systems in which they work. The analyses of Black women's work for the race connect to the present question, since K-12 education is still a field disproportionately staffed by women. So, I wondered, how do the factors that drive African American women to participate in community correspond with those that cause their counterparts in education to participate in race-related activities?

Black Educators

One enduring goal of Black activists that has continued into the present has been the pursuit of educational opportunities for African Americans. Given the assertion of Ginsburg et al. (1995) that educating is a political endeavor and the historical expectation that African Americans work for the benefit of their race, a potential area of activism for Black educators is the attempt to increase the success of Black students in public schools. A much-publicized educational concern in the United States is the achievement gap between Caucasian students and minority students, particularly African Americans. This gap, which narrowed rapidly in the 1970s to late 1980s, shortly after desegregation, has now stabilized and does not appear to be changing significantly, other than in isolated pockets (Hilliard, 1991; Johnston & Viadero, 2000; Singham, 1998). Consequently, there has been much research, often by African Americans, on strategies to eliminate this difference. One example is Ladson-Billings's (1995) model of "culturally relevant pedagogy" which "helps students to accept and affirm their cultural identity while developing critical perspectives that challenge inequities the schools (and other institutions) perpetuate" (p. 469).

The focus on African American student success connects to the career trajectories of minority educators. The increasing significance of accountability in student achievement can be seen in the proliferation of conferences, meetings, workshops, and organizations aimed at expanding culturally relevant pedagogical practices to educators of all backgrounds and closing the achievement gap between White students and minority students. Ortiz (1982) and others found that minority educators tended to ascend into specialized programs rather than more central roles within schools and systems. So, I wondered, in what ways was this so for the participants in my study and what other factors may have impacted their involvement?

Honing from the Literatures to this Research

This background of theory and research provided a rich context for my study. The lives and work of African American activist educators like the participants in my study have not been previously addressed in these related literatures. Investigations of Black activism tend to focus on the lives and activities of political or social participants working for the improved social status of their race. Literature about African American educators also reflects similar reasons for entering the profession. Thus, studying their efforts to support others of a similar ethnic background as activism meant having them relate their experiences, purposes for action, and resulting consequences.

Thus, my research had two purposes, asking: What are the influences that drive some African American educators to participate in race-based activism? How does this participation impact their careers? I embarked upon this project to learn about people like me: African American educators believing themselves to be required to directly impact the academic success of African American children, who carefully chose or designed strategies to achieve this goal while appearing politically acceptable to superiors, and therefore, able to maintain upward career mobility. I suspected that there were numerous "undercover activists" lurking amongst the professional ranks, dancing gingerly between fulfilling the expectations of their race and the requirements of their contracts.

Overview of Methodology

To answer these questions, I used a qualitative research design to elicit participants' experiences through their stories and the meanings they make of them. Chapter 8 has a detailed account of the methodological process for the overarching project that explores the lives of activist educators with wide-ranging involvements, but a brief description of the sample follows.

Targeted respondents for this study were African American educators involved in race-based activism. All respondents had worked in the field of education for seven or more years. To uncover possible career impacts over an extended period of time, it was important to have respondents with greater career longevity. Table 2.1 lists the 10 participants and their attributes. The participants were all African Americans who were either employed full-time as professional public school educators or retired from such a career. All were involved in activities aimed at achieving social justice for others of their race during their careers. The sample included respondents from areas with different percentages of African Americans in the population. By doing so, I sought to illuminate additional barriers or supports that may have been experienced while engaging in race-related activities in varied communities and to focus on demographic diversity in a purposeful manner, as required by the larger project.

The results describe the work lives of these educators and offer insight into supports and barriers experienced by other activist educators with similar involvements, such as work on behalf of other minority groups or people of lower socioeconomic status. Some of the findings regarding driving forces and limitations may not be as easily generalized to the lives of activist educators involved in other causes that are associated with more controversial topics; for example, the rights of lesbian, gay, bisexual, and transgendered (LGBT) persons or those promoting women's reproductive rights (as depicted in chapters 5 and 6).

Inspired by Spirit, Hiding from Shadows

Hearing the stories of the participants was quite a pleasure, as I was able to personally connect with the experiences they shared. My background as a Black educator facilitated entry and elicited responsiveness from the participants. One of the greatest challenges I faced in data collection was to avoid inserting too much of myself and my personal experiences into the interviews. Over and

Table 2.1 Participant Data

Pseudonym	Age	Gender	Most Recent Position	Years in Education	Region	Percent African–American[a,b]
Andrea	37	Female	Assistant Principal	8	Southeast	27.8
Cheryl	40	Female	Principal	17	Southeast	32.7
Diane	49	Female	Teacher	29	Northeast	64.3
Earl	50	Male	Central Office Administrator	36	Southeast	27.8
Edward	50	Male	Central Office Administrator	30	Southeast	27.8
Ernest	60	Male	Superintendent	40+	Mid-Atlantic	44.1
Keisha	33	Female	Central Office Administrator	10	Southeast	27.8
Rhonda	32	Female	Assistant Principal	11	Mid-Atlantic	19.0
Richard	65	Male	State Office Administrator	47	Southeast	21.6
Sharon	43	Female	Central Office Administrator	20	North-west	1.1

[a] US Census data from 2000 giving percentages for population of the city or county in which the school district was located.
[b] This number represents the percentage of African Americans in the state.

over, I heard experiences that triggered thoughts from my life and career. The origins of this project were quite personal to me, and as it progressed it became even more so.

As I stepped back to analyze the data, three threads of inspiration for the educators' activism emerged that intertwined in varied patterns to create a unique activist identity for each of the participants. These primary patterns were race and culture, family and community, and spiritual connections. I expected the first two pairs of driving forces experienced by the educators from my review of the literature. As noted above, research describes racial and cultural beliefs that Black people, particularly those in the middle class, have a duty to uplift others of their race (Gilkes, 1983; Higginbotham & Weber, 1992; McDonald, 1997; Peterson, 1992). Elements of family and community were also relevant components of identity for these educators in their activist decisions. The interaction of race, culture, family, community, and other factors created in each of the educators what I identified as an activist identity, which influenced their activist choices through a continuing process of identity construction and reconstruction (della Porta & Diani, 1999).

In this chapter I will focus on the surprises. First, the aspect of identity that I did not originally seek to analyze, but was raised by some of my participants, was that of spirituality. Spirituality was not addressed in the review of the literature, nor directly investigated in the interview, but it surfaced in several of the conversations as a meaningful component in the commitment to race-related activism. Along with my search for factors that drive African American activist educators, I also sought to illuminate the impact of their efforts on their work lives. Their stories told of contextual barriers, perceived risks, and of strategies they devised to modify their positions or careers to achieve their activist goals. Though committed to improving the school experiences and lives of Black students, they encountered barriers to their desired forms of activism in the arena of public schools. Some of the participants described perceptions of the potential damage that activism could cause to their careers. The limits of their actions evidenced the impact of their assumptive worlds on their professional behavior (Marshall & Mitchell, 1991). Many of the educators addressed such constraints and dilemmas by performing and extending their job responsibilities in ways that helped them accomplish their activist goals, echoing the political nature of the education career described in chapter 1's review of the literature. A few of the educators even went so far as to make their careers activist, strategically placing themselves in positions that allowed them to work for the cause of African American students as their assigned job responsibility, a possible explanation for earlier findings regarding the movement of minorities into and through administration (Ortiz, 1982; Valverde & Brown, 1988). The educators took such great care to make their activist efforts fit their context, and thereby avoid risking elements of their career; however, none of them shared examples of any of the perceived risks becoming reality for them. Through their stories, the African American activist educators communicated portraits of careers carefully crafted to fulfill their activist missions, while evading risks that were not evidenced to exist.

Inspired by Spirit

The role of religion emerged as an unanticipated and noteworthy factor in the activist inspirations of nearly half of the participants in the study. Although the interview protocol (see appendix A for a copy of the protocol) did not specifically reference religious beliefs or background, four of the educators mentioned their faith as a source of drive or support in their activist pursuits. It is quite possible that this number would have been greater, had even one question directly referred to the relationship between their spiritual lives and their activist lives.

The church is one of the strongest and most enduring institutions of the African American community (Sudarkasa, 1997). From the arrival of the first Africans in America, religious participation has been a place of resistance to social domination, even if only in the minds of slaves (Pipes, 1997). During the civil rights movement, Southern churches were centers of movement organization and activity, and pastors filled significant leadership roles (Morris, 1984). Recent scholarship on the relationship of the Black church to Black activism has focused on the impact of church participation on political activism (Brown & Brown, 2003).

The words of the educators included in the present research illuminated their personal spiritual beliefs as inspiration and support for their activism. When Richard was describing how he was able to minimize conflicts that might result from activism, he expressed his drive this way, "You have a mission, almost like a ministry that you do." He also framed the significance of activism in the context of religion:

> I see activism as a moral obligation to anyone who is enlightened enough to understand his or her surroundings. You are morally obligated. It is almost religion as far as I'm concerned, to enlighten whomever you can when you come into contact with them and then you are civilly obligated to do it....

Earl likened his efforts to stimulate parent involvement to sermons, saying:

> In any area that I find myself, I find that I become a kind of advocate for parents becoming involved in their children's education. I kind of, I preach it sometimes, my wife says, just to get people to understand that it's not just the teachers and the principals or whatever.

Rhonda also used the language of her faith to describe her actions in her position as an elementary school assistant principal, basing her model of "servant leadership" on the life of Jesus:

I don't teach students anymore, so I have to use my role to create the best possible opportunity for their teachers to motivate, encourage, and inspire them. It's my job to remove all the barriers that will hinder that teacher in educating that child. Even if those barriers are within that teacher or her classroom, I'm responsible for doing all I can to support her and help her get what she needs to succeed with all children. That's being a servant leader. Even though I'm in authority, I have to "wash the feet," so to speak, of the people I lead. You know, like Christ did for the disciples.

Another assistant principal, Andrea, portrayed her religious beliefs as her encouragement to return to and remain in the field of education. After a brief legal career, she found herself challenged to decide which profession would provide her the opportunity to have the greatest impact on African American youth:

I actually went on a sabbatical for a few days, in the mountains…I went to a little retreat, a place where there were no telephones and no TV's and I went up into the mountains and went into deep prayer and meditation. That was what helped me to make the choice to come back into education so that I could have a more active role and impact in the lives on the lives of young people.

Once back in the field of education, her faith was critical to her survival in an environment unreceptive to her activist priorities:

There are days when I feel very…my heart is heavy, like I'm fighting an uphill battle. It's during those times that I retreat into my office, and I've got my devotion book in desk drawer. So my faith is a real source of strength when dealing with some of these issues. My upbringing, my faith, and my personal background are what I go to, to keep me strong.

Like Andrea, Diane faced a challenging school environment, although it was the circumstances of the students that caused her to draw on her beliefs. When asked if she had experienced conflicts in activist efforts, she stated,

I guess I have conflict with the separation of church and state. I say that because one year, I had five or six hyperactive children in one class and one little boy, in less than a month, had witnessed his mother's murder and her boyfriend's suicide. I had him and some other challenges in the classroom, so I had to bow my head and pray many times.

Richard, Andrea, and two other participants not quoted in this section all briefly mentioned church participation when listing activities in which they were involved. The comments, such as "I participate in a tutoring program at my church," hinted at the church as a potential arena for activism, but did not reveal any significant impact of church participation on their activist drive. The contrast between the importance of their individual beliefs and their church involvement suggests the personal nature of the influence of spirituality on activism. For these educators, their church participation provided a possible arena for activism, but their individual spiritual beliefs were an influential part of their inspiration and activist choices in their education careers.

This section highlights four significant facets of the impetus for involvement of African American activist educators, race and culture, family, community, and spirituality on their self-conceptualization as activists. These activist identities impacted, and were constructed and reconstructed by, their activist choices. The career outcomes of the activists' participation are detailed in the following section.

Hiding from Shadows

This project was birthed from my internal struggle to decide how activist I could be in my efforts to impact the lives of African American students without adversely impacting my long-term goal of becoming a district superintendent. As my wondering was cultivated into research, I became even more convinced that African American activist educators like me were going to great lengths to make their efforts fit the social and political expectations of their positions. My analysis of the data confirmed that the participants also experienced constraints and dilemmas as they attempted to fulfill their activist missions within the politicized context of public education (Ginsburg et al., 1995). The political context of public education was an important factor in many of their approaches to action. Half of the participants made comments specifically referring to the difficulty of being political while being an educator. Richard described it, saying, "Education has not been a favorable environment from which to create activism. There are too many restrictions." Most often, the educators addressed the inherent problems by finding means of further integrating their activism into their work lives. They did this by making positions activist, and some by making even their careers activist. Of interest is that for all these efforts, I did not find evidence that these educators had ever personally experienced any negative consequences to their careers. They were able to detail the risks they feared, but did not note actual occurrences.

Perception of Risks to Career

Attempting to be activists in the education career posed professional risks for the educators. For the more experienced educators, it was less of a consideration than for those in the middle of their careers; however, all recognized the potential dangers. Those who had gained some upward mobility, but were not yet near retirement referred to such threats most frequently. As the educators described their past, present, and potential activism, a bell curve pattern of concern emerged, represented in Figure 2.1. Periods of lesser anxiety about negative career impacts

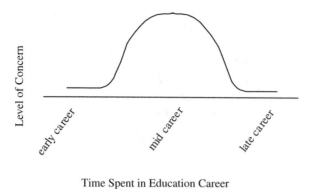

Time Spent in Education Career

Figure 2.1 Continuum of level of concern about risk to career.

occurred at the beginning and end of the educators' work lives, with times of greater worry near the middle. Midcareer professionals indicated that they were concerned about threats to their credibility, security, and mobility.

Credibility

One priority articulated by the educators was sustaining their credibility in their respective positions. Three of the activists talked about being very cautious in their speech and actions to avoid jeopardizing their effectiveness. Andrea, who had returned to education from a legal career, was particularly sensitive to the potential effects of activism on her career:

> Clearly, we have ethical and professional considerations as administrators that prevent us from being able to espouse certain political and ideological ideas in a situation where we're in a leadership role.... In a different life and career…the time may come when I'll be very outspoken about some things that right now I'm just kind of dealing with the way that I can.

Edward also reflected on the need to protect his professional life by monitoring his involvements, even outside of his position. He stated,

> I have to realize first that I am an educator. I am a public servant. I am paid by taxpayers. So I have to keep that in mind when I serve on community type of boards and committees. That is, I can't speak out sometimes, as I would feel that I should speak out, because people don't see me as just a community person. They see me as an educational leader. So whatever I say is generally taken to my profession more than to my community. So I have to be always conscious in whatever I say, because I can't let all my feelings come out in what I say.

Cheryl chose to follow her conscience in monitoring her weighing the risks of her speech:

> I have learned that I'm going to be forced to make choices that I'm going to have to learn to live with. And sometimes I want to speak, but I don't speak for fear of repercussions. And there are other times when, regardless of repercussions, I have to speak.

While discussing her involvement with an African American professional organization, Cheryl mentioned the issue of credibility as one of the uncertainties that affected the participation of her colleagues and her superintendent:

> My work with [a local professional organization for African American educators], has been primarily in building membership because we're in the South, and some of us are reticent about being involved in anything that is going to appear to be too socially radical, especially educators…I don't think you can do it—because even our superintendent, or any other superintendent, if he was seen as too Black, he would never be able to do his job effectively. Every statement he made would be judged on the criteria, "Is he saying that because he wants XYZ for Black people or his Black kids?"

Security

Even the least experienced participants in this research sampling had established stable careers, and, as noted above, the project included only educators with greater than seven years of experience. Job security was a concern expressed by three of the four least experienced participants. As Rhonda explained:

> I think the farther you move up the ladder, the more you have to lose. When I taught, I had more leeway, because you can do a lot in your classroom without anybody noticing, especially if your kids are performing by the end, which mine did. Now that I am an AP, I'm less vocal and more [pause] surreptitious about whatever I attempt to do. I have to frame it so I don't look like I'm trying to help Black kids. I am, and I'm not ashamed of that, but there are many people who perceive that as trying to hinder White kids, which is just not true. I can't afford for that perception to be created.

Cheryl perceived her lack of tenure, which was not available to principals in her system, as an additional constraint to her activism. When asked if she was an activist, she spoke directly to the issue of jeopardizing her career, saying,

> I hope so. I've learned. I think you change. I think you're just very idealistic when you're young. But when you could take a chance on losing a 20-year career or whatever the case may be, I think you become much more careful. I wouldn't say that's true for everyone, but I think it's made me more careful.

In contrast, Keisha had retained her tenure status from her teaching career, but still felt her central office position could be affected by missteps in her activist pursuits: "I could get myself in a lot of trouble, if given the opportunity. I have tenure, but I know that life could be made miserable if I continued on a pathway of just questioning people."

Of the more experienced educators, only Ernest mentioned job security, but not in the same way as the younger participants. He stated that he was aware of the risks, but had not allowed such issues to impact his approach to addressing issues during his career:

> The reason I could do that was because I felt I could get a job somewhere else. I think I looked at it different from most people. When I earned a dollar, it doesn't make a difference whether it comes from the garbage truck or the school system, the man at the grocery store still wants a dollar to pay for the bread. That's a philosophy you have to have. That comes with experience and time.

He acknowledged that other educators might not share this same attitude, but explained that he was able to tolerate a higher degree of risk:

> You also have to think about the personal and professional when it comes to taking stands. If you're seeking upward mobility, you might want to keep your mouth quiet, so that it won't become an issue for you. I have some buddies who wouldn't say a thing. That's not me. You will have to respect me as an individual. I have to feed my family, but I don't have to feed them from here.

Mobility

A third possible career risk faced by activists was limitation of mobility. Research on the careers of minority educators indicates that socialization processes serve to hinder the career advancement of minorities into and up through administration (Ortiz, 1982). From the inception of the idea that led to this study, I anticipated that activism around issues of race might interfere with the progress of African Americans through the education career, but only one participant mentioned it explicitly as a concern. Cheryl spoke of her fears that her activism would or had already hindered her upward or lateral mobility from her position as a principal of a high-poverty elementary school:

> Well, I can say, that I wonder now what impact it will have on me moving up to any role beyond the principalship, because if I've made the wrong person angry, they could stop my career cold, and I'll never know it. I wonder if it now means that I won't be appointed to any other schools that don't look just like mine, because you can be so good at doing something that people forget that you have other talents. Even if I applied for a transfer,

to get closer to my own home, for instance, if he has to choose between principals, and Cheryl is the one who works with the poor kids and she does such a good job with those little babies, then an opportunity to work at very affluent school, Black, White, or otherwise, may not come to me. So I wonder about that, too.

The educators were sensitive to the career risks posed by their activism, regardless of whether they had actually experienced repercussions. For most of them, the perceived risks impacted the form, frequency, and arena of their involvement activist choices, particularly during the middle of their careers.

Making Connections: How Do the Findings Expand from Earlier Literatures to Educators' Lives?

My study focused on a subset of activists who may not always be immediately recognized as such. The African American activist educators at the center of this project may represent an almost invisible population of activists who have been working diligently throughout their careers to fulfill their perceived cultural, community, and spiritual duty to elevate the status of African American students and colleagues. As explored in chapter 1, these submerged networks maintain the energy and momentum of a movement even when that movement has a lower public profile. Prior research considers these educators from various perspectives. For those who are teachers, there has been analysis of their pedagogy. Administrators can find scholarship relevant to their leadership styles and career patterns. Substantial literature is also available to describe the significance of race and class for middle-class African Americans and how those identities intersect to impact their social and political action. I viewed 10 African American educators using a lens through which they clearly saw themselves, though it had been little used by others, by investigating their experiences as educators. I then explored how they could and did engage in activism around issues of race.

Of special interest is my finding that the educators' activist identities were shaped by race and culture, family, community, and spirituality. Another finding of note was how their work lives were distinguished by contextual barriers, perceived risks, and strategies to modify their positions, and, in some cases, even their careers, to achieve their activist goals.

Born of Race, Rooted in Faith

Their identity impacted the choices of these activists on multiple levels. Being African American or being people of faith inspired them to act. Those identities also interacted with each other and additional variables to create in each educator a perception of himself or herself as an activist.

African American racial and cultural identity was important to all participants, which was expected since race was a key factor in the sampling process. Earlier scholarship indicates a strong racial and cultural impetus for the social action of African American educators (Gilkes, 1983; Ginwright, 2002; Higginbotham & Weber, 1992; McDonald, 1997; Peterson, 1992), a conclusion supported and extended by this study. The participants all made comments that directly reflected their awareness of ideology suggesting that upwardly mobile Blacks have a duty to work for the uplift of others of their race.

Spiritual beliefs surfaced as a surprising and important aspect of the drive of almost half of the activist educators. It was quite meaningful because interviews did not directly investigate religion. Based on the number of times spirituality was mentioned without prompting, it is reasonable to predict that additional participants would have also referred to similar influences had they been asked directly about their faith and its impact on their activism. Prior research related to religion and Black activism focuses more on the role of the church and church attendance in the participation of African Americans in political processes (Brown & Brown, 2003). The activists who referenced religion mentioned their participation in church, but spoke more significantly of the influence of their own spiritual beliefs, indicating that the role of faith in activism is far more personal than merely the practice of attending church.

Hiding Activism

The dearth of research framing these African American activist educators as such may be partly a result of the perceived need for great discretion when attempting to effect social and political change within the field of education. Though Ginsburg et al. (1995) declared that educators are political actors by default, educator working conditions do not appear to encourage or promote political action, at least not in the minds of the educators wishing to act. Nearly all of the educators included in this study identified themselves as activists, but they also described barriers and risks that served to shape their activism in significant ways. Their dedication to their activist aims pushed them to find ways to alter their assigned work to accomplish their activist goals, a strategy Jones (2005) referred to as *activising*.

The educators believed there were professional risks associated with activism, although very few of them described experiencing specific instances of such risks. Of all the participants who mentioned the possibility of jeopardizing or losing their careers because of activist missteps, none had actually experienced such a problem. One principal wondered if she might be hindered in the future pursuit of other positions, but had not yet tested her theory. This presents an interesting paradox for consideration in future research. The activists were convinced that they could damage their careers, yet they offered no empirical evidence to reinforce that belief. One possibility is that the activists were so skilled at maneuvering within the educational system while being activist that they were able to avoid placing their careers at risk. Another possibility is that they have an exaggerated perception of the risks associated with their style of activism. My methodological intention—to explore *their* meaning-making—leaves these questions up in the air, for further investigation and discussion.

Still, the greatest impacts of involvement in race-related activism on the careers of Black educators appeared to come mostly from the educators' own calculations and choices. They modified their day-to-day work through the process of activising in response to their experience of the education field as a difficult climate in which to practice activism and their perception of professional risks that could occur. Most respondents spoke in terms of choosing positions at least to a degree to achieve their activist goals. Two respondents had activised not only their jobs, but also their careers by accepting only positions that were partly or completely comprised of the work to which they were committed. This pattern supplements and may even challenge the conclusion of Ortiz (1982) that educators from marginalized groups do not have similar chances for involvement in activities leading to more mainstream socialization as do nonminority male administrators. Analyzing the career patterns of self-identified African American activist educators could offer additional insight into why some minorities tend to receive administrative positions through nontraditional paths and narrowly focused programs that do not lead to higher-level leadership. Deploying an activist model for analysis of Black educators' career patterns could reveal an intentional component to the seemingly stunted career paths of some African American educators.

Implications for Education

While this investigation included only a small sample, the experiences of the educators indicate that much work needs to be done to change the image and the reality of the politics of the field of K-12 public education. There is a federal emphasis on helping students of every demographic group to achieve; yet activists who have a similar mission go to great lengths to keep their aims undercover. Rather than networking with and mobilizing likeminded educators, they avoid overt organizing. Their fear of negative career impacts has made them so good at appearing not to be activists that they are not able to access support and reinforcement to minimize threats to their careers. Further, the development of an activist image has implications for recruiting idealistic young African American educators who may be seeking encouragement to involve themselves in social change.

One implication of this study connects to the theoretical framework of a critical race theory of education. The experiences of the participants indicate that race matters, at least for the African American educators who were interviewed. Critical race analyses of education critique the embedded standards of whiteness within schooling from the perspective of the impact on students (Solórzano, 1998; Yosso, 2002). Extending this analysis to a focus on the perspective of educators may better illuminate their experiences. The care with which the activists executed their activism within their careers points toward the existence of a larger contextual issue that makes involvement in race-related activism risky, such as institutional racism. As detailed in chapter 1, the framework for this project did not include a critical race theory of education as a foundation. Reframing from this viewpoint may offer additional explanation for the educators' belief that being too political, and particularly too Black, would be detrimental to their career effectiveness, security, or mobility. If future research points toward institutional racism as a likely cause for the perceived jeopardy to African American activist educators, that would continue to highlight the necessity of social change.

Within the field, African American activist educators need strategies for support and networking. Despite federal policy demanding achievement, African American educators see it as risky to openly focus on African American students. Their actions are more diffuse, avoiding joint action, one of the five key elements of social movements offered by McAdam and Snow (1997). They stated, "...it is important to keep in mind that the unit of reference is a collectivity—that is, a group of interrelated persons engaged in joint actions—rather than an aggregate of persons acting in parallel but disconnected fashion" (p. xxi). Organizations such the National Alliance of Black School Educators (NABSE) bring African American activist educators together, but joint action is more likely to take place at the local level, where educators are more wary of being identified as part of a group that may attract negative impacts.

Greater organization at the local level might also serve to reduce the perception of risk associated with activist behavior, which was a limiting factor for some of the activists. If activists had more opportunities to talk with other activists and were more aware of what problems, and what successes, had actually been experienced by others within their network, they might feel less inhibited in their actions. Networking locally could lead to sharing of strategies, greater collaboration, easing of personal and career dilemmas, and greater social justice achievements.

Finally, with policy makers and recruiters searching for African American educators, it would make sense to identify motivations that might be nontraditional. There is a tendency within public education to attempt to achieve equality by ignoring distinguishing characteristics like racial identity and religious beliefs, but the activists within this project reflected that those distinctions were central to their decision to get involved. Emphasizing the social justice aspects of religion may be a useful strategy for recruiting educator activists. Expanding the discourse of educational leadership to incorporate and build on the tendency within the African American culture to connect spirituality to matters of social justice could support Black educators as they seek integration of their career aspirations and their identities (Dantley, 2005). By drawing on those valued aspects of identity, change organizations and schools may be able to expand the ranks of educators willing to work for change.

Areas for Future Research

The actions and experiences of African American activist educators have not been adequately investigated. This study highlights the lack of discourse regarding the experiences of Black educators who consider themselves social justice workers on behalf of Black children. There is a need for greater acknowledgment and analysis of this contingent of activists. These invisible activists must be revealed and understood to ultimately enhance the outcomes of their work on behalf of children and colleagues.

One area for future research is simply further investigation of African American activist educators. While they clearly identified themselves as activists, little, if any, research exists characterizing them as such. Literature regarding activism typically places activists within social movements, which does not reflect the experiences of these educators and other activists who carry out their efforts as individuals. Framing their work from a perspective of activism may reveal additional supports, constraints, and dilemmas associated with their choices. Research is needed to create and expand the body of scholarly knowledge on these ignored activists, as well as to provide concrete examples for practitioners on strategies for leadership and change.

Future research into the lived experiences of educator activists around issues of race must seek to determine the roots of African American activist educators' perceptions of the risks associated with their choices. Given that the educators in this small sample were convinced of the existence of significant risks they had not experienced, it is imperative that there be inquiry into the origin of such thinking. Who or what is keeping the risks alive? Are the educators simply hanging on to memories of risks historically associated with Black activism? Are there elements of educator preparation and socialization that perpetuate these beliefs? Is there a broader social foundation for the idea of risks related to African American educator activism, such as institutionalized racism? The perception of career risks for Black educators and Black activist educators is another potential area of research. The risks described by the participants sound similar to issues of concern that, as an African American school administrator, I have heard expressed by my Black colleagues, particularly administrators. This suggests to me that the risks to educators' credibility, job security, and mobility may have more to do with being Black than with being a Black activist, or being an educator, rather than a lawyer. Further analysis may reveal whether such fears play out for other educator activists, or Black activists in other professions.

Another direction for research is into the spiritual inspirations of Black activists, including educator activists. Existing scholarship related to religion and Black activism emphasizes the impact of the church organization on political and social action. The results of this study suggest that, at least for African American activist educators, personal spiritual beliefs are far more meaningful in influencing individual's activist decisions than church participation. An extension of this strand of inquiry would include investigation into the impact of various religions on political and social action. The comments of the educators who mentioned their spirituality suggested that they were Christian, although that was not confirmed. Future research could compare and contrast the influence of different religious traditions on activist choices.

The results of this research demand further analysis of factors impacting minority career patterns. The careers and driving factors of African American educators who follow nontraditional paths through the ranks of administration must be investigated to determine whether the desire to fulfill activist goals can explain the movement of African Americans into special programs and schools with high percentages of minority students found by other scholars (Ortiz, 1982; Valverde & Brown, 1988). While the conclusions of my one doctoral dissertation are not sufficient to disprove existing scholarship in this area, the findings certainly present a reasonable potential explanation for the existing patterns. The words and stories, too, should present inspiration for activists and a challenge for well-intentioned policy makers.

One final area for future study is the impact of activist involvement on the personal lives of African American activist educators. While only one participant referenced an adverse career impact of activism, four people mentioned negative impacts on their relationships with their families or friends. It is possible that these activists are able to preserve their careers at the expense of their personal lives. This problem is worthy of study, but was not within in the scope of this research. It is my hope that future investigations of activism, education, and the work lives of people of color will meet at this intersection to further illuminate the lived experiences of African American activist educators.

3
Activist Women in Educational Leadership—How Likely?

SUSAN WALTERS

When I first began working in the public schools in the early 1970s as a new classroom teacher, it never occurred to me that I could be a building principal. In my experience, principals and superintendents were White males, and although I did not question my competence or ability to do a good job as a teacher or to take on and successfully complete any task assigned to me, I did not question the way things were nor imagine myself, or any other woman, as a principal. Since those early professional years, I have worked in many different schools, in different states, and in different positions. One thing I observed in all of my experiences is that men, usually White, were in education's leadership and management positions while women carried out the day-to-day work of educating children. In all those years, I never heard anyone really question the gender hierarchy, and it was not until the early 1990s that I worked in a building with a female principal. It was at that point that I decided that I wanted to go into administration and thought that I could.

I became part of the Activist Educators Research Project in January 2000 for two reasons. The first reason was to complete my doctoral dissertation; the second was to participate in a research project that really interested me. During my doctoral coursework and research, I began to question the number of female superintendents in North Carolina and then nationwide. This project offered me the opportunity to look beyond the numbers to consider the lives and experiences of the women behind the numbers—the richness and depth of their lived experiences and their identities as women at a time when society was rapidly changing. When I began this study of women in leadership positions in schools, I was interested in understanding if and how other women's experiences as educators were framed by the larger women's movement. As a result, I initially used social movement theory as the theoretical lens for studying women's experiences in education administration. In addition, research on women leaders in education was critical for building a schema for understanding the women and their experiences.

Initially, I chose not to include a thorough review of feminist literature in an effort to keep the study manageable. However, for this text, I brought in feminist theory as another lens for understanding the women in this story, for as I was developing this chapter, the implications of feminist theory as it related to the women in this study were powerful. None of the women in this study identified as strong feminists, nor could they have been considered passionate activists for women's rights. However, as this text makes clear, educators' activism differs from conventional definitions. All of the women in this study worked in quiet and subtle ways to encourage women to aspire to be whatever they wanted to be, to plant the seeds of confidence in women, and to validate and empower women as capable, competent leaders.

Women's Underrepresentation in Education Administration

As noted in chapter 1, women educators remain underrepresented in top leadership positions, and more political activism is needed if we are to effect change for women in the education system. The history and significance of this issue are well-documented in the literature and statistics on women in educational leadership. Early feminist research documented the underrepresentation of women in educational administration (Bell & Chase, 1993; Hansot & Tyack, 1981; Jones & Montenegro, 1983; Schmuck, 1975; Shakeshaft, 1989; Strober & Tyack, 1980 as cited in Marshall, 1993b). Hodgkinson and Montenegro's (1999) survey of the racial and gender makeup of superintendents and school-level administrators found that females held 20% of secondary positions, 32% of middle school positions, and a majority of 53% of elementary positions; only 7.1% held superintendent positions. Although progress has been made in the numbers since 1999, there continues to be a gap at the highest levels of leadership and in positions that are considered stepping stones to superintendencies (secondary school principals).

The conservative agenda of schooling upholds the traditional values of the White, male founding fathers (Timar & Tyack, 1999), while the views of other groups have not been considered important to the education of young men and women. Women educational leaders working in this conservative environment are challenged by the intractability of the system, and their vision of schools as places where all people have a voice and are valued comes in conflict with the prevailing attitudes. Yet at the same time, Schmuck (1995) argued that women educational leaders have to move to the next level in their advocacy of women and begin to be more overtly political if they want to make schools places where all groups are valued and nurtured. So how do women administrators negotiate the educational environment, effect changes that resonate with their vision of schooling, and maintain themselves as viable candidates for leadership positions? What dilemmas, conflicts, constraints, or barriers do women encounter when aspiring to leadership positions in education? Do women in education administration identify with the women's movement now or at other times in their career? How, if at all, has the women's movement affected their thoughts and actions in education? These are the questions that guided my inquiry into the experiences of women leaders in education.

As will be taken up below, in my interviews with women administrators I found that their commitment to children was paramount. I found that these women had a limited view of the women's movement and its impact upon their professional lives. Their understanding of their place in the huge social changes of the 1960s and 1970s was not always apparent, and they experienced a clear dissonance between the promise of the women's movement and their own desires to be wives and mothers. Yet their frustration with "how the system" works was a part of their stories, and many of them benefited from having female role models in leadership positions. Still, taking an open activist stance was not something that most of them were comfortable doing. These women did not see schools as a place where activism would be embraced; rather, they saw it as something that would negatively impact their professional lives.

Throughout my career in public education, I have often thought that public schools are the last places where social justice issues are played out in meaningful ways. We are often reactive to what is going on in the greater society rather than proactive. It is my perception that activism in schools is a double-edged sword. Educators teach students about the American ideals of democracy, representation for all people, equity, and the right to be heard and take a stand. In reality, however, educators are discouraged from practicing what they teach. If schools are to represent what is best about America and endow future generations with the knowledge and tools to continue the American ideals of fairness and equality for all, then schools need to look within their own systems to actively support issues of fairness, representation, and equality.

Understanding the Cognitive Dissonance

The 13 women interviewed for this study came from diverse backgrounds and reached different levels of leadership in education by various career paths. The stories told by these women had some common threads that offer insight into strong, competent women attempting to make their way in the professional world of educational leadership. Like the superintendents in the Bell study (cited in Schmuck, 1995), these women expressed contradictory thoughts and feelings about their professional lives and career ambitions. On the one hand, some of them strongly denied gender as an issue. They did so while at the same time expressing that gender did impact their careers. In addition to this contradictory language, their conversations hinted at the difficulties many of them had trying to assert their competence while maintaining their place in the social and cultural norms of their communities. Embedded in their conversations were thoughts and feelings of gender making a difference in their attaining leadership positions, their own needs to be accepted as part of their communities, and their desire to expand the thinking of young women beyond the cultural norms of the community.

The following data analysis paints a picture of women who were knowingly and unknowingly influenced by the women's movement and other social movements of the 1960s; however, they had conflicted views of their own place within the great changes in social values taking place in the last half-century. Their inability to commit fully to the social movements of the 1960s, specifically the women's movement, was due to the conservative cultural values embedded in their way of thinking about society, the role of women in society, and hierarchal and managerial assumptions about proper gender roles.

The women in this study were very much influenced by time, place, and age. Table 3.1 gives some basic demographic information that will be referred to throughout this chapter. The age range among these women offered a diverse knowledge of and exposure to the women's movement while their professional positions substantiate Ortiz's (1982) research on career paths of women. Their career choices, whether voluntary, self-imposed, or system imposed, are inextricably linked to the women's movement and how women have been perceived in society

Table 3.1 Demographic Information of Study Participants

Name	Position	Age	Geographic Area
Sheila	Area Superintendent	Early 60's	South
Pat	College Professor/Superintendent		
	Search Consultant	Early/Mid 60's	Southwest
Maria	High School Assistant Principal	Late 50's	Southwest
Gail	Curriculum Specialist	Mid 50's	Southwest
Jane	Leadership Academy Staff	Early/Mid 50's	South
Barbara	Director of Career Technology	Early/Mid 50's	Southwest
Sarah	Curriculum Specialist	Early/Mid 50's	Southwest
Claire	Superintendent	Late 40's	South
Carol	High School Principal	Early/Mid 40's	South
Debbie	Director of Grants	Early 40's	Southwest
Jill	Middle School Assistant Principal	Early 40's	Southwest
Karen	Director of Accountability	Mid/Late 30's	Southwest
Anna	Middle School Assistant Principal	Early/Mid 30's	Southwest

Knowledge, Understanding, and Perception of the Women's Movement

> Let's go back I guess even to childhood. Even in high school…. The guys were always the leaders, and I resented that then. And I remember secretly thinking about it, and thinking, hum, this is not fair. But it seemed to be a part of our lives. So you didn't voice it too much…. In the sixties when that feminist movement came along, I have to tell you that I was interested in it. But I also have a side to me, a conservative side to me that said that I am a female and I felt like too many of those women tried to step out of the female role. It's like they almost wanted to be male bashers, and I don't believe in that.

Maria's personal understanding of the social changes occurring in the 1960s and her perception of the women's movement influenced her view of activism. Like Maria, some of the older women had similar perceptions and conflicted feelings about actively confronting gender issues. Touraine (1995) stated that social movements were the result of a rapidly changing world and an attempt to make sense of the great social and cultural changes that are evolving. The women in this study seemed caught in the clash between the conservative, traditional values of the post-World War II era and the social unrest and rapid changes in how society was perceived in the 1960s. There seemed to be less interest in the costs and benefits of actively supporting the women's movement and more concern with simply trying to reconcile those traditional values of their families and communities and the personal values of inclusion and equity for all people.

Pat recalled that she had taken on a position as a reading specialist in a predominantly Black school in the inner city after finishing college. She led the way for the further integration of the staff and became a spokesperson for the integration efforts. After a few years in this position, her principal, a Black male, told her, "I think you really should go into administration. I'm going to recommend you to the University of _____ in a special program they have for school administrators." Although she was unable to attend the program he mentioned, his confidence in Pat's abilities empowered her to work on her administrative degree. Other women had similar experiences of having a male administrator encourage them to move into administration. Some of the women were given mixed messages about their roles and place in society. Gail, for example, was sent the traditional message of the woman's place; however, she was also caught up in the unrest of the 1960s and felt the pull of the message of equality for all people.

> Well, being a child of the sixties, I was probably more influenced by June Cleaver than I was by Joan Baez, but I have my degree in elementary education and part of that stems from a gender issue which is interesting. Because I aspired to be a commercial artist…. I was told that I would have better career opportunities as a teacher…. And I had a guidance counselor

tell me there on campus that I would be better off having a career that would be one that would compliment my husband's career.... I felt like civil rights were civil rights and they were not based just on race, but they were gender based as well. And I felt when that changed it would have a tremendous impact, so I was not a flower child, but I was one who did the protesting as we could do it in a small Oklahoma town.

These women's perspectives and understanding of women working for equal opportunities and recognition were influenced by their own lack of support early in their careers, the conservative, Southern cultural messages that were embedded into the fabric of their lives, their own unwillingness to jeopardize their social and community standing, and in some cases their acceptance of the status quo. Over the span of their careers, their activism played out at the grassroots level and in individual ways that they themselves did not recognize.

Acceptable and Unacceptable Behaviors

"Because you hear all these things about well, if you belong to the NOW (National Organization for Women) group, you're gay." Pat's view of the women's movement was framed by her limited knowledge of its operation at the national level. Pat, along with some of the other women, were greatly influenced by their Southern, conservative roots. Ladies acted like ladies; ladies took care of the home, husband, and children; ladies did not get involved in politics; politics were men's business. Many of the frames surrounding the women's movement at the national level were alien and unacceptable to these women's feelings about the place of women in Southern society. Frames are "slices of reality" within which framers package the message (Gamson, 1990). Frames have to go beyond the traditional cultural symbols; a frame must be fashioned to fit into the target population's value system and needs, and in the case of these women, the frames did not fit. Jane's husband even suggested that she could not emotionally handle an administrative position. When she came home excited about having been offered a principalship in her district, she reflected, "And I went home happy and told him, and he said, 'Do you think your nerves can handle that stress? Aren't you afraid that you're going to have a nervous breakdown?'" When asked what symbol or frame they thought defined the women's movement, they had mixed feelings. Table 3.2 shows how each of the women in this study perceived the symbols surrounding the women's movement. For some of the women, the women's movement was framed by the civil rights movement and federal legislation; however, some of the women saw the women's movement in terms of aggressive women. They recognized a need for greater opportunities and recognition for women, but not at the expense of traditional family values as they knew them.

Framing the issue of women's equity around personal experiences caused some of these women to act individually in ways that would impact the lives of other

Table 3.2 Framing the Women's Movement

Name	Frame Mentioned	Reaction
Sheila	Civil Rights	Positive
Pat	Civil Rights	Positive
Jill	Title IX	Positive
Sarah	Title IX	Positive
Jane	Civil Rights	Positive
Maria	Aggressive Women	Negative
Gail	Civil Rights	Positive
Debbie	Title IX	Positive
Anna	Aggressive Women, NOW	Negative
Carol	Women's Organizations	Negative
Claire	Aggressive Women	Negative
Barbara	Title IX	Positive
Karen	Women's Organizations	Positive

women. These women did not perceive what they were doing as being an activist and did not personalize their actions and see them in terms of their own lives and careers. They saw what they were doing as making a difference for young females coming into adulthood. Jill's knowledge and understanding of women's issues emanated from her early career as a physical education teacher and coach. She expressed a strong desire to give every student equal opportunities in sports and academics. She stated, "When I was coaching I dealt with issues like [coach's mentality] a lot. In fact the athletic director and I butted heads many times over issues. And when Title IX came out, I was singing hallelujah for us, you know. And I used that a few times [Title IX to confront athletic directors]." As an assistant principal at a middle school, she planned and carried out a forum for all eighth grade female students at her school. It was a day-long program with women leaders from the community leading discussions about opportunities for women. Jill's program was unique in her district, and she was very proud of her work with female students. She felt that she was making a difference in their perceptions of themselves and their sense of control over their lives.

Many of these women looked up to women university professors they had met whose major research interest was in gender issues in education. Sarah was more knowledgeable about women's issues than the other women in this study. She became involved with the American Association of University Women (AAUW) during her early teaching years and expressed great interest in the work that organization was doing concerning gender equity in the schools. She recalled how a conversation she had with her teenaged daughter sparked her dissertation topic.

She was in junior high when this happened…. And I walked through the den, and sat down with her for a few minutes to watch an NBC Dateline show with Jane Pauley, and the topic was failing at fairness. It was a news broadcast about Myra and David Sadker's book of the same title, and showed a little girl in the classroom talking about how schools shortchange girls. And I turned to Susan, my daughter, and said "Susan, do you think that girls get their fair shake in school?" And she said, "Oh yeah, Mom, I do." And I said, "Well, why is that?" And she said, "Oh Mom, I'm just obnoxious!" And I thought to myself how sad it was that a girl thought she had to be obnoxious in order to get her fair share of a teacher's attention. So that was the reason for my study and my passion for this subject.

Sarah was knowledgeable about research in the area of gender equity, and recalled the implementation of Title IX in her home economics classes in the 1970s. She had attended conferences highlighting female professors' research, and her perception of the women's movement was influenced by those associations. As a language arts curriculum specialist in her district, she consciously included literature with female protagonists and multicultural views on the reading lists for students. Jill's and Sarah's knowledge and understanding of women's issues did not fit with the patterns of other participants in the study. Although these women became interested in gender issues from different perspectives—Jill from her work with athletics and Sarah with her research and work with curriculum— both of them did push an agenda for the female students in their schools.

The antithesis of Jill and Sarah were Claire and Carol. Carol, a high school principal, was adamant in her denial of knowledge of women's issues as they related to her personally or professionally. She had worked for Claire as an assistant principal before becoming the principal after Claire left to become an assistant superintendent and later superintendent. They both voiced a similar stance about the women's movement and how it related to their lives. Carol stated,

Gender has never been an issue for me. I've always believed in my capabilities, and as a matter of fact, gender was never even a thought for me, until I started my doctoral program. Because I can remember some of the professional staff, some of the faculty, asking me if I felt that there was a glass ceiling, because of the fact that I was a female. And when I started the process [doctoral program], I was an assistant principal. And I can remember being very surprised at the question, because that's never been an issue for me.

When asked what came to her mind when she heard the words *feminist* or *activist*, Carol said, "Probably the first person who comes to mind is Gloria Steinem. I guess I think of a movement which came about to give women an equal opportunity. I honestly don't nor have I ever paid attention to those movements, simply because I felt I could do whatever I wanted based on my own capabilities."

Although Carol stated that she had no identification with the women's movement and it was a nonissue for her, she did admit that "As I have moved up, I have found that that [relying solely on my capabilities] may not always necessarily be true. There are other issues that may have to be considered, when putting people into positions. I think diversity also plays an issue, and it's one thing that is considered when filling positions." Carol's contradiction about gender being a nonissue and diversity playing a part in filling positions confirms what Schmuck and Shubert (1995) found in their study of other high school principals. They found that a majority of the 11 principals they studied denied experiencing sexual discrimination, yet these principals reported being treated differently from men.

Interestingly, there was a great deal of community uproar when Claire became the first female high school principal in her district, and both women's professional ability to lead a high school was questioned based upon their gender. For Claire, at the time of her appointment to the high school principalship, her denial of gender as an issue may have been her way of distancing herself from the controversy. She was a successful principal and mentored Carol during that time; therefore, Carol's responses about gender may have been learned from Claire's experiences. Both women's way of navigating the male world of educational administration was to focus on professional capabilities and to deny gender as a factor. This strategy was successful for Claire; she did become a superintendent. Although unstated, Carol appeared to have ambitions toward a superintendency, and following Claire's model seemed logical and appropriate.

Mentoring, however, was acceptable for all of the women interviewed. Of the three women who had attained superintendent status during their careers, two of them spoke of the need to network, mentor, and become involved in women's issues. These women, Sheila and Pat, were in their early to mid-60s, and they did not have role models or access to women's consciousness raising groups in college or early in their careers. These women began their careers in the late 1950s to early 1960s before there was a recognizable movement at the national level, and the women's movement was not a clearly defined issue for them. Early in their careers there was no structure with which they could align, and the national efforts to organize were not framed in terms that these women could identify. They felt that having mentors during their careers would have offered much needed support as they tried to navigate the male-dominated world of administration.

Civil Rights and Activism

Sheila, a Black woman from the South, felt a stronger connection to the civil rights movement than the women's movement, but she admitted that she could not separate being Black and being female. As mentioned in chapter 1, Black women often felt tied more to the civil rights movement than to the women's movement. Her identity with the Black struggle tied more personally into her value system than her identity as a woman struggling for equality. Sheila may have been responding to the ethos of the 1970s women's movement that was not always inclusive of women of color. She was a member of the National Association for the Advancement of Colored People (NAACP) and a sorority for Black women that did civic work. Sheila stated that at one point in her career she tried to organize the few Black administrators in her district but met with little success. She stated,

> I tried to organize people at one point for them to speak up and be heard. I can remember meeting with other Black administrators, male and female. And of course, you know, there is a schism between men and women. I don't think just between White men and White women or between Black men and Black women. It's between men and women. There is a kind of competition between males and females.

She cited this sense of competition as the reason her efforts to organize failed. "The other Black administrators, most of whom were male, were threatened by me as a female."

Pat, like Sheila, grew up in a segregated Southwestern community, and the issues framing the civil rights movement overshadowed the women's movement. A White woman, she identified with the prejudice and unjust treatment of Blacks in her community, and she left that community as soon as she finished college. She moved to a large Southwestern city and worked as a teacher in an inner city school prior to mandated integration. She did not see the competition between men and women that Sheila spoke about; rather, Pat stated that men more often than women gave her encouragement and opportunities for advancement. She commented,

> I don't think that they [women] meant to hurt each other. It's just that we don't have that model in place that men have in place, of helping each other and networking.... I don't think they deliberately didn't help me. They just didn't know how to help me.

At the time, Pat did not think about the lack of support as a women's issue, and she did not have enough of an understanding of women's issues to think about her career in terms of the women's movement. Both women did have knowledge of the civil rights movement and were comfortable with being identified with that movement.

Costs and Benefits of Participation

An overriding theme that permeated the data was the hesitancy of these women to align themselves with the women's movement. This hesitancy presented itself differently for the women based upon their career positions, their race, and their age. It emanated from their early backgrounds and community norms.

These women lived and worked by the established rules of their professions and communities while they attempted to fulfill the promise of new values and social norms as expressed by the social unrest and the women's movement of the 1960s. They valued home and family and voiced the belief that they should be the primary caregivers. The majority of them saw their role of homemaker and supportive spouse as paramount, and the career positions they attained or aspired to had to fit into the larger picture of their personal lives. The social movements of the 1960s were filtered through the traditional values they had been taught, and the symbols of the women's movement evoked negative connotations for them (see Table 3.2 above). The women's movement threatened to destroy the fabric of society that they were committed to upholding. Yet, like Friedan (1963), these well-educated women felt that their talents were not truly being recognized or utilized to their fullest potential. Unlike Friedan and other outspoken social activists, however, these women found the pull of the prevailing cultural norms and conservative roots too strong for them to take a strong activist stance for women's rights.

The stories told by the participants in this study revealed calculations of the costs and benefits of participation (Ferree, 1992). Table 3.3 shows the costs and benefits mentioned by the women in this study.

The costs of participation in the women's movement did not dominate their talk; however, most of them did consider the professional and personal costs of taking an activist stance.

Maria's recollection of her treatment for being outspoken about the treatment of women in her building was particularly compelling. She even said that she was taking a risk participating in this study. She talked about the hostility that had built up between her principal and herself because she did not always agree with the principal. The situation had deteriorated to the point that she felt she had been ostracized by the administrative team at her school and even by administrators from other buildings and was contemplating moving to another district.

> Going back to your question, do I want to be a principal? I did. He beat me down for two years. I have such a low self-image of my ability and

Table 3.3 Costs and Benefits of Participation

Costs	Benefits
Professional Isolation/Exclusion	Mentorship
No Professional Advancement	Sponsor Approval
Professional Divisiveness	Networking
Labeled as Feminist/Radical	Making a Difference for Women
Loneliness	Upholding Personal Values
Emotional Stress	
Divorce/Personal Relationships	

everything else, and I felt like that was his goal to do that to me. To make me feel like I was a nothing…. I don't know where I stand in this school system…. Now let me end this with saying I am bitter. I'm hurt. I'm frustrated at times.

Maria was very emotional during her interview and expressed very strong feelings of betrayal by her administrative team. They failed to recognize her accomplishments and resented her efforts to give recognition to other women in the school. She perceived that the cost for her participation was lost confidence in her professional abilities and possibly her opportunities for advancement in that system. The other study participants did not have as dramatic a story about the professional costs as Maria.

Those women who aspired to a superintendency perceived that the costs were high, and they tried to balance their desire for advancement with their desire to support other women and speak out on issues of fairness and equity. Karen had thought carefully about belonging to a state organization for women school administrators. She commented on the organization, "I think it's developing informal and formal mentor networks, you know, connecting women to other women leaders. I think there is a little bit of stigma. There is a perception by some superintendents that these [are] women who feel like they've been slighted, who are the Gloria Steinems of the school administrators. And that's not the case at all." Karen was beginning to seek a superintendent position. She had worked in several positions that allowed her to interact with superintendents all over the state during her career, and she had been privy to conversations among male superintendents that caused her to be cautious about her activism. She recalled,

There was a time I was not a member of the [state organization for female educational leaders] and I worked with superintendents at the state level. So there were times when I heard comments about that organization such as "Why do they have to have their own special organization?" I don't think that's a view shared by all male superintendents, but I think there are probably a significant number who do feel like that.

Karen's career had moved very rapidly, and she knew she was in line for a superintendency. If she were perceived by influential superintendents in the state as an activist or feminist, the cost could be reaching her goal of superintendent. She did belong to the state organization at the time of the interview; however, her immediate supervisor was the president of the state organization. She had to consider the cost of not belonging as well. In Karen's case, it was very important for her to weigh the costs of how her activism should play out.

Pat, one of the oldest participants in this study, saw her work for women as a way of making it easier for others to attain leadership positions. She thought that her professional experiences and insights might be helpful to other women. She spoke often in her interview about mentoring and networking with younger women who aspire to superintendencies. She stated, "What I like to do is mentor, not necessarily mentor, but help in any way I can." She expressed pride in the fact that she had placed women in leadership positions when she was a superintendent. Pat recalled,

> We made a lot of progress. It was uphill all the way. But I was able to bring some young women who had never thought that they would ever have a chance of being an administrator along. And now there are eight of those women who are either principals or central office staff.

Pat's desire to make a difference for women was typical of all the women who expressed pride and accomplishment in their efforts on behalf of women.

Six women who did belong to a state organization for women educational leaders expressed a great deal of respect for an assistant superintendent who had encouraged them to join. This woman was the president of the organization, and these six women felt a special sponsorship by her. All of these women felt a benefit in having a powerful district office person advocating for membership.

Carol's thoughts about belonging to women's organizations in education re-iterated her position of gender not being an issue in career advancement. When asked if she saw any benefits to belonging to such an organization, she stated,

> In some respects I think that would be more divisive than anything else. If there was [an organization] I doubt I'd join, because of that divisiveness. And simply because it goes against my beliefs. I don't see belonging to a professional women's organization would be something that I would have to do to move forward in whatever it was I was interested in.

Carol's perceived cost of participation was the creation of a greater rift between men and women, and she saw no benefit for herself personally or profession-ally. Thus, isolated and feeling more punishing costs that benefits, these women educators were not likely to embrace any visible affiliation with the women's movement.

The Vision for Women

Length of time in the education career, along with career level achieved influence the way these women perceived the women's movement, activism, and their actions as educators. Women who had attained higher levels of leadership expressed the need to look at the larger place of women in society and education, while fledgling administrators expressed the frustrations of day-to-day interactions with building level male administrators.

Vision at the Macrolevel

The women in this study who had attained superintendencies were able to look at the larger picture of women in educational administration. Sheila and Pat, two women who had attained the superintendency, were very clear in their understanding that making a difference for women in school administration could only come about as a result of cultural and social changes in how women are perceived. Pat commented on what women need to be doing to effect those changes, "In every organization that women belong to, [they need to] continue to say, 'You don't stop here.' And then to get into as many governing positions that they can get in where they can make decisions that would at least open doors…." Women working with support groups and attempting to raise awareness of women's issues in educational administration, they felt, had been a necessary first step; however, they thought that it would be necessary to become part of the policy making and governmental arenas to effect any sweeping cultural changes.

Sheila, as a Black woman, spoke about wanting to have an impact on decisions that were being made. She recalled early decisions that catapulted her into positions of power and influence,

> I wanted to have an impact on decisions that were made in school, influence policy. Now I couldn't have articulated this then, but that's what I wanted to do. So now I could legitimately do it, and I began to realize that I was pretty good at it. I have a lot of courage. I don't mind controversy.

She used the political and legal system to correct what she perceived as an injustice in her career promotions. When she was not chosen to fill a superintendent position that she thought should have been hers by education, experience, and job performance, she contacted influential politicians to review and intercede on her behalf. She used her knowledge of the political/legal system and laws surrounding discrimination to plead her case, causing her employers to meet her demands of promotion and monetary compensation. She recognized the power of those people in legal and governmental positions and, in retrospect, saw that as perhaps the true avenue to effect lasting social change.

Sheila compared the position of women to that of Blacks in their struggle for equality.

> We cannot say we're there, because when you look at the Senate, and look at Congress, we're not there. That has to be reflected everywhere, not just in elementary schools. You know. I remember that the Black Caucus wanted something in Congress. I cannot remember what the issue was now. But the essence of this thing was, in order for it to be brought to the floor, they needed one senator to sign it. And there was no Black senator, not one out of a hundred. And then you look at how many women senators there are out of a hundred. Then you know we're not there.

Looking at the women's movement from the macrolevel, Sheila saw slow progress and an unwillingness of those in power to share or relinquish that power. She reflected, "I think the people who are in charge, who keep us from getting there, are going to keep on keeping on. If we get there we're going to have to wrest it from them." She was not optimistic in her view of a societal shift in how women are perceived; although, she did admit that there had been some small gains made.

Pat, the other superintendent, began working early in her career for organizations for women outside of the education field. She was on the board for women's groups that mentored young girls and for organizations that advocated for women who were being abused or abandoned by their spouses. Her work with these groups allowed her to meet and negotiate with policy makers and industry CEOs. She, like Sheila, saw the need for women to move into political and policy arenas to move beyond where they have gotten. Pat stated,

> Being in a position to make decisions, like the school board. I'm talking about state boards; they've got a political thing where decisions are made that affect school districts…. So I think women in politics, whether it's the school board, whether it's the state board, whether it's a representative, can really make the difference.

Pat also made an interesting observation when she said, "I think some women think that [at the school level] is where they stop." She reflected that many women did not see themselves in the political arena, and there is a need to help women expand their own visions of themselves as political and powerful. After long careers, both Pat and Sheila were able to see the larger picture of the women's movement as it affects women in school administration, and they felt they could be candid without fear of professional repercussions. Their observations reinforced Schmuck's (1995) view of political action as the necessary step for moving women forward in leadership positions.

Vision at the Microlevel

The women in entry level leadership positions were so stymied by the ongoing confrontations with their building administrators that they found it hard to talk about the larger picture of making a difference for women in leadership positions. As found in Marshall and Mitchell's (1991) work on fledgling administrators, these women found themselves blocked in their efforts to make changes in school procedures and policies by their male peers and superiors. Both Maria and Anna saw the need to make systemic changes; however, they were entrenched in the day-to-day realities of their jobs and the patriarchal hierarchy in place in their buildings that sent a clear message not to challenge the status quo. Their greatest need was support and recognition of their competencies—something they did not receive from their male principals. Maria reflected on her frustration at having no support from male administrators and the system's unwillingness to entertain this lack of support as a problem, "If we want more women at the top, we're going to have to have people who have decided that we need more women at the top…. I saw [the superintendent] all the time being with our male principals, but if he does that for his male principals, why isn't he out visiting females and seeing what we need?" Both women expressed anger at how they had been isolated from decision making, and both saw this isolation as the result of an established male leadership in their systems and cultural norms that reified male leadership skills.

Maria felt she was both physically and professionally separated from the rest of her administrative team. She commented,

> As a curriculum instruction assistant principal, the principal and the administrative assistant principal in the other high schools all work together very, very closely. And they are located in a location together. Because they make the decisions in that building, and they work together to form them. And in my building it's not that way. I'm upstairs.

Her office was on the second floor in a back wing used for classrooms while the rest of the administration was located in the front of the building on the first floor. In addition, Maria expressed some concerns that her age may impact her isolation. She began her career at the age of 40 after her husband died, and she became the sole support for her family. She conjectured that both age and gender may create barriers for her professionally. She acknowledged frustration at being in an entry level administrative position while other administrators in her building are younger and appear more competitive for advancement.

Both Anna and Maria referred to the "coach's mentality" and the "good old boy" network that dominated how leadership was determined and embedded in the schools and community. Maria recounted an incident in which a parent complained about how a coach was teaching her child's class.

> I'm a little concerned about this class. But you know the fact is I don't want to cause any problems for him. Because, you know, Coach Blankety-Blank is a wonderful guy. Everybody loves him, and I wouldn't do anything to jeopardize that, but what can I do because I feel like my daughter is just not learning what she needs to learn.

Maria expressed frustration with a culture that celebrated sports over academic achievements and saw this attitude as one that devalued females.

Anna, on the other hand, saw herself as being used to accomplish her principal's agenda but not getting any credit when she did what he asked. She recounted "When he hired me, he said, 'I want two things, Anna. I want my writing scores to come up, and I want National Blue Ribbon.' And I got him both my very first year." She expressed resentment that he did not give her any credit for these accomplishments or value her contributions to the administrative team. Anna had just returned from a state conference for women's educational leaders, and she was enthusiastic about taking on a more active role in the organization. She thinks that she could make a difference in the professional lives of other women through this organization. She stated,

I have decided that we (another member from her district) want to see more women [from the district] involved in this. At our school there are three teachers going for their midmanagement, and I gave them all the paperwork [to become a member of this organization].... So my goal is to try to get them more involved in this, and to get more assistant principals and principals involved in it. Because it is a good group to come to. They are mentoring each other. I put in to mentor someone.

Although Maria and Anna saw the need for policy, political, and cultural changes to make a difference in how women were perceived, both of them felt unable to move beyond where they were because of the barriers set up by the male dominated system and their inability to move beyond the entry level position of assistant principal. These two women seemed the most vulnerable and unsure of their futures, and their level of vision was limited to the microlevel of individual interactions. Anna, however, as a result of her recent conference with other women educational leaders, expressed a determination to take on an active role in pushing an agenda for women in educational leadership. She saw her greatest contribution at the time of this interview as working individually with other women to encourage and support them. As a result of her meeting and networking with women leaders across the state, she was able to envision her participation beyond individual acts of participation. Unlike Pat and Sheila, who were able to see the broader picture for women, Anna's and Maria's vision was limited by their experiences and a professional culture that discouraged association with the women's movement.

Conclusions and Reflections

Did the women's movement create new identities for these women educators? At the most basic level, women understood that the women's movement played a part in getting federal legislation passed that mandated more fair treatment and equal opportunities for women in the workplace, in educational institutions, and in sports. Beyond the legislation, however, women were more circumspect in their rhetoric about the women's movement, especially if they had aspirations of higher leadership positions. Again, they were caught between the vision of equity and fairness and the reality of the conservative work climate and community norms. The women held strongly to their cultural roots and the values of their communities, and they sought ways of meshing the values of the women's movement with these values. Still, the women's movement played a role in developing a strong sense of self-efficacy felt by female leaders. Increased opportunities to stretch their intellects, fully tap their skills and talents, and influence policies that make a difference for society validated the women in this study as capable and competent people in their own right. Recognition of their contributions through equal pay added to their sense of worth as contributing members of society. Other people's perceptions of their value to society increased with this increased power, influence, and income, thereby further validating their sense of efficacy. Their own sense of competence was enhanced by the knowledge that they did not have to depend upon someone else for their financial security or emotional well-being. All of these factors emanated from the opportunities opened up by the women's movement. With all this being said, the reality of their situations was still one of constantly having to prove themselves to the powers that be (males, conservatives), and often having to tread carefully around contentious social and political issues such as the women's movement.

One of the most powerful stories emerging from this study was the framing of the women's movement and how that influenced the perceptions and activism of these women. The issue of framing in social movement is a complex one. My initial framing for women in educational leadership was oversimplified and it was necessary to take a look at the frames from feminist perspectives to have a better understanding of the complexities. As discussed in chapter 1, the icons of feminism at the national level were not images with which my participants could identify. The participants in this study indicated that the women's movement had been a factor in shaping their identities professionally and personally; however, it was clear that the women's movement did not address the social and cultural needs of women as wives and mothers. In fact, the movement's lack of acknowledgment of these values, at least in the 1970s and 1980s, created a negative connotation for these women. As Stacey (1986) pointed out, no one feminism could speak for all women. Feminist literature in the 1980s and 1990s (Delmar, 1986) did address the lack of a unifying identity around which women could rally, the lack of a cohesive understanding of the term *feminist* or *feminism*, and the negative impact of the more radical factions associated with the women's movement. Mitchell (1986) even argued that for many women in the 1960s and '70s, the idea of being labeled an activist was more appealing than being labeled a feminist. Stacey (1986) went on to state that a feminist backlash has emerged in part fueled by the writings of three well-known names in the feminist literature: Germaine Greer, Betty Friedan, and Jean Bethke Elshtain. Contrary to earlier, more radical feminist writings, these women promoted a profamily stance that viewed sexual politics and the politicization of personal relationships as threatening to the family. In addition, they affirmed gender differentiation and celebrated traditionally feminine qualities. These views clearly align with the views of the women in this study, and had the women's movement been framed around this more conservative, profamily view early in the movement, women in this study might have felt more comfortable with the labels of feminist or activist.

Women seeking equity in the workplace and in society continue to struggle with the embedded values of a conservative community and profession. As argued by women in my study, the male dominated leadership that devalues a woman's perspective is a real barrier to equity for women in educational leadership. This struggle is exacerbated by the political agenda of the conservative New Religious Right, no strong feminist set of values that adequately addresses women's issues, and the diversity of women's views about their identity and place in society. These women's stories remind us that action on behalf of women's equality takes different forms. Even though they rejected the models offered by the women's movement, these women took clear actions to advance women in education administration. Do we call this feminism or activism? Not according to conventional definitions, and not according to the definition of activist set out in chapter 1: *an individual who is known for taking stands and engaging in action aimed at producing social change, possibly in conflict with institutional opponents.* And not according to the women in this study. It is the public dimension of activism that is problematic in education systems so entrenched in conservative norms. How likely are we to find activist women in educational leadership? All of these women worked in quiet and subtle ways to encourage girls and women to aspire to be whatever they wanted to be. They nurtured women's confidence and validated women as capable, competent leaders. Still, until education administration as a field can make room for practitioners' public advocacy that challenges the status quo, women administrators will likely continue their quiet, subtle activism.

4

Approaching Activism in the Bible Belt

GLORIA HINES JONES

Student-to-student sexual harassment in the K-12 setting is a topic for open discourse and immediate action for educators. Educators have the capacity to lead the charge to stop student-to-student sexual harassment, but at what risk? This chapter explores the efforts of public school educators to raise awareness about occurrences of student-to-student sexual harassment in their classrooms, hallways, schools, and school systems. It is about their reasons for getting involved, their closeted activism, and about the influence of the conservative geographical region in which they work as a key factor impacting their activist choices.

My desire to investigate student-to-student sexual harassment as an issue needing immediate attention was due to the daily charge of building level educators to provide a positive, nurturing, and safe learning environment. As a middle-school classroom teacher and school-based administrator, I have witnessed first hand the emotional turbulence that students endure as they struggle with issues of physical, social, emotional, intellectual, and sexual development and the myriad of growing pains resulting from these developmental stages, the most common of which are inappropriate student interactions. I have dealt frequently with reports of sexual harassment among students resulting in he-said, she-said situations because no adult could corroborate the victim's account; witnessed perpetrators suspended for the remainder of the school year and relocated to alternative settings, without rehabilitation; and testified in court, recounting testimony, hoping the perpetrator would receive help and the victim reprieve and the chance to return to school and learn free from harassment. Peer sexual harassment exists in schools, elementary and secondary, and incidents are occurring at a rampant pace. It is a prevalent social problem that poses a threat to individual victims and perpetrators and to schools and school systems. I wanted to understand the activism of those who might take action to mitigate the problem.

Conceptualizing the Research

My research explored educators' lived experiences as activists to thwart student-to-student sexual harassment in the K-12 setting, and the underlying beliefs, values, and assumptions that inform those experiences.[1] I defined harassment as physical or verbal behavior of a sexual nature inflicted on students by their peers in the public school setting.[2] I was particularly interested in how and why educators emerge as activists to stand against student-to-student sexual harassment in the public K-12 setting, and what professional and personal dilemmas confront them when they choose to engage in activism to alleviate student-to-student sexual harassment. Drawing on identity theory, social movement theory, and related educator activist literatures as explained in chapter 1, I expected to find that both personal and professional resources and factors frame how educators identified with the issue of student-to-student sexual harassment (i.e., time, money, energy, talents, skills, goals, values, profession, family, career mobility), and that identity factors drove their activism to intervene and stop sexual harassment. I also considered the historical significance of sexual harassment, including definitions of harassment, litigation, recognition, legislation, and subsequent policies.

As will be elaborated below, interviews with activists revealed three emergent themes: educator activists bring diverse impetuses to their involvement in intervening in student-to-student sexual harassment; educators do activist work to prevent peer sexual harassment; and educator activists against harassment encounter confounding dilemmas. The information presented in this chapter will discuss these emergent themes and patterns, naming the "wow" factor, "aha" moments, provocative practices, and sustained discourse of activism to prevent student-to-student sexual harassment.

Activists' Context: The Legal and Political History

The activism discussed in this chapter is situated within the context of student-to-student sexual harassment. What follows is a snapshot of existing theoretical and legal literatures framing student-to-student sexual harassment. The term *sexual harassment* traveled through many arenas and frames as a topic of discourse and debate before its introduction in the K-12 setting. Its trajectory through social, political, legal, and educational arenas has been nothing less than turbulent. Influential legislation in the conceptual development of sexual harassment includes the 14th Amendment to the U.S. Constitution's guarantees of life, liberty, and property; Title VII of the Civil Rights Act of 1964 made discrimination based on sex illegal; and Title IX of the Education Amendments required gender equity in school funding. These and numerous other state and civil statutes all recognize sexually discriminating and harassing behavior as illegal and wrong (Jones, 1999; Moore & Rienzo, 1998). Subsequent persistent activism at the local, state, and national levels resulted in legislation recognizing sexual harassment as illegal in the workplace, and then in educational settings, first on university campuses, and most recently, in primary and secondary school settings (Marshall, Taylor, & Gaskell, 2001; Stein, 1999).

A myriad of studies and surveys has substantiated the severity of student-to-student sexual harassment in K-12 schools. *Secrets in Public* (Stein, 1993b), *Hostile Hallways* (AAUW, 1993), and *In Our Own Backyard* (Permanent Commission on the Status of Women,1995), along with subsequent countless and nameless state, national, and international studies, surveys, and reports examining student-to-student sexual harassment noted similar findings (AAUW, 1993, 2001; Crisci, 1999; Fineran & Bennett, 1998; Moore & Rienzo, 1998; Stein, 1999; Yaffe, 1995). According to Yaffe (1995), "Most significantly, they revealed just how large a portion of the student population had been subjected to unwelcome sexual behavior" (p. 6).

Three U.S. Supreme Court cases set legal precedence for subsequent sexual harassment cases in schools pursuant to Title IX. *Franklin v. Gwinnett County Public Schools* (1992), *Davis v. Monroe County Board of Education* (1996), and *Gebser v. Largo Vista Independent School District* (1998) resulted in significant implications for school districts and schools in the K-12 domain that failed to address issues of sexual harassment (Berlin, 1996; Cahill, 2001; Francis, 2001; Hotelling, 1991; Stein, 1999; Wetzel & Brown, 2000). Yet despite the legal prohibitions, sexual harassment is still a problem in the K-12 setting. Schwartz (2000) encapsulated the issue: "peer sexual harassment among students is a complex and widespread problem with significant effects on the perpetrator, the victim, and the school environment" (p.1).

Impact of Student-to-Student Sexual Harassment on Individuals and School Systems

The impact of peer sexual harassment on individuals, schools, and school systems is extensively documented in the literature. Student-to-student sexual harassment is a frequently occurring problem in schools around the country (Stein, 1999; Yaffe, 1995 as cited in Moore & Rienzo, 1998). Randy, the only practicing school counselor among this study's educators, substantiated this claim when he stated, "[I], being a counselor, see that student-to-student sexual harassment does indeed go on every day." The impact of peer sexual harassment is a growing concern in schools, affecting students' social and academic progress and daily attendance, contributing to student truancy and teen suicide, and significantly impacting the victim, the perpetrator, and the educational setting (Human Rights Watch, 2001; Rowell & McBride, 1996; Schwartz, 2000; Stein, 1999 Wetzel & Brown, 2000).

Wetzel and Brown (2000) stated that individual victims might experience "psychoemotional, psychosocial, academic, behavioral, and even physical consequences" including "an increase in self-consciousness, decreased self-confidence, decreased self-respect, and decreased self-esteem" (p. 5) after experiencing sexual harassment. Some students are absent or tardy more frequently, experience a desire to drop out of school, move to a new school, withdraw from required classes, find it difficult to focus on studying, put forth less effort completing academic work, maintain lower academic standards in general, or no longer believe they are intelligent enough for college (Burstyn et al., 2001; Lumsden, 1992; Stein, 1999; Wetzel & Brown, 2000; Yaffe, 1995). The impacts on the social and physical well-being of students include headaches, stress, nausea, pervasive feelings of anger, fear, embarrassment, vulnerability, and confusion as well as doubts about their popularity status and ability to develop a healthy intimate relationship (Fineran & Bennett, 1998; Jones, 1999; Moore & Rienzo, 1998; Stein, 1993a; Wetzel & Brown, 2000; Yaffe, 1995). Stein (1999) noted more specific "behavioral consequences as avoiding the person, staying away from a particular place, changing seats in class, withdrawing from a particular activity or sport, changing group of friends, and changing route to and from school" (p. 26).

Lumsden (1992) characterized sexual harassment as an "issue that can undermine the effectiveness of your school system as an organization and your staff as a team" (p. 1). Given the nature of the clientele of schools, educational institutions are prone to incidents of sexual harassment. As Ramsey (1994) noted, "no other entity deals with large numbers of volatile, energetic, and hormone-driven young people confined in limited spaces for long hours every day" (p. 141). Repeated sexually harassing incidents create a hostile environment. Given existing laws, schools can be held liable if they know of behavior and fail to report it. Therefore, schools and school systems are charged with developing a whole school-district approach to dealing with sexual harassment. The activists in the study embraced this charge through a multiplicity of efforts.

The Activists

Eleven activist educators were interviewed for this research, representing an array of positions, age groups, years of experience, states, and geographic locations (see Table 4.1). These participants initially identified themselves by positions held in their respective school systems. However, as they engaged in candid discourse regarding their concerns about the persistent problem of sexual harassment among students in the K-12 setting, multifaceted identities were revealed. The educators disclosed diverse orientations driving their activism, how they identified with student-to-student sexual harassment, and their motivation to work to deter sexual harassment among students. Their voices and experience provided the raw data used to generate understanding of their activism. I will display some of their diverse perspectives of activism and motivations for their activist work to stop student-to-student sexual harassment. This chapter will provide sound bites and brief glimpses of many of the educator activists and broader profiles of others.

Diverse Impetuses for Involvement

The educators in this study identified with student-to-student sexual harassment at varying levels and to varying degrees. This section names three factors that

Table 4.1 Educator Activist Profiles

Pseud-onym	Race	Age	Victim of Sexual Harass-ment?	Total Years Experience in Education	Position Held in Education when Interviewed	Geographic Location of Work Site	State of Previous Work in Education
Sara	White	20s	Yes	"Since age 16"*	Graduate Student	Piedmont, NC	NC
Lorraine	Black	40s	Yes	21	Assistant Principal	Piedmont, NC	
Tim	White	50s	No	31	Principal	Piedmont, NC	NC
Mike	White	40s	Yes	27	Counselor	Piedmont, NC	
Randy	Black	20s	No	3	Counselor	Northern VA	NC, VA
Tonya	White	40s	No	23	District Office Administra-tor	Piedmont, NC	NC
Kerry	White	50	No	3	Teacher	Piedmont, NC	FL, NC
Janet	White	20s	No	6	Teacher	Southeast GA	GA
Doris	White	30s	Yes	10	Teacher	Southeast GA	TX
Kim	White	40s	No	7	Teacher	Southeast GA	GA
Glenda	Black	50s	No	27	Instructional Leader Teacher	Southeast GA	CA, AZ, MO, IL, TX, GA

*Note. The respondent explained "since age sixteen" as follows" "I began 'teaching' (i.e., counselor) at day camps and after school programs at age 16-21. I did my student teaching my senior year in college. I then taught English for four years.

served as impetuses for educators' activism: (1) career obligation; (2) victimiza-tion; and (3) socialization. The meaning and importance that these respondents attached to beliefs, values, individuals, and experiences comprised these impe-tuses. Subsequently, these impetuses influenced the educators' personal, social, and professional choices related to their activism.

Victimization as an Impetus

An educator's identification with teasing and harassment in schools can lead to activism. Victimization had not been discussed or framed in the literature as an impetus for involvement, but it was part of what led to the decisions of four of the educators to act. By their accounts, one male and three females were either a victim of and/or a perpetrator involved in degrading name-calling, sexual comments about gender and body parts. These findings are consistent with the results of numerous studies on peer-to-peer sexual harassment conducted in schools indicating that victims of harassment, in turn, often become perpetrators, harassing others (AAUW, 1993, 2001; Crisci, 1999; Fineran & Bennett, 1998; Jones, 1999; Moore & Rienzo, 1998; Stein, 1993a; Yaffe, 1995).

The educators articulated their personal experiences of sexual harassment impacting their decisions to lead the charge. Mike disclosed being bullied during his youth. For Doris, teasing was broader in scope as illustrated in her statement below:

> I was teased for different things. I was teased for not having a dad. I was teased for developing early. You know, all of those awful things that kids will find…just anything that they can pick on. I've felt so insecure after being picked on.

Doris also disclosed that her insecurity following her own victimization led to her teasing a female classmate. Lorraine, spoke poignantly about her victimization:

> …from high school being involved in a date rape and he did exhibit the sexual harassment behaviors prior to that, but in wanting to just be his friend, I overlooked it. But now, if anyone makes me feel uncomfortable or gives me a look that I don't appreciate, it sort of triggers that moment. That has certainly affected me personally and my involvement.

Equally poignant, Sara rationalized her victimization from a spiritual perspective:

> I think my work is my life and it comes from my life experiences. I can remember experiencing sexual harassment as a student in public education. I might not have called it that at the time, which is even more the reason why I wanted to be particularly aware of paying attention in my classroom because I think a lot of times some of my students might not realize sexual harassment for what it is. I was raped at age 20, and that enabled me to pick up a lens and start to see the world in a very different way and start to pay attention and understand systemic oppression of various groups of people, but especially women…I notice I'm trying to sensor and filter this spiritual part of my being, but I feel it's part of my path… that I was given these experiences of sexual violence by the creator to use and integrate into my work.

Educators' own victimization motivated their desire to affect change at the microlevel by putting a name to student-to-student harassment and framing it as a social problem and a public issue, thus strengthening their need to become involved.

Career Obligation as an Impetus

Glenda stated with conviction, "I believe as an educator, I have to support the system that supports me." Her belief succinctly captured the sentiments of many of the participants as to why they engaged in activist work—career obligation. Title IX assigned schools the legal responsibility of developing policies and procedures to protect employees and students against sex discrimination (Cahill, 2001; Fineran, 2002; Francis, 2001; Marshall, Taylor, & Gaskell, 2001; National Coalition for Women and Girls in Education [NCWGE], 1997; Yaffe, 1995). Yaffe (1995) stated, "In the eyes of the law, administrators, teachers, and other supervisory school personnel are equated with employers in that their positions give them the kind of control that creates the opportunity for harassment and the responsibility for redressing it" (pp. 2–3). This legal mandate was reflected in the mission statements of the schools in which these educators worked to provide a safe, caring, and orderly learning environment.

Although all of these educators worked or had worked in public K-12 schools, only five cited career obligation as having a major influence on their decision to get involved with student-to-student sexual harassment activism. For them, doing so was part of their contractual responsibilities as described by Randy: "As part of our countywide counseling and guidance curriculum, we are required to address sexual harassment." The following comments illustrate the views of other educators in the study who explained that their activism evolved from federal, state, and local mandates and expectations. Lorraine expressed her job allegiance this way:

> I would say that my membership in the social movement regarding sexual harassment is directly from my job through Title IX and the sexual harassment policy that is from a federal mandate. That is how I see myself working actively in this particular arena…that's how I participate. I think the only true choice that I have made regarding sexual harassment is that I have chosen to fulfill my role and my obligation as an administrator in enforcing the policy.

Tim echoed the obligatory sentiments of the other respondents:

> I got involved actively to reduce any type of sexual harassment the day I walked into a classroom. We do have county policies that speak to the inappropriateness of sexual harassment in my county. We have had those in place many years. In fact, we basically have a no tolerance policy toward sexual harassment, physical harassment, and abuse of any nature. The reason that I'm involved with it is because of being in education.

This "activism by career" attitude impacted these educators' commitment and level of participation. They described their activism as limited and were only involved to the extent that they had to be to enforce the policy. Career obligation was an important variable in that it could potentially place limitations on an educator's willingness to do the work and the effectiveness of the work.

Socialization as an Impetus

As separate impetuses, socialization was most dominant in terms of impacting educators' decision to engage in activism. Socialization and career obligation as primary impetuses aligned with past research that found educators exercised their voice or acted out of contractual responsibilities and obligations, while others did so because of personal or moral obligations (Sachs, 2000). The significance of career obligation and victimization were deemphasized when examined individually, but fortified when interrelated with socialization.

Socialization is the process through which "individuals learn to behave in accordance with the expectations of others in the social order" (Pearce, 1995, p. 41). Nine of the 11 educators shared realizations about the impact of their own childhood socialization on their decision to engage in activism. Specifically, beliefs, experiences, ideologies, and lessons learned related to dimensions of family, education, gender roles, morals, values, and sexual orientation emerged as key constructs of socialization as cited by one or more respondents as an impetus for activism to stop student-to-student sexual harassment. Some dimensions, independently or interlinked with other dimensions, emerged as more salient to some respondents than others. The interrelation of values and morals presented the most significant and provocative influences although the educators recognized aspects of family background, values, gender, and sexual orientation frequently. Unexpectedly, socialization was also significant in unpacking a critical influence on the activism of the participants—the Bible Belt. The brief accounts chronicled here are the interpretation of educators' beliefs, perspectives, stories, suspicions, feelings, anecdotes, lived experiences, and additional insights about their activist agency and capacity. These personal accounts frame the Bible Belt's influence as it restrained and loosened the educators' ability to engage in activist work.

Familial Influence and Gender Roles Four educators credited familial influence and learned gender role expectations as having impacted their decision to do activist work. They specifically noted the values and traditional gender roles that had been instilled in them by their parents. Kim, Lorraine, and Sara shared how family lessons fueled their desire to educate their students about appropriate behavior toward self and others. Kim emphatically stated:

> I'm the youngest of four children. And because I was a female, there were a different set of standards that my brothers [had] and how they were allowed to engage with one another versus how they were allowed to interact with

me. I was raised as a young lady and the boys in the family were to treat me accordingly. So, I think that definitely affects how I want the young ladies in my classroom treated. I want them treated with the same level of respect that I grew up with. And, I want them to know that it's important the way that that was communicated to me growing up as an adolescent. Watching the young women that I teach in my classroom, it definitely has affected who I am and how I kind of view society. And, it gives me a much better understanding of what young women in this day and time are going through as opposed to maybe how I was raised in the sixties.

Kim also commented how her learned respect for young ladies and traditional gender roles led her to use gender stereotypes in her classroom as a proactive way of stopping student-to-student sexual harassment:

I look at student-to-student sexual harassment from a one-sided perspective. I really watch to keep the boys in check when it comes to sexual harassment. That probably is a stereotype in and of itself. But, I really watch the boys and what they say and how they behave in my classroom.

Sara, too, expressed the use of learned gender role stereotyping in her classroom. She paid close attention to the interactions between students in the learning environment, but having witnessed sexual harassment between two boys; she knew that peer-to-peer sexual harassment was not always cross-gender.

Through family conversations, Lorraine learned a similar lesson about traditional gender roles, which impacted her view of sexual harassment:

I would say family background has affected it because of my mom and how she would always tell us in growing up, you should be treated like a lady and a lady is not called certain names, a lady is not touched in a certain manner, a lady is not even looked at in a certain way, so that has definitely affected how I view sexual harassment and played a big part in how I enforce it as well.

Righting Wrongs Familial influence continued to weave itself through the lived experiences of these educators connecting to other dimensions of socialization influencing their activism. Not all activism stemmed from positive experiences related to family background. Sometimes activism stemmed from negative socialization experiences, but had positive outcomes as explained by Sara who spoke emotionally about the existence and influence of oppression in her family on her activism:

I come from middle-class background. My parents both grew up in poverty. I see a relationship to that and sexism and sexual violence.... I know from my mama's experience growing up with child abuse in the house and domestic abuse, and all of that wisdom and I think her life experiences especially kind of affected my ability to empathize with people, and my sense of what's fair and what's not, what's ok and what's not, what's acceptable behavior and what's not, what's treating somebody with dignity and respect and what's not…how people should be treated…how men treat women in the family.… Mama gave me that sensitivity toward other people and that empathy toward other people.

Divorce motivated Doris to rethink the way she treated others. Doris's parents divorced when she was 9 years old. She barely knew her father as a result of the divorce and rarely saw her mother who worked to take care of the household. Positive role models at home were lacking in Doris's life. Doris shared that being the product of a broken home contributed to her low self-esteem, which resulted in her being teased, and in turn, her teasing others out of fear of being bullied more. Doris stated that she often shares her story and reads books about bullying to her students. Doris and Sara turned dysfunctional family impacts into positive motivation and participated in activist work to empower their students to make better choices than they did.

Values and Morals Sexual harassment has been framed in the literature as a moral wrong (Francis, 2001). One reason these activist educators became involved in student-to-student sexual harassment activism was out of a sense of moral obligation. This perspective is supported by della Porta and Diani's (1999) more general work on collective action and values in which they stated that an individual's values influence and shape morally acceptable goals and strategies employed and "provide the motivation necessary to sustain the costs of action." (p. 62). The interwoven dimensions of morals and values were influential in shaping perceptions of several educators. Glenda echoed Kim's earlier reference to being raised in the 1960s, denoting an implied understanding and connectivity to those two decades. As illustrated in Glenda's quote below, growing up during the 1950s and 1960s influenced her activism:

I have strong moral values because I am a child of the fifties and sixties. So, I love to talk to students up and down the hall…about their values and where society is and maybe where they should be, and where their values will carry them. And that applies to sexual harassment. So, that's where I see my role there.

Tim later refers to the significance of socialized community values. This thread of family, values, and morals connected to a seam of conservatism as educators spoke of working in the Bible Belt, the generally conservative southern region of the United States, as discussed in chapter 1.

Socialized Community Values The three male educators spoke about the influence of their conservative communities rather than their own values or familial influence. Tim spoke about his job to support others' value systems, stating, "I tell parents basically that we are there to support their value system, and they… are the main teachers of their children." Like Glenda, Tim used the phrase "value system" as if its meaning was universal as he did not disclose any explanation or provide examples of values. Tim and Glenda, too, referred to conservatism and the Bible Belt:

> We have a very conservative community, which makes it easier to work with dress codes and so on. We're in the Bible Belt, but we're getting a more and more diverse society. (Tim)

> I've been in the South twenty years and in that twenty years, I've seen the South, which has been very conservative about children and manners and things of that nature swing…I was very impressed with yes ma'am, yes sir. That's gone. That whole moral fiber, although we consider it the Bible Belt, it's changing, I can see it. (Glenda)

Two of the educators shared that their education influenced their decision to get involved. Kim commented on the importance of her level of education:

> I think the higher (level) of education you have lends itself to your ability to interpret law to understand concepts that are going on in society and so obviously I think my level of education does affect my ability to understand a particular issue and therefore affects how I choose to be involved.

Sara spoke about education as having a broader influence in terms of personal growth and understanding of social justice issues:

> I think my women's studies classes really kind of opened my eyes to the issues about social justice.… For me to kind of come to grips with and not to categorize and stereotype and generalize, but also to acknowledge how might sexual harassment between White students differ from sexual harassment between minority students who are different, and how do the cultures look different if they do and in what ways does that affect sexual harassment? Those kinds of education classes got me reading and thinking about these issues and you know how they cross lines, and intersect, and how they might look different than my own experience or similar to my own experience.…

For Kim and Sara, their education was an important factor in their ability to better understand societal issues and laws governing them as well as the intellectual capacity to do the work necessary to bring about change.

Sexual Orientation Another significant dimension of socialization important to sexual harassment activism of the educators interviewed was sexual orientation. Two educators noted this dimension as a key factor in their decision to engage in activist work. Kerry's activism could be described as antidiscriminatory and empowering for students whose sexual orientation was gay or lesbian. She embraced and supported the gay and lesbian students by agreeing to be the advisor for the gay and lesbian alliance club.

Only one educator disclosed his sexual orientation. But, his sexual orientation packed a powerful punch on his involvement. He internalized his gayness, his fear of being outed, and his conflicted struggle to hug or not to hug his elementary students. His goal was to protect himself from peers, protect his prominent family, and protect his job. So, he left the profession. His sexual orientation shaped these experiences. Now he uses these experiences as a platform to speak out against student-to-student sexual harassment. There are other activists, like Mike, who are nondisclosures when it comes to their sexual orientation. However, Mike used his agency as a gay man to establish networks and supports aimed at reaching others. Sometimes activism requires taking it out of site as discussed later in this chapter.

The Intermixing of Socialization Dimensions As shown in these educators' quotes, each dimension of socialization was interrelated with other facets of socialization. Educators could not completely compartmentalize the dimensions of family, education, gender roles, morals, values, and sexual orientation, because for many of the respondents the dimensions were interwoven. The ways individuals think about gender, and frame human interaction, and value traditions of civility in general impacted their desire or need to get involved and how they chose to capitalize on their activism. Sara's sentiment, "You know, it's just incredible to me how we try to compartmentalize our education and our life and our values" demonstrated her expressed disbelief that one would even attempt to separate the various dimensions. Kim gave a more concrete example in her quote:

> I think my background, my level of education, and growing up in the sixties…adds to how I feel about sexual harassment and how I deal with it with my students. I can't segment myself as a woman, as an educator, as a wife, as a mother.

Social movement theorists suggested that various facets of individuals' lives and activities impact each other as discussed in chapter 1. These examples are representative of the educators' recognition of the significance of their childhood socialization to their participation in student-to-student sexual harassment activism. These dimensions of socialization comprised a recurring pattern of beliefs among these educator activists and constituted a major impetus for involvement.

The Bible Belt Impact

All of the educators interviewed lived in the Bible Belt (see Table 4.1). Dorough (1974) stated, "To some the Bible Belt is really a term that reflects an attitude, a type of conservatism that is not confined to any special section of America. It might apply to the city as well as to the country" (p. 17). Typically, however, the term *Bible Belt* refers to a geographic region comprising a swath of states in the southeast United States. This area of the South is characterized in chapter 1 as resistant to progressive, provocative causes and having conservative religious beliefs and political views. As this research progressed, the influence of the Bible Belt and its conservative religious values became pronounced among activists regarding student-to-student sexual harassment. The educators in this study did not specifically mention religion in their interviews, but what they did mention was a conservatism which is suggestive of religion or religiousness. Their conservative views and conservative communities impacted the way in which they deployed their activism. Marshall and Oliva (2006) spoke of, "…the on-going matter of selective silences regarding religion and public education" (p. 7). It is a powerful silence.

Lorraine had come to the realization that part of her activism had sifted through a conservative screen:

> For me, it's the…realization that I am very much a conservative and I have to watch and be careful of how I want to put my belief system on others or how I believe that my belief system is the correct one and that others are false or incorrect.…We have conservative versus liberal for the most part. So, I have to make sure that I keep my own personal perspective in place and in the right perspective.

Genette shared, "I think my role of addressing student-to-student sexual harassment has probably come mostly because of the dress code, trying to enforce the dress code." Whereas earlier Kim targeted male students, Genette disclosed that she filtered her activism of enforcing the dress code through her conservative views of how girls should dress, thus targeting female students. Tim stated that working in a conservative community facilitated his activism. For Randy, his conservative school community complicated the deployment of his activism:

> One thing I would say that has made it harder, even though we are in [a metropolitan] area, my particular school division is very, very conservative. The things that I hear that they are doing in other counties, we have yet to implement it, probably due to some opposition that we would expect to get. And sometimes, that kind of puts your fire out, or your energy out, or your enthusiasm out.…

The term *Bible Belt* is suggestive of an approach that can be described as conservative. For Gennette, Lorraine, Tim, and Randy, living and working in the Bible Belt was a significant factor related to their activism. Their activism was impacted by their perception of their conservative school community or conservative self in terms of facilitating or complicating the work.

Educator Activists' Work: Closeted and Cloaked Activism

> I learned how to do it more effectively, how to finesse the situation very gently in a way that will prod somebody to learn, challenge the system they are working from, the assumptions they are working from, but in a way that does not cause a huge self-crisis that throws up the defense mechanism and burns the bridge between your ability to reach them at that moment and in the future. (Sara)

As discussed in chapter 1, activists' work, individual and collective, may be represented by many forms ranging from symbolic gestures such as wearing buttons to public displays of support such as front line picketing. The activist work of these educators was conservative and carried out under mandates, curricula, and pedagogical cloaks. In my dissertation (Jones, 2005) I suggested that educators "activised their roles" (p. 93), highlighting the ways these educators' embedded activism in their work through daily routines. Their activism was aimed at making their schools safe, raising awareness, and enforcing sexual harassment policy and procedures. Sara spoke about the daily charge of making schools and classrooms safe and her desire to create safe hostility-free learning spaces for students:

> I want my classroom to be a safe classroom. I want the school to be a safe school…to focus on creating and maintaining a safe space within my room really, really paying attention to interactions between men and women, girls and boys…to pay attention to (because I think sexual harassment doesn't have to be cross-gender), I see a lot of sexual harassment especially between boys-to-boys. I'm not sure about women-to-women, if I have seen that as much.

Administrators and teachers are expected to manage safe, nurturing, secure, disciplined, and hostility-free schools in which students are able to transition about without fear of being bullied or sexually harassed by their peers (Shuttleworth, 2003). The educator's quote above illustrates recognition of this expectation and the commitment to making it happen.

The first significant site of activism for these educators was in the classroom and point of entry into activist work was through the curriculum. This finding is supported by previous research on educator activists that discussed how schoolteachers used their capacity as educators to work outside of their schools as political agents as well as engaging in political action through their curricular choices (Dove, 1995; Ginsburg et al., 1995).

Curricular and pedagogical strategies and methods were employed to disseminate information and create spaces for discourse about sexual harassment and related topics within their workspaces—classrooms, offices, hallways, and other arenas within the school building. Most frequently, the classroom was used as the primary hub for their activist work as evidenced in the following excerpts from Sara and Kerry:

> In my classroom I teach English. I see that as a vehicle to talk about…kinds of violence and issues around social justice. Research papers give [students] opportunity to explore some of these issues, and ask questions, and think about it. I can use literature as a way to tap into different forms of sexism or sexual harassment or let's look at this or talk about this, those are ways that I can bring it in. Opening space to explore issues and to think about them is a type of activism. That's how I bring it into education into my classroom. That's my work. It kind of looks like that. (Sara)

> Well the first week…all the students were saying, "that's gay" to everything. And this was an honors class that I am getting ready to talk about, their honors 11 American Lit class.… Then we started reading *Middle Passage*. I don't know if you remember the opening of that book, part of it is the cabin boy and the captain, and the cabin boy comes scrambling out of the captain's quarters pulling his pants up. It's very graphic. It's the only thing in the book that's a little bit off, you know. But, it is on our list, and as soon as you get by that little paragraph, it's all right. But, that brought the conversation back up again, homosexuality, gay, what is ok and what is not ok. And, through the discussions in that classroom, two boys and one girl actually came out just from that little conversation we were having. One of the boys came out all the way because he was afraid to at home. (Kerry)

Educator activist literature frames educators as having power and agency to challenge and question existing social structures as discussed in chapter 1. Sattler (1997) concluded that "teaching is subversive, political, and activist…and education is inherently political…[the very essence of] teaching children to ask questions, to question their beliefs and sex-role stereotypes, and to examine silences in their school curricula" is political (p.162). The activist work discussed here is not described in terms of parades and protests traditionally associated with activism. As these teachers, principals, counselors, and central office level staff actively worked to make their schools safe, to educate students and staff about sexual harassment, and to enforce school sexual harassment policies, their activism was quietly done. There was, however, the establishment of networks at the microlevel. In school sites, teachers collaborated with the counselor; the counselor enlisted the help of the school resource officer; the administrator utilized materials and workspace of staff; the principal facilitated school community meetings. The networks were established based on the shared goal to raise awareness about student-to-student sexual harassment. This notion that shared beliefs are at the center of social networks is supported in the literature (Diani & Eyerman, 1992).

Most of the educators preferred working, individually, one-on-one with students or in small groups when addressing student-to-student sexual harassment. The majority of the study participants described their student-to-student sexual harassment activism as a part-time, one person at a time endeavor, only engaging in activist work while in their educator role. The majority of their activist work was pedagogical in nature and conducted in the confines of the school site, collaborating mainly with those individuals with whom they worked.

Activists' Confounding Dilemmas

If I was completely honest, that's part of why I'm back in [graduate] school right now...because I have to figure out a way to negotiate the conflict and navigate my path as an educator and the system and learn how to do this work.... I think talking about any of these issues around social justice in the public schools is more difficult because there's such a push on the curriculum, there's such a push on the standard course of study, on teaching for our tests....

As Sara reflected with deep introspection in the above quote, educator activists must tread carefully as they negotiate their activist path through the assumptive world of education (Marshall & Kasten, 1994; Marshall & Mitchell, 1991). Reflective practitioners by trade, these activist educators shared the personal and professional strains and tensions they encountered as they attempted to negotiate a balance between their work and their activism. Fear was a common feeling among these educators. These educators' fears had roots ranging from possible misinterpretations of their activities, their embarrassment regarding sexual language, and fear of job loss as evidenced in the quotes below. First, Kim:

I wouldn't go to the administration and say "I beg to differ on your interpretation of the law and I think that you handled it very flippantly," and that's why it's so pervasive in society because of that exact feeling of how they are treating it. But, I wouldn't go to the administration because I would feel backlash.

Kerry's activism impacted her professional relationship with colleagues:

I lost a lot of contacts in the faculty.... They stopped talking to me. I tried to have conversations with them. I tried to let them know that the purpose was strictly to have a safe place to talk about issues. That was really all it was about from my perspective. But, they weren't going for that and it was...it was awful really. They would go to the other side of the hallway to avoid saying anything to me. Certainly not everybody...but a good percentage of the faculty...and that was odd...I thought. This is an educated group, right?

Although their fears and limitations impacted their activist work, these educators did not let fear paralyze their activism. In fact it motivated two educators in the study to pursue other venues for their activism. Sara was one of two educators in the study conflicted in her decision to remain in the classroom given the limitations placed on her activist work. Both decided to leave the profession. The lack of time and lack of creative control in administering the curriculum was the determining factor for Sara.

The decision of the second educator to leave teaching was prompted by his own admission: "My fear and internalized homophobia caused me to really be sick all the time." Mike, a gay male physical education teacher, had experienced first hand sexual harassment in his youth and as an elementary school educator feared close interaction with his elementary students:

> I would have been active earlier because I was certainly feeling the pain, even though in elementary school, [being gay] was a lot easier to get away with. [My sexuality] was never an issue, although, it was always in my mind. Kids, I know, needed hugs so bad—but it was hands off. Don't even get close; don't even think about it. I'm naturally a huggy person. They're safe with me, so I turn to the side and give a side hug, you know.

His second reason for leaving the classroom was due to the desire to broaden the arena for educating more people about the issues of sexual harassment.

Moving Out of School Sites

Sara and Mike felt it necessary to relocate to educational arenas that were more conducive to their activist work as their activism grew outward. Mike's work after leaving the classroom, writing health education curriculum and conducting related workshops, enabled him to potentially inform more individuals about this issue:

> I got out of the classroom and tried to influence [sexual harassment issues] from the teacher level versus the one-on-one with students, although, I love working with students. Obviously, if I can influence 12 teachers, they in turn can influence 400 kids each. Then we've got something done.

Mike's activism was the most broad-based of all the educators in this study as he had engaged in activist work at the local, state, and national levels. Sara agreed that working in a nonpublic school site facilitated activist work:

> I think that a program that's designed specifically to recognize this oppression and to serve students in a way that empowers them and educates them about these issues is going to be more acceptable and open to talking about different kinds of violence and issues around social justice. I had more leverage and more room in there to really bring these issues in and talk about them in an open way.

Although Lorraine did not leave the profession, she visualized greater involvement for herself:

> I could see myself working beyond the school setting because it is a passion of mine. It's something that I would personally want to lobby the senate; the state senate, about in regards to getting or bringing more attention to [student-to-student sexual harassment] in the same way that they brought more attention to bullies don't belong in the classroom. You know, pedophiles and students that sexually harass others; they don't belong either. Yes, I can see myself continuing to be involved and my involvement would probably be heightened after I left the field of education because I would not feel that my hands would be tied or I would have to be careful as to how vocal I was on this particular subject and there would not be consequences for me later.

Leaving the classroom facilitated Mike and Sara's activism. Working in arenas more conducive to their activist work enabled them to enhance the discourse and speak more openly and to a wider audience about the issues of sexual harassment or oppressive social issues. For Lorraine, leaving the school site to bring the issue of student-to-student sexual harassment to the top of the legislative agenda is her vision.

Insights and Revelations

Interviews for this study revealed an abundance of rich, descriptive detail about educators and their activist work. Significant findings included recognition that both personal and professional resources and factors frame how educators identify with the issue of student-to-student sexual harassment; that identity drives educators' activism to stop the harassment, and that involvement in student-to-student sexual harassment activism impacts the educators involved. In addition to my initial hypotheses that both personal and professional resources and factors frame how educators identified with the issue of student-to-student sexual harassment, that identity drove their activism to stop harassment, and that there are consequences of their decision to participate, I also expected to find that these educators were working to stop student-to-student sexual harassment because their job requires it pursuant to Title IX legislation.

Through interviews with activists, I also found additional personal and professional impacts unique to the activism of the educators in this study. For example, victimization, or having experienced rape or sexual harassment, emerged as an impetus for involvement in student-to-student sexual harassment activism. These educators were involved in direct activism given that they were on the front lines doing the work in their classrooms, schools, and related jobs yet they were nonparticipants or distanced participants in any organized social movement group. Also, these educator activists indicated that male students were watched more closely than female students in classrooms, which took the onus of student-to-student sexual harassment off of the females. Another fascinating discovery was the way the Bible Belt seemed influential in this increased supervision of males as Bible Belt norms both facilitated and complicated the deployment of activism of these educators.[3]

Other new insights about the student-to-student sexual harassment activism of these educators emerged as a result of this research. In addition to the influence of identity in activist work that I expected to discover, these interviews revealed the importance of educators' knowledge of Title IX and sexual harassment law to their actions to stop student-to-student sexual harassment. That knowledge impacted how educators identified with student-to-student sexual harassment, their activism, and how their activism was deployed. Knowledge of Title IX and sexual harassment policy was useful when dealing with sexual harassment, although policy was not often used as a point-of-reference for initiating discourse about student-to-student sexual harassment. These educators' diverse interpretations of the law resulted in varying degrees of enforcement of the school's sexual harassment policy. Their interpretations ranged from disregarding what the law stipulates, relying on the victim's interpretation of the harassment, to enforcing the policy to the letter of the law. Educating administrators, staff, students, and other members of the school community about Title IX and the school's sexual harassment policy, and ensuring that the policy is being enforced in a standardized way increases the chance of effective and efficient implementation, and are first steps to stopping sexual harassment (Francis, 2001; Macgillivray, 2004; Paludi & Barickman, 1998). These educators suggested a need for a comprehensive, effective, and efficient framework for educating school stakeholders. The cornerstones of the framework include continuous discourse, training, curricular strategies, and support all aimed at identifying, addressing, and stopping student-to-student sexual harassment through understanding Title IX and related school policies. It also indicates that residing and working in the Bible Belt affected their activism as illustrated in the educators' stories.

I asked these educators to share their stories about activism to stop student-to-student sexual harassment, and out of these stories emerged a surprising insight. The common language and expectations of conservatism that permeate education in the Bible Belt region, along with the varied impacts of this conservatism on the educators' activist work led to the insight that conservatism binds activism. For some of the educators, stories of religion intertwined with the conservative nature of their communities, for others it was their own conservative upbringing or conservative political stance that complicated or facilitated their activism.

This chapter is a snapshot from the study. It is not meant to cause an alarmist movement, but rather an awareness movement. If schools are to ensure that all students receive an education and participate in school activities in an environment free from any unwelcome or unwanted sexual behavior, sexual harassment must be addressed. Peer sexual harassment occurs most frequently *in* school, and extinguishing harassment falls squarely on the shoulders of the site-based educators. A wealth of resources pertaining to effectively confronting student-to-student sexual harassment is available from a variety of reputable sources, so why is the work not being done? This chapter, describing specific ways these educators activised their career roles, can be a beginning. This work demonstrates that it behooves educators to lead the charge and raise the level of consciousness. The work of the activists in this study was performed at the microlevel with little or no supportive social networks. Some educators did not want to risk being too activist out of fear of backlash and related repercussions in their work lives. Others put it all on the line, testing job limitations, their will, and their spirit, to ensure that the learning environments and lives of their students were free of sexual harassment.

For those individuals who choose to involve themselves in social movement activity, there is often a struggle with the decision to enact social change at the risk of nonconformity with institutional practices and norms. As discussed in chapter 1, every organization has its own organizational identity, its own culture, and its own rules, and this is true in education. Those who challenge the existing social structures or culture of the school may be subject to personal and professional risks dependent upon the impact of their actions on the organization (Hogg & Terry, 2001; Lofland, 1996; Owen, 2001). Educators must be concerned about personal and professional risks ranging from social stigma to job dismissal to loss of life in some instances (Lofland, 1996). Those who are administrators also worry about being tagged as troublemakers, which can result in stifled career mobility (Marshall & Kasten, 1994; Marshall & Mitchell, 1991).

As they faced personal choices and dilemmas, these educators highlighted professional strains and tensions that they contended with in choosing to do activist work. These tensions included compliance-related frustrations, fears of parental repercussions, administrator backlash, and the trouble, isolation, and embarrassment that can accompany activism. These activists articulated clear concerns about the professional risks of activism on educators' careers, and they cited the lack of a culture of support for their activism against student peer harassment. Embedded in their talk, these educators revealed factors that would facilitate their activism: (1) public discourse about ongoing issues of sexual harassment; (2) teacher and administrator training to recognize and confront harassment; and (3) appropriate curriculum that supports educators' work to confront student-to-student sexual harassment. Educator activists are searching for support in their profession. The challenge for policymakers, school districts, and individual schools is to provide a comprehensive framework of supports for educators, thus creating space, affording latitude, and building capacity for activist work toward stopping student-to-student sexual harassment in schools.

Notes

1. See "Site-Based Voices: Dilemmas of Educators Who Engage in Activism Against Student-to-Student Sexual Harassment" (Jones, 2005).
2. The terms peer sexual harassment and student-to-student sexual harassment are used interchangeably.
3. In chapter 8, note the description of my reframing to guide data analysis. As I listened to the stories that emphasized conservative values, I realized the need for wider framing.

5
Surprising Ways to be an Activist

WANDA LEGRAND

I was inspired to study educator activists as a result of the experiences of one of my good friends. My friend and I started teaching at the same school at around the same time. We received our masters' degrees in education administration from different state universities; they had a similar program of study, and both had a good reputation in the state. After receiving those degrees, we were both hired as assistant principals within the same school district in which we taught. As assistant principals, we were considered up-and-coming leaders within the district and were often asked to do presentations for other educators who wanted to pursue administration. Up to this point we appeared to be following similar career paths, but after two years as assistant principals, things began to change.

I was selected to be a principal, but my friend was not, and there is one difference not yet mentioned that, I believe, prevented him from getting a principalship. He was a gay male, and I was a heterosexual female. As I embarked upon my dissertation research and decided to join this group project studying the lives of educator activists, I was inspired to study educators who are activists for lesbian, gay, bisexual, and transgendered (LGBT) rights because of what I believe happened with my friend. I was convinced that his sexual orientation was the reason he was never given a principalship.

This chapter highlights the surprising ways that educators can be activists—even activists for LGBT rights—that I uncovered during my dissertation research (Legrand, 2005). When I began my study, I did not believe I would find public school educators who were activists for LGBT rights. Educators are often expected to obey a hidden set of rules that serve as preconditions for their employment or advancement (Marshall & Mitchell, 1991; Sattler, 1997), rules one might expect to preclude activism. And activism for LGBT rights seems especially risky, for despite advances in civil rights for African Americans and women, for example, LGBT individuals have found civil rights slow in coming.

Societal and Legal Progress for LGBT Rights

Educator activists are functioning within a context of slow societal and legal support for LGBT rights. Two hindrances for advancement in civil rights for LGBT individuals are the lack of civil rights and the oppressive reactions to gayness (Goodman, Lakey, Lashof, & Thorne, 1983). Civil rights protections for LGBT citizens are limited. As of July 2002, only 3 states had codified LGBT civil rights protections, with 11 states offering lesbian/gay/bisexual (LGB) protections (Lugg, 2003). Typically, this legislation bans discrimination against any individual based on his or her sexual orientation in employment, housing, and public accommodations, sometimes extending to select other areas. Yet passage of such legislation meets many challenges. State legislators in New York, for example, were first asked in 1971 to amend existing human rights laws to include the words *sexual orientation*, yet did not ratify such protections until 2002 (Rothenberg , 2001).[1] Oppressive reactions to gayness include the various reactions that LGBT individuals experience when their sexual orientation is revealed or known (Goodman, Lakey, Lashof, & Thorne, 1983). The best-known example is the "Don't Ask. Don't Tell" policy of the U.S. Armed Services, by which LGBT individuals are allowed in the armed services as long as their sexual orientation is not known or disclosed. When their orientation is known, they are relieved of duty.

However, the armed services are not alone in their oppressive actions toward LGBT individuals. The medical system has proven to be quite oppressive as well. Goodman et al. (1983) found that historically, the field of "psychiatry is the worst offender" (p. 18), citing psychiatrists' efforts to try to find the cause of homosexuality, and thus advance such cures as electric shock treatment and aversion therapy. It was not until 1973 that the American Psychiatric Association (APA) voted to remove homosexuality from its list of sexual disorders.

Oppressive reactions to gayness in the medical field are evident outside of the world of psychiatry as well. Rothenberg (2001), for example, shared the story of Michelle DuPont, a lesbian who sought a new primary care physician. When DuPont filled in the name of her partner of three years in the appropriate space and "domestic partner" as a choice for marital status on a medical registration form her physician told her that he did not approve of her lifestyle and suggested that she make her next appointment with another physician in his practice. When sued by DuPont, the attorney for the doctor denied that his client discriminated against DuPont because he did not refuse her medical care but made other arrangements. Still, documentation of the DuPont-like challenges to oppressive reactions to gayness and the lack of LGBT civil rights—one of countless examples—encourages activism for the rights of LGBT people. Where laws and courts provide little protection, social movements are ignited for collective action.

Many scholars date the start of gay rights activism and its ignition as a social movement to the June 27, 1969 police raid of a gay bar called the Stonewall Inn in New York City (Lugg, 2003). During this raid, Stonewall patrons fought back by beating policemen and smashing patrol cars: the fighting continued for five nights. The fact that these marginalized citizens actually fought back so violently changed the vision and perception of LGBT people forever (Lugg, 2003).

The contemporary gay rights movement began with the incident at the Stonewall Inn, and led to the emergence of two prominent groups: the Gay Liberation Front (GLF) and the Gay Activist Alliance (GAA). GLF wanted to end oppression for all people and worked with other groups such as the Black Panthers to do so. In contrast, GAA was only focused on securing basic rights for gay men and lesbians (Lugg, 2003). The GLF—also referred to as the Gay Liberation Movement—was developed from the encounter between the Homophile Movement and the New Left (Armstrong, 2002). The Gay Liberation Movement, or Front, was the first to advance the political strategy of "coming out" (Armstrong, 2002, p. 57; Lugg, 2003, p. 64). Armstrong (2002) explained this strategy:

> Gay liberation, on the surface, is a struggle for homosexuals for dignity and respect, a struggle for civil rights. Of course, we want to "come out" (that is, to end our hiding), to forbid such terms as "faggot," "dyke," and "queer," to hold down jobs without having to play straight, and to change or abolish those laws which restrict or denigrate us. (p. 30)

This recent history provides the background for the societal struggle for LGBT rights. The struggle within education is complicated, in part, because even well-intended, progressive policy makers and educators who in general care about human and civil rights, still shy away from LGBT issues.

LGBT Educators Join the Fight

Certainly this societal and legal turmoil affected educators concerned about LGBT rights. Potential activist educators were made uneasy by the U.S. military's "don't ask, don't tell" policy; by the negative intervention of courts and state legislatures in the personal lives of LGBTs; by the oppressive treatments for LGBT identification by psychiatrists and other medical personnel. At the same time, the national movements in civil rights generally, and in LGBT rights specifically, emboldened a few activist educators.

Bolstered by the solidarity following the Stonewall riot, LGBT educators joined other LGBT individuals in public demonstrations for their rights. In New York City in 1971, the first demonstration took place at the Board of Education (Harbeck, 1997). LGBT educators picketed and "presented affidavits concerning discrimination against lesbian and gay male teachers" (Harbeck, 1997, p. 236). Chancellor for the New York City School System, Harvey Scribner, convinced the group that it was the State Board of Examiners that created school policies, leading to a sit-in by LGBT educator activists in the Examiners' offices. This protest was the first reported incident of LGBT educators collectively risking their jobs for their rights.

LGBT individuals pursue (at least) two goals at once: dealing with a sexual orientation that is not widely accepted and also acknowledging their membership in a minority group that is largely invisible (McCarn & Fassinger, 1996). To complicate this focus, LGBT educators are often involved in an "evolving dynamic where they struggle to present themselves authentically" while also protecting their jobs, physical safety, and emotional well-being (Kisen, 1993, p. 20). LGBT educators must both establish their images as professional educators and also cope with the emotional strain of leading a double life as an LGBT individual and as an educator, often working to prevent the two from intertwining. Kisen (1993) posited that LGBT educators often exist in a "glass closet" where they establish an authentic identity as a professional educator while protecting their own safety from harassment, isolation, social condemnation, and job loss (p. 3).

Insights from this history of societal and legal struggle provided me with the grounding I needed to understand my friend's experience in not receiving the promotion to principal that he deserved and to begin my exploration of those who are both LGBT activists and educators.

Enacting Activism

Contrary to my initial expectations, I learned that there *are* educators in public schools who are also activists for LGBT. As shown in Table 5.1, my 10 study participants were between the ages of 22 and 60, male and female, who were (or had been) practicing K-12 teachers or administrators in public schools in the United States between 1970 and 2002. The participants were gay, lesbian, or allies and worked in various school districts; some worked in districts with nondiscrimination policies that included sexual orientation while others did not. This chapter will tell the stories of educator activism for LGBT rights, illuminating their work independently or in groups, within their schools and school systems, and beyond their workplaces.

Activism as Individuals

A central component of social movement theory posits the importance of collective actions taken against powerful opponents in order to right societal wrongs (Tarrow, 1998). This was the theoretical base from which I considered how the educators in my study not only participated in collective actions as members of the gay community, but also participated in individual activism. How did the activists in my study view collective action? My activists for LGBT rights were at diverse points along a continuum that ranged from solo activities to those working as members of activist organizations.

At one end of the continuum were solo activities conducted by educators working as individuals. Fred, Carl, and Joseph all took individual initiative and participated in activist activities such as protest marches, AIDS fundraising walks, and writing to policy makers to share their views on LGBT rights. For

Table 5.1 Participants

Pseudonym	Sexual Orientation	Job/Position	Policy	Race	Number of Years in Profess
George	Gay	Principal	Yes	Black	12
Mary	Straight	Teacher	Yes	White	23
Kimberly	Straight	Teacher	No	White	27
Fred	Gay	Asst. Principal	No	Black	6
Carl	Gay	Counselor	Yes	White	8
Joseph	Straight	Teacher	Yes	White	9
Lucy	Lesbian	Teacher	No	White	3
Raven	Lesbian	Retired Teacher	No	White	33
John	Gay	Teacher	No	White	22
Tameka	Lesbian	Teacher	Yes	Black	4

Note. Policy indicates whether school system where they worked the majority of their career had an anti-discrimination policy that included sexual orientation.

example, Fred reported, "I'm not out there with signs…or the bullhorn…. My strength is writing. I can write something and let policy makers know that I don't appreciate what [they] said…. I make people think." Although he spoke of avoiding the visible activism, and, in that sense as being "in the closet," he viewed behind-the-scenes activism as viable. Fred also considered his interactions with his friends as activist activity. He said,

> I don't let them know about my personal situation, but I let them know you may need to rethink what you said [about lesbian, gay, bisexual, or transgendered people]. I try to relate [gay] rights to our rights as African Americans and minorities because at one point people would say, people still say, "You shouldn't get this or that because you are African American." I said "How would you feel on that? It's the same as that type of thing. You've got to protect all people's rights."

When asked about his activities, Carl explained, "I think I probably lead more by example than anything else. I don't really talk about my private life with my students or faculty and staff in the schools in which I work." Still, he believed that just being an openly gay man was a quiet but effective activist strategy.

Although Fred avoided "[letting others] know about my personal situation," and Carl avoided "[talking] about my private life," they still chose to speak out about LGBT rights issues. So, although public stands and public collective action were not always viewed as safe or comfortable, individual activism was still possible.

School Activism

All participants in my study indicated that they participated in activism for LGBT rights within their schools. When asked specifically for ways to be an activist within the system, George provided this explanation:

> By creating safe spaces for kids…one good way really is through curriculum. Something as simple as reviewing the books that are found in the library, making sure that the ones that are purchased reflect the population, and give kids good places to go for good information, because there's a lot of misinformation out there. Bringing in presenters, speakers, having discussions, having conversations.

Additional forms of school activism included making faculty members aware of and sensitive to the needs of all children, assuring that literature discussions include homosexuality if it appears to have impacted the work being presented, and reviewing library books to make sure they "reflect diverse populations." George, Mary, Fred, Joseph, and Tameka explained that within the school they participate in activism by creating and maintaining a classroom that is safe for all students and free from gay-related slurs or insults.

School activism in Mary's classroom was based on "just the basics of treating people fairly" and incorporating character education. She declared:

> A lot of LGBT teens are so harassed. It's just an obvious sort of opportunity. I always make a very clear stand in the classroom if there is ever any kind of derogatory remark made or anything like that. I immediately bring it up to focus and then just move on.

For Fred, activism also included immediately addressing any issue where students were harassed by stereotypical and harsh comments. He said he would not "let it slide as some teachers have done." Joseph concurred that "gay-related slurs or insults" and "negative comments about gays as a group" were not tolerated in his classroom. In Tameka's classroom, she "enforces school rules and discipline" by not allowing students to call each other gay or lesbian under the rule governing "name calling and respect." In addition to making her classroom a safe space, Tameka also worked to assist students dealing with day-to-day concerns about being gay or lesbian. She confided:

> There are several students who come and talk to me about their lifestyle and the impact it has on their life. These students are troubled every day because of how they are treated at school and home. They are stereotyped because of how they dress and who they hang around with. I try my best to keep these students focused. I let them know without encouraging the lifestyle that it is nothing wrong with doing what they believe in. I talk with them because I can see their frustration. I can listen to them and give them advice without telling them I am a lesbian.

The day-to-day concerns about being gay or lesbian that Tameka's students endured are similar to the oppressive reactions to gayness expressed in the literature (Goodman et al., 1983). According to the literature, others' negative reactions to gayness often encourage activism for the rights of LGBT people, and this is clearly the case as described by Tameka.

Three participants started a Gay Straight Alliance (GSA) at their school, while three others incorporated activities into their lessons such as discussing diversity, "treating all people fairly," and providing character education. As a fighter for social justice on a personal level, Lucy took that position one step further and empowered her students in her social studies classes to do the same. She said:

> I try to live what I preach within my classroom and try to help students see that they too are a part of the political process in creating change in the world. I think being honest with kids in this day and age is sort of being an activist in the classroom. A lot of kids think that maybe because they're in sort of the margins of society they don't have a means or the intelligence or whatever they think they need to be an activist. If you can help them to see that and help them foster that ability to create change then they'll really sort of grasp hold of it. Because they're not satisfied with the way things are. I mean you can ask any of my kids, and there's something that they would change. It's just a matter of helping them understand that they can be a part of creating that change.

Joseph elaborated a similar point:

> An effective thing I've done with my students is, when issues come up, when there is some kind of discussion about gays and lesbians and what their "proper role" is in society—the students have very defined ideas of how gays and lesbians should operate in society. When I challenge that, I try to challenge it on an intellectual level. "Tell me what basis, on what legal basis, on what moral basis are you going to exclude these people? You need to make that case for me. You can't simply operate in fear. If you are acting in fear, you have to recognize and address that."

Such actions illustrate the political and activist use of curriculum to address oppression, especially as shown in the actions of Joseph, Lucy, and Tameka. Although educators' actions may be predicted as part and parcel of their political power (Ginsburg, 1995), these educators' activism illustrates how educators have an opportunity to flex their political muscle through curriculum decisions, pedagogical actions, student evaluation, and research.

Group and Community Activism: Going Public for Larger Societal Change

While many of the educators participated in individual activism, 8 of the 10 had been or were current members of groups that support or advocate for LGBT people and their rights such as Gay Straight Alliance (GSA), Gay Lesbian Straight Educators Network (GLSEN), Human Rights Campaign (HRC), and Parents, Family and Friends of Lesbians and Gays (PFLAG). Collective actions of social movements are distinct from individual actions because they bring the resources of groups of individuals to bear, challenging and threatening established groups and carrying the potential to effect social change—recall our chapter 1 review of social movement theory, especially Oberschall (1993). Collective actions are an "ongoing process in all social movements struggling to overturn existing systems of domination" (Taylor & Whittier, 1992, p. 510). As members of groups that support or advocate for LGBT people and their rights, participants have acted as individuals and as educators; as individuals by taking part in rallies, socials for queer educators, marches, fundraisers, and support groups, and as educators by involving or supporting students in activities that included alternative proms for LGBT students, Day of Silence, and World AIDS Day.

Career Dilemmas in Nonsupportive Work Environments

The educators in this study participated in activism as individuals and in groups. However, they were not working within supportive workplaces. As predicted by the literature surrounding educator activism, the activists in this study faced career dilemmas. Given that educators navigate hidden sets of rules in order to remain employed and achieve career mobility, they encounter and attempt to overcome many barriers in their careers (Marshall & Mitchell, 1991; Sattler, 1997). Being at all political in the education career is suspect, but acting to assert LGBT issues increased the risks of these educators' activism. Activism created career dilemmas for the participants in this study, including decisions pertaining to degree of involvement in activism, whether to "come out" at work as lesbian or gay, attempting to make their activism manageable, and seeking support for their activism.

Tempered Choices

The educators in this study reported that they tempered their activism choices as educators in their careers. The adjustments for these educator activists involved decisions about their participation and degree of involvement in activist activities, about coming out at work, and about their role in activities. Seven of the educators in this study shared stories of the kinds of choices in deciding to participate in LGBT activism. Reflecting recognition of education's assumptive world rules (Marshall & Mitchell, 1991) these educators modified and tempered their activist choices, "limiting risk taking to small and finite projects" (p. 397). In this case, "small" was a subjective concept, and its definition varied in different schools and school districts and from educator to educator. They knew that they needed to display loyalty to the dominant values, to avoid presenting divergent ideas and demands, and to keep problematic issues quiet, within school walls.

Some of the LGBT educators appeared to consciously have assumptive world rules in mind as they made decisions about their actions, while others appeared to ignore the rules and throw caution to the wind in order to effect change in the schools where they worked, and were willing to continue their activism for LGBT rights when necessary.

Degree of Involvement Carl made a conscious choice to be the advisor of the first GSA in his school system. While reflecting on that moment, Carl stated:

> I remember rolling that around in my head for a couple of moments before I said yes. Probably a total of five to eight seconds; it didn't take me long to say yes. I thought it was fascinating. I think that's what got me more than anything else. I remember thinking that having one of these [groups] show up is really going to blow the roof off this place.

By agreeing to start the GSA, Carl gained satisfaction in realizing that he paved the way for other GSAs to start at other high schools within his school district. While Carl's activism led him to start the first GSA in his school district at the high school where he worked, Joseph had to "temper the choices" he made as an activist because of his job. He felt that his concern to keep his job "squelched" his desire "to fight the issue." He stated his concern this way:

> I don't think I work in an overly oppressive environment where I can't speak my mind, but I do know that I am probably liberal to a fault. I know that sometimes I have to pull back from what I would like to do in order to maintain participation in the mainstream.

Lead the Parade or "Sit Back?" Each of the seven educators who shared that they had made deliberate choices in deciding to participate in activism for LGBT rights also indicated that they made choices regarding their level of involvement. George admitted that he did not "always advocate" but sometimes, "like many adults," he will "sit back" on occasion. In describing his level of involvement, George used a parade analogy: "Most people would think I fit the role of the grand marshal." However, George rejected that role, as well as the roles of band member, clown, and spectator, like "someone…holding a baby up in the air watching the parade." Instead, George said he would be the "person sitting off to the side who orchestrated the whole parade, planned…[and] did all of the setup." He indicated that this was the role he preferred and one that he would play in the future regarding his activism. He described it as "not totally behind the scenes, but very much the architect."

Having decided to bring LGBT activism into their careers, educators found that it could create conflicts with their careers. Joseph, for example, learned that parents expressed concerns about some of the things he revealed in class or his "attitudes towards gays and lesbians," although he indicated that he felt "the comfort of falling back" on his curriculum "which does seem to make it easier." His curriculum included the study of ancient Greece and Rome, which, he believed, made gays and lesbians "legitimate topics of discussion." While Joseph felt he had the safety net of his curriculum, John admitted to having to move to a new school more than once because of conflicts with administrators and his activist activities, having no safety net or policies to support him. As noted above, Carl chose to lead by example in a more subtle form of activism, choosing to be "not nearly as active as some other people."

Choices and Ulcers

A common activist story was the frequent choices they made in deciding "to act or not to act" based on the situation at hand. George revealed that as he got older he decided that if he did not "say something" or "stand up…there may come a time when there's no one to stand up and say and do." With that in mind, he tried to say what was on his mind and tried to advocate. According to Raven, her "choices regretfully have been made later in life." She confided:

> I think that's due to fear. The choice was to stand up for what I believe, no matter what the consequences. When I was younger, and the income was vital to exist, and acceptance was something that was a big part of, you know, being in your 20s and 30s, that was, it was too scary to come out and to be an activist. When I got older, it's like, what the hell? What damage has this done being silent? How many ulcers do I have? How many opportunities have I lost? I think you just, regretfully; you get to a point in your life when you're older when you just say the most important thing is to be truthful. I'll never forget a saying that someone was talking about that when you're in the closet all you do is live with lies, secrets, and silences. So many secrets and silences: So I would say that in my youth, I didn't lie, but I kept secrets and silences.

Even though Raven kept her activism and role as a teacher separate, she refused to "let things go by" that she thought were unfair or harsh. She liked to speak of herself as a teacher of the whole child, not of her subject area. Still, she struggled with being whole herself, perceiving that she could jeopardize her high status as a respected educator by any outspoken LGBT activism.

"Choosing From that Point On to Do the Right Thing" (George)

What pushes LGBT activists over the edge in the decision to speak out and get involved in action? Even with idealism about fairness and liberatory pedagogy, educators sensed a need to keep their concerns for LGBT issues or their sexuality quiet. Raven struggled with this through a decades-long career as an award-winning teacher. But watching two same-sex friends' ordeal over trying to have their church celebrate their union made her say, "What am I afraid of?" Seeing their courage when people hurled hateful words made her think, "I could certainly stand up and support them…you can't not speak up." The decades of repressing had become a habit, though, so her compulsion to speak up was strongest among friends, not in the public arena of the politics of schooling.

At school, though, several stories reveal educators deciding they *must* speak up. After years of coping with the strain, George "came out" to a history class when students were making derogatory comments about homosexuals. "I finally just had enough and sat down with the class," he said, reminding them that "every time they called someone a fag or a sissy, it hurts me." Similarly, John's determination came as he was struck by the unpleasantness of the rampant antigay comments as he walked the middle school halls. Joseph had always had gay friends but the two neighbors who developed HIV also introduced him to ways to support the community through a community health and education project. For others, it was the suicide attempt of a best friend from college because of family pressure about her lifestyle, or friendships that led to being a "sounding board for lesbian friends who talked about their personal battles with oppressive treatment." For all, it was grounded in a sense or fairness and human rights and, as Mary said, "the idea of education precludes any feelings of 'you are not acceptable, you are not worthy of learning'…I don't know how anybody…could be a serious educator and exclude a student on any basis unless they are acting horribly."

Avoid Being a "Nut" in the Classroom

Joseph and Tameka also spoke of having to temper their activism choices in order to keep their job, indicating that fear sometimes squelched their desire to fight for the cause. Tameka believed that because of her "lifestyle" she was taking a chance with her job by participating in activism. She confided, "I choose to help these students because I believe I can make a difference. At least one less teenager will be lost to suicide." Even though he did not consider his working environment to be overly oppressive, Joseph admitted he made choices to "pull back" from what he would like to do in order to "maintain participation in the mainstream, and not just come off as being an absolute nut," adding that "nuts are not necessarily good for the classroom." Joseph and Tameka's fears are validated by previous research (described above). Participating in activism violates the restrictive and conservative rules for the behavior of public school educators outlined earlier in chapter 1's literature review.

Making It Manageable: Merging Educator Work with LGBT Activism

In order to participate in activism and work as public school educators, all the participants in this study devised ways to do both. Initially, Mary indicated that she separated her activism from her class work, but then quickly changed her mind: "Ah, no, I don't." She admitted that doing both is "a tricky thing because you…you want to be content-appropriate when you need to be, but part of the content in my classroom has to do with just the basics of treating people fairly, and character education too." Kimberly explained that she takes advantage of any "moment in the curriculum that's appropriate" to shed light on the sexual orientation differences of the authors or characters in literature, citing the study of British literature, Edward Albee, and James Baldwin. She also reported that she "always makes a clear stand in the classroom if there is ever any kind of derogatory remark made." Five other educators described activism that involved students or classrooms that they thought was a natural part of being a teacher. For example, as mentioned earlier, Joseph and Tameka banned all negative comments about others, including gay-related slurs. Tameka maintained that when she faced major problems with LGBT issues concerning students and their families, she talked to the student's counselor: "I allow the counselor to make any parent contact needed. I have dealt with students verbally abusing each other down to parents verbally and physically abusing their child, all because they thought they were gay or lesbian." Such were the strategies used, in their minds, to manage their identities, their sense of the need to make a difference, and their need to avoid calling attention to any activism.

George said that as an administrator he "sees advocators for kids, and advocators for kids who are gay, lesbian, bisexual, and transgendered as being one and the same, as an advocate for kids." He surmised that he managed being an activist and an educator by "looking for the similarities [of both roles] instead of trying to draw them out and making them separate things." Joseph also explained how it works for him:

I don't become overly preachy to the students in that I am constructing an agenda to indoctrinate students into my way of thinking. I am just very firm that this is the way that it will be in this classroom. If the students themselves want to know why that is, then I will explain my motivations, but usually what I do is just, that is the rule, the established rule and that's just the way because I say it is. If they are interested to know why, I tell them.

Lucy did not have to think about managing participation in activism and her work as a public school educator; activism appeared to be second nature to Lucy. She indicated that she always did what needed to be done and whatever she did, she did wholeheartedly to the best of her ability: "I think it's my job as an educator to be an activist, especially as a social studies educator because I am teaching kids about society." Tameka also tried to relate any situation in her classroom to real-life. By way of example, Tameka said, "I do not allow students to call each other gay/lesbian. You are not even allowed to use the word [gay] out of context. I tell students they never know who they might be offending especially since half of them don't know what being gay/lesbian really means."

Unlike many of the other participants in my study, Raven managed being an educator and an activist by keeping the two roles separate and also combining passion and humor with her activism. In her opinion, humor diffused many problems in the world, and she believed that if a person cannot laugh at some situations he or she will be "in the corner crying." She said, "And when you're in the corner crying, you are by yourself. And you're not getting much done." All of the participants in this study made activism manageable in various ways ranging from making it a natural part of their educator roles to totally keeping the two roles separate, while being activist only in their personal lives.

Steps for Supporting LGBT Activism

Findings from my research project on educators who are activists for LGBT rights have implications in many areas such as policy, educator training, educator networks, and administrative procedures. When educators find they have to hide key elements in their identities, they may simply leave their careers (or never enter education in the first place), no matter how much they care about schooling and children. They may feel they have to avoid leadership roles since their identities would be more visible and open to community and professional scrutiny. This is a loss, especially when they could be excellent role models and advocates, especially when they, more than most education policy makers, have a sense of just how unsafe and unwelcoming schools are for children who do not meet the strong messages that heterosexuality is *the* normal way to be.

Policy

According to these activists, one of the most strategic actions school districts could take to support LGBT educators is amending nondiscrimination policies to include sexual orientation. Such policies provide legal job security for educators who are activists for LGBT rights and are lesbian, gay, bisexual, or transgendered themselves. This protection could reduce the hesitancy some LGBT educators and their ally activists feel because of their fear that activism could endanger their jobs or generate questions about their sexuality. Eventually, the fear is that those questions and suspicions could evolve into persecution, and potentially job termination, solely based on sexual orientation. Educators working without nondiscrimination laws are very vulnerable in their jobs. The existence of a nondiscrimination policy that includes sexual orientation not only protects activists who are LGBT, it also establishes the school system as an inclusive environment for all people, including those that are LGBT. That inclusive feeling could have an effect on LGBT allies who would feel that their collaboration in activism is not only accepted but even supported in such a workplace.

While 6 of the 10 educators who participated in this study worked in school systems that had nondiscrimination policies that include sexual orientation, this study did not uncover a pattern of behavior that differed between those who worked in school systems with those policies and those without them. Thus, the policy is not the only answer. Further study is needed to explore what other factors, besides policies, make a difference in creating supportive work environments. Future study could compare the working conditions and activism of educators who work in school systems with nondiscrimination policies that include sexual orientation, and those that do not.

Educator Training

Educator training traditionally includes only curricular and pedagogical topics. The topics that are not emphasized include sexuality, sexual orientation, gender, seeing oneself as a whole person, empowerment, and rights as a citizen. And educators' professional preparation certainly does not lay the groundwork for their thinking of themselves as leaders in activism for rights of the marginalized LGBT students and professional educators. Such topics are uncomfortable, even taboo. While 9 of the 10 activists in this study saw a natural fit between being an activist and an educator, how many others do not make the connection? Those who do not see the connections between education and social justice work could decide to avoid activism as public school educators, or avoid becoming public school educators. They could leave the profession, finding more likely arenas in which to pursue their activist passions. If educator training included more explicit discussions about educators' activism, future educators could see role models and learn of strategies to use so that they could participate in the activism of their choice. In addition, overall educator training programs might appear welcoming to activists who do not want to hide or abandon that aspect of their identities in order to serve as a public school educator.

Educator Networks

Support of educator networks was mentioned as a necessary condition for activism for LGBT rights by participants in this study. Several national organizations such as the Association of Supervision and Curriculum Development (ASCD) and National Association for Secondary School Principals (NASSP) have networks or subgroups that support various social justice issues including LGBT rights. However, those organizations have not reached out to support activism by their members. Organizations can support LGBT activism in several ways: by enhancing organizational outreach efforts; demanding that LGBT issues be addressed in preservice and in-service professional training; including literatures on websites and in publications that promote LGBT networks; and making connections between LGBT rights and other civil rights more explicit. While many participants in this study mentioned that educator network support would make provide great comfort, only one participant specifically mentioned knowing about such support.

In all my years moving up "the ladder" in education, I did not know of the existence of LGBT networks, nor did I know of policies and programs of professional organizations. Conducting my own research on this topic, I had to actively pursue information on such networks within professional organizations as it was not readily accessible. In addition to national organizations, local education networks and school boards must also provide support and encouragement for activism for LGBT rights. It should not take an adolescent's suicide or an educator quitting the profession to get this ball rolling. My study shows that those who *would* take on the issues face too many dilemma-laden choices to be the only ones leading the parade.

Administrators' Attention and Procedures

LGBT rights are too easily ignored. My study found a yearning among activists for administrators to provide tangible and symbolic support for LGBT educators, students, and activism. Building principals and assistant principals, as well as central office staff members such as directors, executive directors, assistant superintendents, and superintendents should have competency requirements that include direct action against LGBT discrimination and homophobic remarks and behaviors.[2] Administrators can send strong statements to the community by assertively verbalizing public support for LGBT rights, demonstrating support through hiring and promotion practices, and giving space and other outward encouragement for LGBT programs and safe spaces agendas. Even passive agreement, such as an administrator allowing activism to take place without interference, would be an improvement over the experiences of some LGBT activists and educators. Researching the connection between administrative support and educator activism more closely could provide more specific information and strategies to assist administrators in various types of school systems in knowing what they should and should not do to support their employees who desire to be activists for LGBT rights.

Could the findings of my research project have prevented my friend from leaving public education? It is too late for him because he has absolutely no desire to return. Understandably, he could take only so much isolation, discrimination, and suppression of identity. I hope my research can save other fine educators who can give so much to children.

Notes

1. Complicating activists' challenges of amending state laws to include civil protections against discrimination based on sexual orientation are the existence of state sodomy laws that oppress LGBT citizens (Goodman et al., 1983). Although these laws apply to all individuals, no matter their sexual orientation, they primarily serve to make homosexual acts illegal. Lugg (2003), for example, detailed the experience of Michael Hardwick, who was arrested in his home for consensual sodomy with a male houseguest. Aided by the American Civil Liberties Union (ACLU), Hardwick was prepared to fight his arrest until the district attorney dropped the charges. Hardwick was not satisfied and took his case to federal court in order to challenge the constitutionality of Georgia's consensual sodomy statute. In a 5 to 4 decision, the Supreme

Court ruled that Georgia's statute was constitutional, thereby ruling that homosexuals have no constitutional protection for consensual sex with a same-sex partner, even if it occurs in his or her own home (Lugg, 2003).

2. Marshall and Ward (2004) found that national-level education policy makers acknowledged that their associations avoided calling attention to or putting resources into LGBT issues, saying that the issues made their constituents uncomfortable.

6

Is There Choice in Educator Activism?

AMY L. ANDERSON

Terms of the Debate

Safeguarding reproductive choice and insuring a woman's ability to make decisions about her body are defining issues of the feminist movement and expressions of women's sexual and political rights. "My body, my choice," "Keep Abortion Legal," and "Pro-choice, and I Vote" are slogans that adorn posters, bumper stickers, T-shirts, and placards in the ongoing fight to preserve reproductive freedoms.

Though legalized in 1973 in the landmark *Roe v. Wade* decision of the United States Supreme Court, access to safe and legal abortion has come under persistent attack since *Roe*'s passage. As recently as April 2007, the U.S. Supreme Court upheld a 2003 Congressional ban on a particular late-term abortion procedure. This ruling represents the first significant challenge to *Roe* to become codified in law, what Justice Ruth Bader Ginsburg decried as "alarming" and "irrational" in her dissenting opinion in the cases of *Gonzalez, Attorney General v. Carhart et al.* (05-380) and *Gonzalez, Attorney General v. Planned Parenthood Federation of America, Inc.* (05-1382).[1] Speaking of the majority decision to permit the ban of so-called partial birth abortion, even in cases where the mother's health may be at risk, Ginsburg wrote: "This way of thinking reflects ancient notions about women's place in the family and under the Constitution—ideas that have long since been discredited." She continued:

> It tolerates, indeed applauds, federal intervention to ban nationwide a procedure found necessary and proper in certain cases by the American College of Obstetricians and Gynecologists (ACOG).... And, for the first time since *Roe*, the Court blesses a prohibition with no exception

safeguarding a woman's health.... Revealing in this regard, the Court invokes an antiabortion shibboleth for which it concededly has no reliable evidence: Women who have abortions come to regret their choices, and consequently suffer from "[s]evere depression and loss of esteem.".... The solution the Court approves, then, is not to require doctors to inform women, accurately and adequately, of the different procedures and their attendant risks.... Instead, the Court deprives women of the right to make an autonomous choice, even at the expense of their safety.

Justice Ginsburg's dissenting opinion reminds us of how the government has infantilized women in its legislation, and she expresses her concern that this recent ruling reeks of patriarchal notions of womanhood. Ginsburg's argument serves as a reminder that for all the freedoms women enjoy in contemporary U.S. society, patriarchy endures and works to limit women's freedom of privacy and freedom of choice.

Reproductive choice is a contentious issue in American social, religious, and political life, and while the subject may be avoided during polite dinner party conversation, it is an issue about which many citizens have strong opinions. Candidates for office are expected to take a stand as either pro-choice or pro-life—for it is an issue around which there is little neutral ground—and a candidate's political stance can be a make-or-break position for single-issue voters. Companies also enter the debate through decisions about what procedures or medications are covered in insurance policies as related to reproductive health (e.g., coverage for birth control, maternity or family leave policies).

Private citizens, however, are rarely compelled to take a *public* stance about reproductive choice. Nevertheless, some individuals do choose to engage publicly in the reproductive choice debate. There are many options for pro-choice activism, from fundraising to acting as a clinic escort, from public awareness campaigns to major marches and demonstrations, from running for elective office to supporting comprehensive sex education. My own participation has ranged from joining marches on Washington, to supporting friends through their choice, to writing letters to members of Congress. In my professional life, however, I have not had to censor my pro-choice beliefs for fear of losing my job—or even risk losing favor in my job. However, pro-choice activism maintains degrees of risk for many, and concerns about job security can amplify the perceptions or realities of risk.

If individuals find issues of reproductive choice contentious in their private lives, these dilemmas are amplified at the level of public schooling. Educators, although presumed to have opinions about reproductive choice as individual citizens—as well as opinions on hosts of other political or controversial issues—typically check those opinions at the school door. Debates between pro-choice and pro-life activists and politicians may play out in the court of public opinion, in courtrooms, in the media, around dining room tables, and in front of women's clinics, but as this chapter will show, it is not a conversation taken up by colleagues in schools. As first noted in chapter 1, educators are socialized into silence (Anderson, 1990) in regards to some issues, and this is one of those issues. The same patriarchal notions Justice Ginsburg decries as infantilizing women are also well-documented in education (e.g., Cammack & Phillips, 2002; Grumet, 1988; Leck, 1990; McRobbie, 2007; Weiler, 1988); I argue that patriarchy is evident in light of the silences among educators that surround controversial issues. School leaders set the parameters for educational discourse and silence those discourses that fall outside accepted norms. This keeps discussions of pro-choice activism beyond school walls.

Patriarchy is also evident in regards to the abstinence-only policies that govern students' access to information. While schools have long played some role in edu-cating young people about reproduction, sexuality education curriculum remains the subject of public debate about what children need to know, when, and from whom. Sex education is the placeholder in public middle and high schools for conversations about students' sexuality, most recently controlled by the current fetish with abstinence-only sex education. According to the Alan Guttmacher Institute (2007a), the United States has one of the highest teenage pregnancy rates in the world; Ventura, Mosher, Curtin, Abma, and Henshaw (2001) found that between 800,000 and 900,000 teens in the United States become pregnant each year. Forty-one percent of teens who have children before the age of 18 never com-plete high school (National Campaign to Prevent Teen and Unwanted Pregnancy, 2001). Schools function in part to help students engage with and interpret issues and debates through academic disciplines, providing information to promote students' problem-solving skills, and facilitate students' decision-making skills, yet current federal initiatives work to limit students' access to information about sexual health. In spite of the federal push for abstinence-only sex education, its efficacy in preventing unwanted teen pregnancy and sexually transmitted diseases is widely disputed.[2] Advocates of abstinence-only sex education argue that comprehensive sex education sends messages to teens that sanction their sexual behavior, yet the National Academy of Sciences' Institute of Medicine (2001) found that neither sex education nor access to condoms in schools increase sexual activity among teenagers. In fact, compared to abstinence-only programs, comprehensive sex education has proven effective in delaying initiation of sex among teens (Sexual Information and Education Council, 2005). Students suffer when the sexuality education they receive is filtered through a conservative politics that limits their access to comprehensive information.

As a political and moral issue, and thus a contentious one, reproduction can be dangerous ground for educators pressured to present politically neu-tered personae and follow educationally sanctioned discourses. While state- or district-mandated curricula set parameters for what is covered in public school classrooms, as citizens and moral beings, educators also have personal opinions about what children—and the public—need to know about reproduction and reproductive choice. What dilemmas do educators who would be activists for choice confront when that activist stance comes in conflict with their roles as educators? As public figures with personal beliefs, what conflicts do educators face when personal beliefs come in conflict with the sanctioned curriculum?

This chapter shares the experiences and dilemmas of current or former educators who are or have been activists for reproductive choice as a means of describing how eight women worked to find balance between often competing priorities—honoring their commitments and expectations as educators *and* honoring their commitments to act to protect reproductive freedom. If social movements are characterized by "public, nonroutine dimensions…that challenge and threaten established groups, and…[have] potential for being an agent of social change" (Oberschall, 1993, p. 1), how do pro-choice educators—who are conventionally expected to be routine and nonthreatening in their public role as educators—pursue private activism for choice? As this chapter will demonstrate, at this moment in time there is little room for overlap in the public and private commitments of these educators regarding abortion rights activism. They are as committed to safeguarding reproductive choice as are other educators in this text to advancing racial equity and eliminating sexual harassment. But to the extent that activism as it is conventionally understood requires public action, the women in this chapter felt tremendous pressure to divide their teaching lives from their activist lives. Although the personal may be political, educators seem to enjoy limited freedoms to take public positions as choice activists.

Educators as Pro-Choice Activists

When I became a member of this research group, I chose to study the lives of educators active for reproductive choice for several reasons: protecting reproductive choice is important to me as a woman and as a feminist, it is clearly an issue on the progressive spectrum we chose for our work, and activism in this domain seemed a dilemma-laden pursuit for educators—and thus an interesting case for this research. As indicated in chapter 1, the guiding questions I brought to this work included:

- What does an educator's activism for reproductive choice look like?
- How public can educators be with their activism for reproductive choice?
- How do educators reconcile their pro-choice activist politics and identities with their identities as educator?
- Given that reproductive choice falls outside the domain of sanctioned curriculum in the schools, how do activists for reproductive choice compare to activists for more sanctioned areas?

As soon as I began trying to establish contact with educators active for reproductive choice, however, it became clear just how contentious—or dangerous—the issue is for educators.[3] A teacher who chose not to participate in the study sets the stage for my challenges in finding teachers to interview:

I am trying to think of educators interested in reproductive rights. No one really comes to mind…. I have lots of nonteacher friends who are active with Planned Parenthood, etc. But I can't think of any teacher buddies who are. It is interesting that we don't really talk about it much at school—really pretty much ever. So many of our colleagues are sooooo conservative… that I think we try to stay on common ground as much as possible. (Sylvia, nonparticipant, 30s, elementary schoolteacher)

As Sylvia suggests, this is not a topic that is discussed at school, and as a result, recruiting participants for this study was slow and difficult; ultimately I completed only eight interviews (compared with 10 or more completed by other participants). As noted in Table 6.1, all of the participants interviewed for this chapter were women; six were White women, two were African American. Their ages ranged from 26 to 62, and their time in their careers as educators ranged from 3 to 30 years. All of the women interviewed taught in a Southern state. Of greatest significance for this study, they all identified as pro-choice, but not all consider themselves pro-choice activists; as will be shown below, activism for reproductive choice and a career as an educator are often viewed as incompatible among the women in this study.

Seven of these women: Karen, Molly, Anne, Ashton, Rebecca, and Shantal were still in the profession. Joanne was a veteran of 30 years in the classroom, retiring as a high school English teacher. While Hilda left teaching to return to graduate school, limitations on pro-choice activism were not the primary reason she left the classroom. These limitations did, however, contribute to a generalized sense that teachers were asked to, as she said, "check too much at the door." Hilda described her return to graduate school as a part of her efforts to find other ways to work for social justice in education; this also facilitated a return to more active work for abortion rights.

Table 6.1 Participants' Demographic Information

Pseudonym	Age	Discipline/ Grade Level	Years in Profession
Karen	36	HS Physical Education/ Health	14
Molly	28	HS Biology	7
Anne	48	Assistant Principal	25
Ashton	43	4th grade teacher	22
Joanne	62	Retired	30
Hilda	26	Former teacher, Current graduate student	3
Rebecca	30	6th grade – Math	6
Shantal	39	8th grade – Language Arts	17
Sylvia	Ea 30s	2nd grade – Non Participant	10+

In the state where the women in this study taught, sex education and STD/HIV education are mandated for students (Alan Guttmacher Institute, 2007b). In both cases, abstinence is the stressed policy, with no requirements to cover contraception. Abstinence-only is the approach in 85% of the state's counties, with state statutes indicating that all lessons should stress "a mutually faithful monogamous heterosexual relationship in the context of marriage" (Winn, 2005). Districts wishing to offer more comprehensive sexuality education can do so only after a public hearing and a public review of instructional materials (Donovan, 1998).

What follows gives insight into the challenges these women faced in honoring two dimensions of their identity: educator and activist. Many components factored into the equation. As suggested by chapter 1, conservative influences, which included being in the South, issues of religious conservatism, and the silences around educators' politics, were influential for these women. Also important to these educators were the achievements and sacrifices of feminist forebears who fought to make reproductive choice an option, and those generations of women who experienced illegal abortions. While factors that *got* these women involved in abortion rights vary, the factor that *keeps* them involved, at least at some level, is their belief in the importance of protecting a woman's right to make choices about what happens to her body and in her life.

Choice is Worth Fighting For…

Being pro-choice, it's just a part of who I am. Maybe it's the time I grew up in…I can remember when *Roe v. Wade* was handed down. But this issue is so important, and I'm not sure younger women today appreciate how significant it is. (Anne, administrator)

The theme that unites the women in this study is their passionate commitment to reproductive choice, and each of the women avowed its importance and declared their commitment. Molly echoed Anne:

This is such a dicey issue, but it's so important. My roommate in college had an abortion when we were sophomores.… I went with her to Planned Parenthood, and I was so nervous, and scared for her…but I also felt like she was in really good hands.… It just makes me crazy that people who have no idea about what a woman faces when she has an unwanted pregnancy—I mean it's usually White men you see arguing against abortion, right?—these people who have *no idea* want to tell women what they can and can't do, and it's just not right. There has got to be a choice. Can you imagine having to go back to illegal abortions in this day and age? Can you imagine them really arresting a woman for having an abortion?

Molly introduced many themes here that keep people active for reproductive choice, referencing the trauma of facing an unwanted pregnancy, naming the irony in the demographics of many vocal anti-choice supporters, stating the importance of maintaining access to safe abortions, and lamenting the potential consequences of making abortions illegal.

During the course of the interviews for this study in the spring of 2007, the U.S. Supreme Court handed down its ruling that banned a particular later-term abortion procedure, and this context framed Joanne's remarks:

> I'm so troubled by the people, policies, and laws this administration has been able to put in place. It was truly a shock when the Supreme Court handed down their ruling, and I had an anxious feeling in my stomach for days afterwards. Given the current climate and the justices currently seated on the court, it seems we might be entering a crucial period when attempts to chip away at *Roe* come more and more frequently…and that stuns me, it really stuns me…. I have to believe that the people of this country will not stand for *Roe* to be overturned, but when I look around, I rarely see events aimed at public awareness…. I worry that we're too complacent and letting the Right win the day. But surely when the time comes we will rally to protect *Roe*, surely we won't be so complacent?

Among the participants, only Joanne was of a generation of women who came of age when abortion was illegal, although Ashton and Anne have some memories of the passage of *Roe v. Wade* in 1973. Given her memories of learning about others' illegal abortions, for Joanne the stakes were highest and threats to *Roe* most heartfelt. As Joanne indicated, there was concern among these educators that despite the rhetorical positioning of abortion in the United States that returns it to public attention with each election cycle and each Supreme Court confirmation proceeding, there is too much complacency in regards to protecting choice. Anne, Joanne, Ashton, Shantal, Hilda, and Molly all expressed concern that many younger women take access to abortion for granted and fail to appreciate the threats to reproductive choice. Yet even though these women acknowledged that future court rulings could jeopardize abortion rights, they remained incredulous that access to abortion might actually be denied in their lifetime; these educators had faith that women would rise up should any serious threat to abortion emerge.

Getting Involved Women come to pro-choice activism in various ways and for various reasons, and the same is true for these women. As noted above, Molly's involvement started with a roommate's abortion. Two of the women, who will not be named, had had abortions. Karen was close with someone who had an abortion, though her involvement with the pro-choice movement predated that relationship. Karen grew up in an activist household, "a cause a month club," with choice among many progressive issues the family supported:

> It always seemed we were off to protest something. But it was more than just being out there shouting or carrying a sign…. Dinner was never a

wasted time. My parents saw this as a prime opportunity to talk about important issues—abortion rights, environmental issues, animal welfare. We were always discussing something. There were times growing up when it was embarrassing to have friends over for dinner—you never knew what might come up. But mostly I'm thankful for that training.

With one exception, all of the women interviewed had a close personal connection to someone who had had an abortion, either friends or family members, and each referenced this connection as influential in her desire to become a choice activist.

Only Anne had no intimate connection when becoming a pro-choice activist. Initially, hers was an intellectual connection to the issue. She remembered hearing arguments about abortion among her sister's friends while growing up, arguments that challenged her thinking about right and wrong and who decides. College discussions in women's studies courses and among feminist friends nurtured her pro-choice beliefs, although Anne reflected that it was likely that abortion had touched at least one of those friends. Anne's touchstone was Margaret Atwood's (1998) *The Handmaid's Tale,* a work of fiction that describes a dystopian future in which women's reproductive lives are manipulated and controlled: "I can't tell you how important [that book] was to my thinking about women's rights. Women were so oppressed in that book, and it helped open my eyes to just how close we are to that exaggerated condition." Anne's connections to choice activism were strengthened through participation in the abortion rights movement, grounded in her personal beliefs, and not intimate connections:

I really didn't think I had any close friends who'd had an abortion. It was only recently that a friend told me she'd had an abortion as a younger woman, and she was a good friend I'd known her for years. It's just such a personal issue, not only for the conflicting personal feelings around making the choice in the first place, but because you never know how someone will react if you tell them. No matter what you think you know about someone's politics, you don't always know where they stand on abortion.

Unless we choose to be on the front lines and put a deliberate face to pro-choice activism, we are rarely compelled to make our beliefs public; no set of demographic data can predict beliefs about abortion—there are pro-choice Catholics, for example, and women who oppose abortion. As Anne indicated, you cannot make assumptions about an individual's position on abortion.

...But "Choice is Loaded"

The women interviewed in this research did not underplay or undermine differences of opinion when it comes to abortion. Molly described her divided identity in relation to abortion rights:

I'm pro-choice, but even among my friends it can be a tricky thing. I have, like, two sets of friends. With one set I'm just nice Molly—a schoolteacher, newly married to her college boyfriend, she likes gardening and scrap-booking in her spare time—so these are my upwardly mobile, yuppie-ish friends, and I guess it's the upwardly mobile, yuppie-ish me!... But I also have this more radical group of friends from college—from when I lived in the dorms and we had all kinds of late-night deep conversations. That's the group I'm pro-choice, anti-Bush, anti-war with. [My husband and I] agree, and are both more liberal than many of our friends—I guess that's part of the problem, that neither of us works in professions where you have those more radical conversations.

Molly went on to indicate that in part she maintained these divided rela-tionships out of self-protection, fearing that she would be shunned by current friends if they knew of her more radical past. She maintains some of the college friendships, but having moved away from those connections into a community of young professionals, she chooses to nurture perceptions that connect her to new friends, while suppressing "more liberal" conversations. As will be taken up below, Molly is one of the educators who question whether she can be considered a choice activist. Although she supports choice organizations, pro-choice activ-ism is not a part of her public life.

There was also some recognition of the conviction and emotion behind others' intense opposition to abortion. Rebecca, in particular, was sympathetic to others' principled pro-life convictions. Her objection was when those convictions re-sulted in actions that jeopardized women's lives—through clinic protests, threats to doctors, and threats to *Roe v. Wade*. The educators' intellectual recognition of the complexity of the abortion debate, however, did not diminish their com-mitments to keeping choice legal and available.

The semantic differentials around issues of choice were referenced by four of the women in acknowledgment of how significantly discourses shape the terms of the debate. As Shantal indicated:

I say I'm pro-choice, because I want to make it clear that I respect whatever choice a woman makes: the choice to end the pregnancy, or the choice to continue the pregnancy. We have to keep abortion legal, and safe, but I don't say I'm pro-abortion, I say I'm pro-choice.

Molly also identified as pro-choice, and took exception to the opposition's use of "pro-life" language:

I'm pro-choice, but it's not like I'm not pro-life too. I support a woman's right to choice, because her life *matters too*. They say, "It's a child, not a choice," but where are they when that child is born to a poor single mother? Whose life is rescued anyway?

Karen's language reflected her focus on the maintenance of reproductive free-dom and reproductive choice. As a health educator, it was important to Karen to keep her language close to the languages of the curriculum: "We already talk about reproduction in schools, so the move to talking about reproductive choice isn't such a leap. It's important that students get good information from a reliable and safe source. I try to be that source." As an educator in a school district with a comprehensive sex education policy, Karen did not feel silenced in talking with students about options, but believed she had limited freedom to talk about her own pro-choice convictions: "It just isn't a topic I'd want to get into at school. I don't think anyone would be surprised at my stance, but I don't believe they'd want to hear about it either."

Given their beliefs about the importance of maintaining abortion rights, yet their concerns about broaching the topic in their daily work lives, what forms of activism did these educators pursue?

Is This Activism?

As first noted in chapter 1, early in this activist educator project we developed a working definition of an activist as *an individual who is known for taking stands and engaging in action aimed at producing social change, possibly in conflict with institutional opponents.* Given our collective experiences in education, we de-cided to temper our conceptions of what it means to be an activist and to avoid constructions of activism that required dramatic and public action by outspoken citizens, for such models of activism would be out of character for educators. The term *activist,* however, is laden with associations and stereotypes, many of which held for the pro-choice educators in this study. In conversations, it was clear that these women embraced the idea that activism is legitimized through some sort of public action or stance, and for the most part they were unwilling to be public with their pro-choice convictions. Taken discretely, each of the terms "fit," as Hilda said. She went on, "I'm an educator, I'm pro-choice, and I consider myself an activist. But there is no way I'd consider myself a pro-choice educator activist. That combination doesn't work, and doesn't fit any educator I know of." As noted previously, Hilda left teaching after three years to pursue graduate study in education, and once out of the classroom she felt freedom to express her pro-choice convictions.

> Now I can wear my "I'm pro-choice, and I vote" T-shirt proudly and in public. I wouldn't have dreamed of doing that while teaching. There are so many taboos... who knew it could be risky to buy wine at the grocery store? That's not my story, but I have friends in [another county] who cross county lines to buy alcohol! For me, it was taboo to be identified with abortion rights, even if just meant wearing a T-shirt.

Hilda's reflections captured the sentiments of the other educators who were also pro-choice. Some went a step further and suggested that although they were educators and pro-choice, they questioned their activist credentials. Several framed it as a "then" and "now" issue. Molly, for example, indicated that although she was pro-choice now and kept informed and involved in the larger movement, her activist days happened "then," and were over, given her "yuppie-ish" friends and current life. Molly considered herself an activist in the past, when she supported a college roommate through an abortion, when she sat up talking and planning with "radical" college friends, and when she marched in Washington, DC in support of abortion rights. Yet Molly is a high school biology teacher, closer to curriculum related to reproduction and human sexuality than most educators. Molly was committed to providing her students with accurate information in regards to reproduction, but she shied away from going beyond disciplinary boundaries into debates and beliefs about abortion.

Anne also participated in an abortion rights protest march as a younger woman, but relegates this involvement to her past:

> I went to a NARAL March on Washington sometime after college—sometime in the late 80s maybe? Anyway, that was great to be a part of, such an exciting weekend—finding, yourself [in DC] among all these other women—mostly women—chanting in unison and signing petitions and listening to speakers…. And for a while I got the NARAL newsletter in the mail and continued to feel connected to something larger, but I cannot say I was ever active in a *movement*. Being active, being an activist, for me has certain connotations—you spend weekends doing things for the cause, you write letters, you talk to others. I still have friends I talk to about choice issues—it remains an important issue in my life—but it cannot be a part of my life as an educator, especially not now that I'm in administration.

As will be elaborated below, the perceived risk of associating with abortion rights was too great for Anne because of her position as a school administrator.

Among the educators still teaching, Karen and Ashton were most active for reproductive choice, although in their case the term *educator* was bracketed when it came to identification. They identified as pro-choice activists, but not in the same spaces as they were educators. For Karen, growing up in a progressive household nurtured her activist identity before she became an educator, and it was important for her to find ways to remain connected to choice activism. Karen supported NARAL and the National Organization for Women (NOW) through letter-writing campaigns to state legislators, and she volunteered "behind the scenes" at a Planned Parenthood clinic to avoid seeing, or being seen by, students. Ashton was also connected to national organizations that support reproductive choice, although she too kept her choice activism separate from her teaching life. Both of these women have friends outside education with whom they discuss and pursue choice activism.

As a retired educator, Joanne was most comfortable integrating all the labels, educator, pro-choice, and activist. Joanne carefully followed details about events in abortion legislation, and was most knowledgeable about pending legal challenges; she contributed to several pro-choice organizations, and was also active in contacting legislators with information and opinions about issues including health care legislation, and nominations and confirmation hearings for federal appointments. "I've always been active for choice, even during my 30 years as an educator. This doesn't mean I was always public in that activism, but I marched then, and I'll march now given the chance."

Karen, Ashton, and Joanne each referenced the 2008 presidential elections and the likelihood that a candidate's position on abortion would again emerge as a factor in their electability. All were certain that the campaign would return abortion discourse to the public domain, but only Joanne indicated her intention to campaign for a pro-choice candidate.

As this section has shown, for those still in education, involvement in pro-choice activism is distanced. They will write letters, donate money, and might participate in a march if occurs outside their community. However, they would not choose to appear at a local and public pro-choice event, would not sport a pro-choice bumper sticker or T-shirt, and would not introduce pro-choice conversations among colleagues at school. Although clearly stating that choice is worth fighting for, lamenting others' complacency or ignorance about struggles to protect access to abortion, and worrying about its protection amid persistent legal challenges, abortion rights was not a cause that bridged the space between these women's private lives as activists and their daily lives as educators. Ashton echoed Sylvia's contention that abortion is not a discussion topic among colleagues in schools:

> There is just no way I would talk about abortion in a group at school—not even as a philosophical issue…. First of all we don't have much time to talk together at school any more, at least not that kind of talk. Second of all, who would I talk to?…. I couldn't name anyone at my school who I would call pro-choice. There are some younger teachers that might be, but I just don't know. This is the kind of thing I talk about with friends from college—not teachers at school.

As will be taken up again below, a persistent theme among educators active for choice was that the topic was deemed too controversial for school, among colleagues, or for the curriculum.

Education's Silences

> Good Lord, no, I wouldn't talk about pro-choice activism at school. And I'll talk about most things! Childbirth? Divorce? Yes. Abortion? Not a chance. [Abortion] is so controversial outside school walls, why would you want to bring it in? (Rebecca)

Like Ashton and Sylvia above, Rebecca named the silence that surrounds abortion in schools. None of the women in this study believed they would be recognized as pro-choice activists by most colleagues at school. As described in chapter 1, and elaborated above, colleagues in education avoid engaging in potentially contentious issues. Even among long-standing colleagues, the issue of abortion is given a wide berth. Their reasons for avoiding contentious issues are diverse, including fear of offense and fear of sanction.

Fear of Offense As indicated previously, these women educators work in the South and six of the eight were raised in the South. At the risk of overgeneralization, within this brief description are keys to their circumspection in regards to choice activism, for as educators and Southerners, they are subject to lessons that encourage respect and discretion in the face of controversy. It could also be argued that as women they are socialized to silence, although these women embraced feminism. Rebecca, however, acknowledged the public sentiment that "being a feminist can be as offensive as being pro-choice in some circles!"

Nevertheless, three of the women indicated that not wanting to offend other colleagues' beliefs kept them silent about their own pro-choice stance. Like Ashton and Rebecca above, Molly was reluctant to introduce abortion as a topic for conversation among colleagues. Because it is an issue that is socially controversial and cloaked in silence in schools, educators remain unsure of their colleagues' beliefs and find discretion preferable to offense.

Fear of Sanction Another significant constraint to activism was the fear of sanction, felt particularly by Anne and Shantal. As noted above, Anne considered her activist days behind her, especially given that she was an administrator:

> I still have friends I talk to about choice issues—it remains an important issue in my life—but it cannot be a part of my life as an educator, especially not now, now that I'm in administration. My fear is that if I participated in something publicly that I'd end up with my picture splashed across the front page of the newspaper holding some "pro-choice always!" banner. I don't know, maybe I'd be pleasantly surprised and find administrators and parents supportive of my activism, but…no, actually there is no way that would happen….

Although allowing herself a moment of hope that others might support her pro-choice activism, Anne quickly retreated to a skeptical position, choosing to restrain her activism for fear of possible sanction. While quick to reflect that she was unaware of any educators being sanctioned for pro-choice stances, she also conceded that she was in fact unaware of practicing educators who were also public pro-choice advocates:

I'm sure they're out there, and maybe I even know some of them without knowing I know them! But really, this isn't an issue that has any place in school as we currently know it. Really the only thing you hear about is abstinence-only education, based on the short-sighted but pervasive policies of our president.

Shantal also expressed fear of sanction as a factor in her silence about choice and choice activism. As one of two African American women interviewed in this study, Shantal indicated that to labels of educator, pro-choice, and activist, she also would add African American and feminist, "they're all important to who I am and how I am in the world." Yet Shantal was sensitive to perceptions that her actions were filtered through others' perceptions, and even stereotypes, about Black women.

I can take on issues of racial disparity in education. That's expected, and I think others hope I will so they don't have to. But I generally stay away from abortion rights issues, and even women's issues, when I get on my soapbox. Neither of them has much traction these days. Teen pregnancy is a big issue, a life-changing issue, but we just bury our heads and preach abstinence. As if telling a kid to "just say no" to sex ever worked. But for me to get out ahead on abortion rights? I think that would just invite trouble.

And so issues of choice are enclosed in an area of silence in schools (Anderson, 1990). It is, in effect, a nonissue. Nevertheless, in addition to fears these women had about threats to legal protections for abortion, they also shared Shantal's concerns about the consequences of education's silences for students' access to comprehensive sex education. Give the opportunity, they would willingly petition school board members or district personnel to advocate for comprehensive sex education for students. Yet as this section has made clear, identities as educator and pro-choice activist remained incompatible for most of the women in this study. Framed as a contest between the two, the educator identity wins.

Implications for Policy and Practice

Women in the United States have not always had to fight for access to legal abortions, although the safety of the procedure can only be understood in relative terms. Abortions up to the fourth month of pregnancy were performed legally in this country from its founding,[4] and were not made illegal in all states until the turn of the 20th century (National Abortion Federation [NAF], 2007). The American Medical Association (AMA), in its infancy at the turn of the 20th century, played an important role in criminalizing abortions as the organization worked to "establish for themselves exclusive rights to practice medicine" (NAF, 2007, ¶6), thereby dividing midwives and homeopaths from "trained" medical professionals. Ironically, even as medical procedures were being made safer through technological advances, women were driven to illegal, unsafe, and unregulated abortions. "Back alley" abortions, therefore, were the only option for most women in the United States from the 1880s to 1973, although some states made exceptions to save the life of the mother, in cases of rape or incest, or in the case of fetal malformation. The landmark *Roe v. Wade* decision of the U.S. Supreme Court in 1973 made states' antiabortion laws unconstitutional on privacy grounds, ruling that a woman's right to choose pregnancy was protected by her right to privacy. *Roe v. Wade* made it possible for women to get safe and legal abortions from trained medical professionals. However, if reproductive choice through access to safe and legal abortion was guaranteed to citizens of this country with the Supreme Court's 1973 ruling in *Roe vs. Wade*, among the issues taken up in this text, activism for reproductive choice is unique in its relationship to practices and policies in schools.

As a nation we have determined that discrimination based on race and gender are unacceptable and we have passed legislation ruling that discrimination based on race or gender (including sexual harassment) is illegal and punishable by law. Increasingly, protections are also being extended to prevent discrimination based on sexual orientation. We have also gone steps further to prevent discrimination through laws and policies that extend to public schools. As Legrand showed in chapter 5, activists and policy makers for gay rights are expanding these protections for gay, lesbian, bisexual, and transgendered students and educators, because explicit school policies make a difference. Curriculum development eventually follows these legislative mandates, if only through the efforts of educators and curriculum developers who insist on revealing hidden curricula that offer a homogenized, whitewashed version of events and issues. Previous chapters have shown that activist educators make sure that expansive histories and biographies make it into classroom conversations (see chapter 5), and that protective policies make it into school hallways and practices (see chapters 2 and 3). Thus, for them, on-the-job curriculum and programming activism is possible.

However the case for reproductive choice, specifically abortion, is somewhat different. Although access to abortion is guaranteed by law, there is no national consensus that this is an inalienable right; as a result, access to abortion faces ongoing legal challenges. And so the issue of choice, per se, is an area of silence in education, given little to no place in public school policy or curriculum. In fact, education policy makers and systems rarely get to issues of reproductive choice, preferring to contain the controversy by limiting conversation to choices teens make about sexual behavior. By asserting that teens must be abstinent until marriage, no matter what we may know about teens' actual choices, policy makers and educators declare that sex education and abortion are not issues for schooling. Thus the current approach to sex education in the United States can be identified as one of denial and control: if we limit students' knowledge of and exposure to competing discourses on sexuality and reproduction in education, we can control their behavior. We presume that if students do not see, hear, or speak of reproduction and sexuality, they will not engage in related behaviors. This approach can also be see as one that separates the public from the private: the public role of education and the private lives of students. This separation of the public and private is mirrored in the lives of educators invested in protecting reproductive choices through pro-choice activism such that the public face is the educator, the private face the activist. The educator can be public and private, but the choice activist has no public face, or a masked face at best.

Educators' silence in regards to reproductive choice is learned, shaped by conservative values in education that value discretion in the face of controversy. Although there is no explicit injunction against speaking out for choice, the perceived risks are great enough to inhibit that speech. It is also worth remembering that for these women the lack of a strong national voice advocating choice makes it even riskier for educators to step out on this issue. Political candidates' pro-choice stances are not sufficiently protective to invite educators' public participation. Educators also indicated disappointment that neither NOW nor NARAL keep choice discourses on the public stage between elections. The concern was that activists and potential activists had to go looking for information, resulting in complacency among younger generations who fail to appreciate the pre-*Roe* conditions.

Thus abortion is one of those public controversies that do not penetrate school walls, akin to silences around issues of don't ask, don't tell in regards to sexual orientation. At the school level, silencing begins with our sexuality education curriculum and in how we talk with children about reproduction. At this point, most schools talk about pregnancy prevention through the prophylactic of abstinence, but this has proved to be an unreliable barrier against unwanted pregnancy. As discussed above, research indicates that the alternative to abstinence-only sex education, comprehensive sex education, has greater success in preventing teen pregnancy, but hopes of its adoption at a national level remain distant. In other chapters in this text we learn of educators "activising" their work, embedding their activist work in their work lives so that they mesh and complement each other. For the women in this study, such practice was limited to educators' commitments to providing accurate information about sexual health and reproduction. Neither health/science educator would refuse a student's content-based question, but neither would choose to reveal her pro-choice activist commitments.

That this study did not uncover educators working publicly to protect choice does not mean these educators do not exist. As indicated in chapter 1, the educators in this study worked in a conservative profession in a conservative part of the country such that issues of choice remain outside sanctioned educational discourse, tied to an individual's politics. Educators are not alone in being asked to check their politics at the door, but any snapshot of the political landscape in the history of the United States reveals that what we consider political is not a static, bounded system. Until such time as the pendulum swings and choice politics move from *Roe vs. Wade* legislation to sanctioned educational policy, this is likely to remain an area of silence. Schools do not take the lead on pressing against contentious issues, instead waiting for policy to settle at the national level and trickle down in the form of school policy. This means that educators cannot expect protections for speaking up and out outside the bounds of sanctioned discourse.

Each of the women in this study had "choice" friends, people with whom they could share their pro-choice passion, but the friends are people they know outside of school, or select colleagues with whom they have long-term relationships and assured safety. This isolation is perhaps another consequence of educational practices that either value a teacher only to the extent that she is successful in her classroom, or force her retreat into that classroom as her preferred sanctuary from persistent pressures to perform according to particular accountability measures. Teachers' isolation is not a new phenomenon, yet it is another enabler of the conservative culture of schooling.

The status quo is not without consequent sacrifices. At the level of pro-choice activism, remaining silent concedes free speech protections, sacrificing personal politics to school politics. When imagining ways to blend education and choice activism, these educators have found that the best alternative is to press for adoption of comprehensive sex education policies that at least leave doors open for educators to acknowledge the existence of alternatives beyond the abstinence-only curriculum. Because abortion has become such a nonevent in sanctioned school discourses, for these educators it is critically important that pro-choice activists work at the national level to ensure continued access to reproductive choices. These women indicated that there is little room for private commitments regarding abortion rights to overlap with public commitments as educators. For these women there is no choice in educator activism.

Notes

1. Excerpts from Justice Ginsburg's dissenting opinion are presented here. The full text can be found at http://www.supremecourtus.gov/opinions/06pdf/05-380.pdf.
2. In 2004, for example, the U.S. House of Representatives Committee on Government Reform published findings indicating that abstinence-only programs have never proven effective in delaying the onset of sexual activity among teens.
3 My participation in the Activist Educator group was unique among the other participants in that my first involvement was as a graduate assistant to Catherine Marshall. I was interested in this research for social and political reasons, but I pursued dissertation research in another area While Gloria, Annice, Susan, and Wanda worked with Dr. Marshall and their committees—in addition to our collective work—to conduct their dissertation research, my pace was somewhat different. I was a graduate student in another program but sustained my involvement with this group after my assistantship work with Dr. Marshall. As a consequence, I delayed recruitment of participants until my own dissertation work was nearing completion, assuming that when the time came, I would catch up with the other women in our group. Given the silences around this issue, this proved to be a risky choice, limiting the number of participants interviewed.
4. According to historical and anthropological research, abortion has been practiced in every civilization studied.

7
The Activist Professional

CATHERINE MARSHALL

What does all of this say about educators and activism? Chapters 2 through 6 have detailed the major findings and examples from the rich description of the individual case studies. Williams's study (chapter 2) accentuates the moral and spiritual dimension, coupled with race identity, as inspirations that enabled African American activists to persevere. Furthermore, there were instances where educators' leadership for equity actually facilitated their career opportunities! Legrand's activists (chapter 5), when working on GLBT issues, did find spaces within schools to introduce them in liberal conversations and in curricula; however, being "out" and being overt leaders in the community were not viable choices for her educators. Similarly, Walters and Jones (chapters 3 and 4) found that educators who wanted to prevent barriers to girls' opportunities and the harms of sexual harassment found ways within the context of their jobs. They found some support from laws and policies that empowered them, although sometimes only in small ways, to take action and initiative. Nevertheless, these educators sometimes sensed that their behavior could be considered strident. Also, with all of these carefully carried out modes of activism, there were worries—about the health-threatening stress, about consequences to their careers, about being seen as weird or unnatural. From all of the studies, the coping strategies are instructive: they ranged from taking part in public demonstrations and networking away from home, to finding safe spaces with like-minded colleagues, to confining their activism to modes that very clearly fit within their job descriptions. Still, the starkness of the limits on activism is demonstrated in Anderson's activists for women's reproductive rights. Her cases in chapter 6 vividly illustrate the activism within a context of perceived backlash. If we have seen variations in form, nonetheless themes have emerged from this rich array of activism enactments.

Beyond the powerful descriptions of the lived experiences of educator activists, the original research design multiplies the significance of our research. The chapters above provided insights into particular social movements and causes, as experienced by our participants. Now we will display patterns in the findings that emerged as we analyzed the accumulated material, which consisted of five social movements and the career experiences and identity development of 52 educators.

To truly capitalize on the wide range and in-depth cases reported in previous chapters, we asked questions of the data, in cross-case analyses (see appendix C). These questions came from our collective knowledge of social movement theory and theories of educators' careers, as well as literatures on specific social movements. The questions came, too, from the addition by the researchers of insights from critical theory and empowerment literatures. Recall, for example, Williams's and Walters's realization that their data required them to use feminist and critical race theory and Jones's work that helped us all see that Southern culture added another layer of conservatism. This chapter describes:

- The overarching patterns and themes identified across topics;
- How theory is expanded or challenged by our research; and,
- What educators, policy makers, and citizens should learn from our research.

Identifying Patterns from Cross-Case Comparison

From day one and throughout this project, this research was conducted to maximize the viability of cross-case comparison. Our reflections and our methodology are detailed in chapter 8. For now, it is important to say that our shared interview protocol (see appendix A) made possible the cross-case analysis of the educators' experiences presented in the preceding chapters. The protocol was organized to facilitate analysis of commonalities and differences in a variety of domains including: membership in a social movement; defining moments that led to activism; ways activism is or is not practiced in schools; and conflicts confronted when deciding when and how to work for change. Throughout data collection, our research group met to identify emerging themes and query each other regarding the ways in which theory did or did not work.

We searched, through our cross-case analysis, among educators active in a variety of social issues, asking, for example, what practices do LGBT activists share with those involved in race-related activism? How do activists for reproductive choice differ from those working to prevent student-to-student sexual harassment in schools? Did any activists face legal or contractual constraints regarding activism? What were common perceptions of risk? How did varied career contexts, identities, and options available in the "cause" affect actions? How did activists work through dilemmas?

Some initial findings are:

- A family heritage of obligations to promote fairness and a sense of identification with the marginalized are very much a part of the inspiration for educators who work for social justice.
- Where Bible Belt community values are strong, social justice activism must be either closeted or tailored to accommodate those values and the power of interest groups.
- Educators, foregoing promotions, credit, and visibility, *are* working on social justice projects, quietly and creatively.
- Educators use pedagogical opportunities for activism, which is conducted at a micropolitical level more often than as visible acts of political contestation in more macropolitical arenas.
- The fear of backlash and of being labeled is a career constraint for many.
- In some instances, the fear of reprisals for one's activism is the inhibitor, not the reality of reprisals.
- When enacting activism, educators, even when they know that laws and job descriptions support their efforts, sense limits from organizational and professional conservatism.
- Activism seems less risky for those in top leadership or near retirement.
- Social justice activism is fragmented: activists often feel isolated, unaware of activist colleagues.
- For some activists, national movements (either historical or present day) still hold potential for expanding their social justice values-identification and participation.

These patterns will be clarified and then illustrated with selected excerpts from the data from across the cases.[1]

The Impetus for Activism

No one incident or role model alone inspires choices. Various facets of individuals' lives and relationships drive choices, augmented by degrees of identity salience (Stryker, Owens, & White, 2000). Our educator activists' inspirations came from an intermixing of socialization, identity, and the social movement choices available to them. They did not compartmentalize sources of their identity development, but expressed interweaving identity and activism. As Kim in chapter 4 said, "I can't segment myself."

The Complex Intertwining of Identity and Social Movement Membership

Our activists were inspired to become active for social justice by empathy that arose from seeing or experiencing victimization; a sense of identification coming from community heritage and family values; ideals about educators' roles; convictions about women's rights; and a sense that one's personal spirituality is interconnected with issues of inequity and intolerance.

Victimization

Identifying with or knowing of the harm done by inequities and intolerance inspires activism. We have several examples of this from GLBT activists (chapter 5), such as Sara seeing a friend driven to attempt suicide, and Raven reflecting on the ordeal of two lesbian friends who wanted a church union, and were abused by members of the congregation as a result, which made Raven decide that it was just time to stand up. Recall Mike saying, "I didn't want kids to have to suffer through what I'd suffered through." Among the activists against harassment (chapter 4), educators were motivated by being victims of harassment and a desire to redress abusive and deprived family histories, some also wanted to atone for having been bullies themselves. It was important for these educators to turn these experiences into positive motivation to empower their students to have a wider number of options from which to make better choices. In chapter 6, many women first got involved in pro-choice causes because a close friend or family member had an abortion. Although having an abortion does not necessarily constitute victimization, educator activists' fear of the Religious Right's power and tactics to terrorize women energized these activists' commitment.

Interestingly, African American activists did not speak of the victimization theme, although it may have been taken for granted, and understood, especially with an African American researcher eliciting their stories. Generally, too, the women in chapter 3 did not see institutionalized racism and sexism as affecting them but they did see how it could hamper kids and mentees. We wondered whether they really were activists or is denial of victim status evidence of a way to exercise agency? That is, by not dwelling on the ways that racism and sexism had affected them, they instead became activists.

Aha Moments

Defining moments, critical events, or, sometimes slow-building awareness inspired activism. African American activists' clarity of mission seemed provoked by aha moments, as Edward, one of chapter 2's participants, experienced when he testified before his State Board and got the Board to agree to his dropout prevention proposals, and realized how much he had to give (Hood, 2005). Or Diane's seeing through other educators who say they "don't see race, just children," and thinking about her ancestors (Hood, 2005). Or Keisha, realizing how, long ago, her middle school African American history class had role modeled a student to be a teacher and an activist (Hood, 2005). Similarly, from chapter 3, recall how Anna attended a conference and was energized to "stick my neck out," and how Sarah's passion for gender fairness was kindled upon seeing Myra and David Sadker on TV. GLBT activists' aha moments were more like George's when he finally told his students: "every time you call someone a fag…, it hurts me." Pro-choice activists indicated that an accumulation of significant moments opened their eyes to the importance of their involvement. These moments included participation in women's studies courses and being close to someone needing an abortion, and the 2007 Supreme Court decision regarding late-term abortions that challenged *Roe v. Wade.*

While some activists had aha moments, often the identification with social justice activism was inspired, primarily, from upbringing and values embedded in family, community, and religious life.

Inherited and Learned Responsibilities

Time and again, we heard that family and educational background were strong bases for educators' activism. Their very sense of identity and self was propelled by involvement in social movements, or at least interventions against inequities. For one woman, activism was "in her genes,…instilled by family" rather than a conscious choice (Legrand, 2005, p. 63; and see chapter 5, Lucy). In chapter 4, Kim spoke of her higher education giving her the ability to be an activist against sexual harassment (Jones, 2005). She was brought up to believe that you are a part of the problem if you see injustice and back away. She spoke of parents who worked in the Civil Rights Movement so preventing sexual harassment was a natural continuation. Education enhanced understanding of social justice issues for Sara too, whose eyes were opened in women's studies to the intersectionality of racism, classism, sexism, homophobia.

Family traditions in civil rights and education careers were especially evident in the stories of African American activists, who drew support from a sense of history blended with strong community patterns. Andrea's mother was the "foundation" (Hood, 2005, p. 57), while Keisha's family legacy of "mission" drove her activism (p. 57; see also chapter 2 for Andrea and Keisha). Contrast this with Cheryl's unsupported inheritance as her family avoided talk about civil rights (Hood, 2005, p. 59). Role model fathers who supported Blacks, parents involved in civil rights, Black history, and more gave many a message that the educator activists were never free of some responsibility for others.

Educators' Ideals as Role Models for World Citizenship, Empowerment, and Fairness

As we compared our participants' talk about inspirations for their activism, patterns emerged centering around a sense of right, of moral obligation. Although this was not a dominant theme, this sense was expressed as a desire to participate as citizens contributing to a better world. Often, though, participants' talk honed in on how being educators created obligations and opportunities to enact social justice activism, as was predicted in literatures reviewed in chapter 1.

Activists in chapters 2 and 6 were more likely to describe their social activism as interwoven with identification with wider social, economic, and political ills. Those in chapter 6 were working within a context where poor women had less access to abortion and where the military had withdrawn funding to pay for abortion. They were most alarmed that challenges to *Roe v. Wade* would jeopardize women's rights and access to abortion. Recall Joanne's lament at the new makeup of the Supreme Court: "It seems we might be entering a crucial period when attempts to chip away at *Roe* come more and more frequently…and that stuns me." Interestingly, the most public issue, race (chapter 2), and the most risky and controversial issue, abortion (chapter 6), engendered the strongest sense of moral obligation among activists in this research.

African American activists' words often reflected a realization that their educator-citizen stances would affect all of society. Edward, for example, said he considered himself as an activist for *all* children which would, in turn, help Black children. Earl, noting the responsibility of Black men to mentor young boys, was embracing a philosophy emphasized by Dillard regarding the "history of communal responsibility for African children" (1995, p. 551). Diane shared this commitment, choosing to work in schools with high numbers of minority children and by weekend volunteering for life skills and career exploration programs for minority students to "see themselves as college students" (Hood, 2005, p. 53). The value placed on broad community support for social mobility is a distinction of racial-ethnic communities (Higginbotham & Weber, 1992). In addition, the sense of activism as "doing good" was more likely to be found tied to spirituality and religion among African Americans (as will be described later).

Instances of activists' framing their involvement in an educator-citizen's wider struggle for rights, world improvement, and fairness inspired activists. A stronger pattern showed activists' values tied to their beliefs that education makes the difference for children learning about justice and equity. Richard said, "How they learn has more to do with what we do here, than it has to do with what they bring here" (Hood, 2005, p. 81; see also chapter 2).

Activists for GLBT equality, too, spoke often in terms of education's purposes. George spoke of teaching being about liberation, about freedom. And Joseph's wording is revealing: "The idea of education kind of precludes any feelings of 'you are not acceptable, you are not worthy of learning'…. I don't know how anybody reconciles that, how anybody could be a serious educator and exclude a student on any basis" (Legrand, 2005, p. 53; see also chapter 5).

As indicated in this section, one's individual values influence and shape morally acceptable goals and strategies employed and "provide the motivation necessary to sustain the costs of action" as della Porta and Diani said (1999, p. 62). Indeed, many of our activists did understand their moral and role modeling responsibilities as educators in the larger political system, as citizens themselves and as those with the power to make a difference in challenging oppressive historical forces. Where did that understanding come from?

Spirituality and the Pushes and Pulls of Religion

The influence of religion was presented differentially among activists. For some, religion provoked proactive activism. For some, activism was in reaction to conservative religion. For many, religion was simply not mentioned.

The role of faith and the importance of the church was a strong, proactive theme inspiring African American activism. "Preaching" activism motivates and strengthens, from a tradition of resistance to domination, reminiscent of the Civil Rights Movement coming from the churches. Andrea and Diane in chapter 2 found strength for activism from their faith, and Richard spoke of it being about defining oneself "as somebody who has a higher purpose" (Hood, 2005, p. 60).

Inspiration and support from spirituality and the church was not a theme for activists beyond chapter 2. However, some expressed belief that their activism was centered and was inspired by their own personal ethics and morals. And, among pro-choice activists, while holding fast to their convictions that protecting choice was the ethical stance, all of the women made reference to the moral debates surrounding choice, to varying degrees expressing understanding about why *others* find abortion immoral. Several pro-choice activists knew their families did not welcome their pro-choice activism, for example. All shared the sentiment that the Religious Right was the source of contentious politics. Activists' awareness of and engagement with moral and spiritual debates, however, did not offset fear of the Christian Right's power to mobilize against their movement. GLBT and pro-choice activists spoke of religion and spirituality primarily as providing power to the forces of personal and political repression from the Christian Right. For these activists, activism was often a reactive response to the press of conservative politics.

Thus, for some, organized religion was an inspiration and support to rising up against oppression. Personal morality inspired others. However, conservative social morality hampered activists for GLBT and for choice. Also, as we will show in the next section, conservative social morality can provide a rationale for those who wish to keep women and girls socialized to embrace traditional and limited feminine roles, and to deny full GLBT rights to expression and identity.

Inhibited Identities Shaped by Conservative Professional and Community Values

Community and professional socialization could inspire activism. However, we found more evidence of such socialization creating barriers to educators identifying with and committing to social movements.

Southern Propriety, Gender Role Socialization, and Deference to Traditional Power Structures

Chapter 1 touched on the cultural norms of the South. Culturally conservative socialization in rural southern and southwestern communities is referenced as influential to personal and professional choices, especially among women recalling emphases on wife and mother roles, being "talked out of ambitions," and finding themselves in quandaries over how to mesh career demands and desire for family. Frequently their internal resolution was to activate for girls in schools, but to a much lesser degree, if at all, for themselves or other career women. Although their social convictions and Title IX supported girls having equal opportunity, even female role models, and even empowerment, the maternal (and responsible educator) roles fell short of any attack on institutionalized patriarchy. Community values reinforced the idea that the women's movement was too radical.

Similarly in chapter 4, several educators' upbringing framed their interventions against sexual harassment as respect for young ladies; traditional gender roles meant "keeping the boys in check," and monitoring girls' clothing, reflecting lessons about traditional genteel ladies as we noted in chapter 1. Valuing propriety then, framed interventions against sexual harassment, but also framed rules of decorum that undermined affiliation with the feminist movement. Also in chapter 4, the three male educators emphasized their activism as being framed by their job of supporting their community's value systems , and Glenda referred to conservatism and the Bible Belt valuing dress codes and "yes ma'am and no ma'am" gentility (Jones, 2005, p. 80).

However, most pro-choice activists spoke less about Southern culture inhibitions framing silences in terms of the power of the Religious Right to influence policy and curriculum and also threaten choice activists with tactics ranging from social ostracism to violent attacks. Anne spoke powerfully about the cultural-political context which conveys a clear message about the patriarchal authority of the Religious Right, fearing for her job security should she be identified as pro-choice, much less a choice activist..

Recall chapter 1's literature on Southern cultural norms, especially among White Baptist traditionalists, framing as disruptive such outsider influences as labor unions, gay rights, feminism, and civil rights. Modernizing and progressive influences in the South were more accepted when accompanied by economic benefits and slowest when challenging race relations and assumptions of male domination in the family and the workplace (Luebke, 1990; also Fleer, 1994; McFadden & Smith, 2004). Governors and education leaders have, therefore, concentrated on economic incentive packages and technology training more than on getting at the root of racism or setting up conditions for women and girls' empowerment. Thus, the cautiousness of our activists is indeed a reflection on dominant values.

Conservative morality was a theme with many complexities and variations. It was interwoven in discussions of family, values, and morals as educators spoke of working in the generally conservative southern region of the United States known as the Bible Belt.[2] Southerners see themselves as more traditional, conservative, religious, and well-mannered than other Americans. Administrators like Tim in chapter 4 felt a responsibility to his conservative southern community to enforce traditional sex roles. Glenda, who had worked in six states from California to Georgia, spoke of the conservatism and strongly tradititial moral values of the South, limiting discussion of anything that had to do with sex. Thus, for many of our activists, their familial, community, and professional socialization originated or was stuck in a conservative culture that created significant conflicts for their activist interests.

Ironically, religion provides a positive impetus for social activism in, for example, the moral and social energy for the civil rights movement in the South, and the sense of morality to stop the harm and impropriety of sexual harassment. Yet it is interwoven with the conservative cultural norms that inhibit women's identification with the "radical" women's movement and their sense that feminism undermines family and even challenges the boundaries of Christianity (as when Maria, a woman in education administration said, "I come from a Christian background, and I felt like they [women activists] overstepped some of the boundaries").

Thus, sometimes influences of socialization into Bible Belt conservatism facilitates activism, sometimes it supports a sort of conservative activism, and sometimes it crystallizes activists' identification with social movements.

Conservative Messages in the Profession

Professional socialization shapes identities, values and understandings that frame educators' professional ethics. For many of our participants, the primary brake on activism was their socialization as educators. For example, pro-choice activists' careers socialization shaped them to heed policies and avoid controversy so they strictly avoided acting on their personal beliefs in their professional lives.

One might expect, though, that enforcing laws would be part of administrators' job descriptions. Ironically, this did not always hold true for enforcing progressive social justice and equity laws. Recall, for example, the activists preventing sexual harassment. With policies dictating that they had to intervene, we found reports that that some educators weren't even aware of the policies. This speaks to a disconnect between early teacher and administrator professional socialization and limited social justice in-service training options.

Activist Risks and the Management and Positioning of Activism

The interweaving of constraining contexts in community and professional conservatism makes educators feel they are taking risks by identifying with social movements. Sometimes the constraints seem so powerful that if confronted the educators fear the loss of professional identity and status along with the perceived effects on their personal lives. For some, the fear and perception of risk were enough to dampen or even thwart educators' identification with a social movement.

Risks and Losses

The dilemmas of risk faced all participants in this study, some more, some less, some quite tangible, some inferred or internalized.

Professional One kind of fear came from socialized discomfort with sex. Recall Randy, from chapter 4, worried that students would repeat to their parents what he told his class about "grabbing private parts" (Jones, 2005, p. 112), and the parents would misconstrue what he had said. Janet feared the mom's reaction when calling home to tell about the student making sexual noises (Jones, 2005, p. 113). Sara believed that because of her lifestyle she was taking a chance with her job by participating in activism. Cheryl in chapter 2 shared her fear of the possible repercussions from speaking out, which could include being accused of reverse discrimination and even being warned to avoid becoming identified too narrowly because of her interest in issues of race (Hood, 2005, p. 74). Recall Kerry, in chapter 4, who found that many colleagues stopped talking to her, as the person who assisted gay students. She knew of teachers who were lesbian who shied away from the whole issue, worried about getting into trouble with parents. In chapter 6 we saw a perceived level of risk so high as to inhibit teachers' public activism for choice.

So, an activist educator may lose professional credibility by appearing too Black, too obsessed with sex, too queer, too feminist. However, in rare instances, there are career opportunities from one's activism (for example, one of Hood's (2005) participants imagined a career based on the No Child Left Behind Act and the achievement gap providing positions).

Personal Many participants described personal losses related to their idealism and ambitions, particularly family losses. African Americans worried that they neglected their own families when devoting so much to the movement. Two women mentioned in chapter 3, attributed their divorces as coinciding with moving up the career ladder. (Walters, 2003). Jane's explanation was that spouses cannot handle powerful women. Recall Maria's (chapter 3) feeling of being ostracized by administrative team members and isolated physically and emotionally. In chapter 6 two activists mentioned family tensions over their pro-choice politics. The only safe spaces for these women are in the private sphere; but even there they had friends with whom they would not talk about abortion.

So, worry about loss of face and status in one's community, social, and family because of activist identity was an inhibitors, even while, as stated above, for some, especially those in chapter 2, community and family provided impetus for activism.

Language and Labels Educators learn to avoid displaying divergent values (see chapter 2). It appeared worrisome for our participants to be labeled as troublemakers or as people who advocated "aberrant" values. They worried about being seen as "a nut" or a "bra burner," or a "male-basher." One participant from chapter 4 about being seen overly focused on sex (Jones, 2005) for even thinking about, and calling attention to harassment. Labels were risks to professional status and identity, as often reflected in participants' concerns about perception of being too in to the cause. Cheryl avoided public participation, while making decisions regarding NAACP activities, and marching. She said: "…they see me marching, and now my students' parents are going to behave differently towards me." (Hood, 2005, p. 69; see also chapter 2) She also described her dilemma this way:

> I am the principal or a teacher all the time. I never get to be just [myself]. So those things parents fear I'm very vocal about, will then impact how I respond to their children..... You can advocate to the point where you look like a single cause. As I was going though my master's program, one of my White professors actually pulled me over after my comprehensive exams, and said to me, "I want to caution you about one thing. Be careful about becoming pigeonholed as a single-cause person."…because I've always advocated for poor and minority students whom I thought were not be done justice in the public school system. He said that sometimes you can scream so loudly for the cause that people think you have nothing else going for you. (Hood, 2005, p. 69)

Cheryl also stated, "You have to be very careful about how you say it, and you have to talk very quietly to people, pull them over, not put them on the defensive, not become *labeled*" (Hood, 2005, p. 70).

Recall in chapter 3 that the perceived radical slant of the feminist frameworks did not help the women identify positively with the women's movement. We heard Joseph saying he held back so he could "maintain participation in the mainstream, and not just come off as being an absolute nut" (Legrand, 2005, p. 88; see also chapter 5). In chapter 6, educators chose to identify as pro-choice, avoiding controversy by avoiding the language of abortion rights. Thus, one's status in the profession could be undermined when professional colleagues and community members could find reasons to apply derogatory activist labels.

Assessing Backlash In chapter 6 we saw that activists' fear of the Religious Right led to them to focus on concerns about the physical safety of abortion providers; however, the perceived risks about identification as a pro-choice activist were reflected in sentiments that one cannot be an "out" pro-choice activist and retain status as an educator. In this cause the personal is *not* political or public because of the perception of risk. In contrast, some activists in chapters 2 through 5 found a few safe spaces within and near their professional identities and even their job descriptions. It is perhaps a measure of the gains of the gay rights movement that GLBT educators feel greater freedom than do pro-choice activists, although as we will see, legal protections for GLBT educators are emerging that give greater sanction to their efforts. An emerging theme in this section is there may be a continuum of perceived level of risk: from extreme physical threats to career risks and losses *actually experienced*; to career risks and losses, as *perceived or assumed*; to perceived and actual personal risks and losses (as in social nonacceptance by community, friends, and family.

Perceived risk was greatly affected by the intensity of the public and professional discourse for or against one's social movement. Some issues "caused a ruckus" by mere mention. Some (e.g., pro-choice and GLTB, sexual harassment) were uncomfortable and unmentionable, and some labeled or considered fixed (e.g., civil rights for racial minorities and women's rights). Some of the educators in chapters 3 and 4 felt that, with laws for sex equity and against harassment, there was little public or professional cultural demand or support for redressing these issues. This was based on assumptions that they were no longer issues, so that a push to expand rights or tighten social justice agendas regarding sex and gender issues was deemed unnecessary. Thus, the degree of professional and public discourse and valuing of their cause were factors as activists calculated the consequences of their activism and the possibilities of having any support if they encountered backlash. A nuance shown in chapter 6 is the concern that there is not enough intergenerational dialogue, and not enough recognition of the historical fight for abortion rights. As indicated by choice activists, if younger women remain complacent about access to abortion, abortion foes might succeed in overturning legal protections. The older women in Walters's study (Walters, 2003), also expressed concern about the need for younger women to know about the history of women's struggle for equality. Younger women interviewed recognized the historical importance of the women's movement, but did not see a strong connection for them.

Thus, the public and professional discourse surrounding educators gave signals that shaped their assessments of activism risk. The widened and public discourse of the historical civil rights movement that supported the seasoned and secure educators in chapter 2 is in marked contrast to the narrowed discourse supporting gender and harassment activism. The result was the very carefully chosen undercover or careful safe actions of educators who sometimes even denied their activism. Then we saw more and more narrowed, even forbidden discourse around GLBT and choice, where identification and activism on the job certainly was risky and was more often than not relegated to hidden private and personal spheres.

Identity, Age, Career Status, and Social Movement Participation

How does perceived level of risk change over the course of a career? Does involvement evolve along a continuum? Is an individual likely to be more of an activist while young, after finding strategies and spaces for intermixing social movement with education career, or will her or his activism increase after attaining desired positions in receptive locations?

Career Continuum

We have discussed activists' sensitivity to being labeled as such because the public discourse affects career status and mobility. Doris, in chapter 4, spoke of wanting to learn more about being an activist, indicating that activism had not been part of her teacher education and offering confirmation of chapter 1's literature on the assumptive world rules about avoiding risk-taking and being a troublemaker. Call to mind Cheryl in chapter 2 being warned in her university program about overidentification with Blacks and poor kids, and Keisha saying that, early on she learned that she couldn't keep quiet—that silence is acceptance—so she made a "conscious choice to speak out (Hood, 2004, personal communication).

In chapter 2, Williams's activist job continuum depicted the level of congruence between participants' job assignments and their activist identities. The farther up the career ladder, the more there is to lose, until attaining top leadership positions. Activist risk is least at the very beginning and at the end of career, she found.

The power and visibility of higher positions makes activism both possible and risky. Chapter 2's senior Black men embraced visible activism. But Keisha still felt vulnerable even though she retained her tenure status from her teaching career. She felt her central office position could be affected by missteps in her activist pursuits. Cheryl, knowing about the reticence in the South about appearing socially radical, said "even our superintendent, or any other superintendent, if he was seen as too Black, he would never be able to do his job effectively. Every statement he made would be judged on the criteria, 'Is he saying that because he wants XYZ for Black people or his Black kids'?" She asserted her belief that, "you will have to leave what you're doing if you plan to make wide, sweeping changes…to take it beyond [quiet microactivism], I do believe that you have to become the leading expert on it and become a consultant or something more" (Hood, 2005, p. 75).

Figure 7.1 portrays the forces affecting our activists at various career and life stages. We found this career continuum useful for analyzing experiences of most of our participants, as they made choices about career, identity, and social

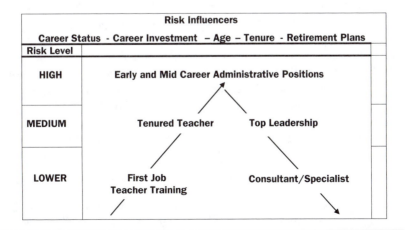

Figure 7.1 Correlation of risk influencers and career positions.

movement participation. Certainly the risk level varies depending on one's cause, and public support for one's cause as one reaches any particular status. Recall chapter 5's Raven's reflections:

> [Early in my career] it was too scary to come out and to be an activist [for GLBT]. When I got older, it's like, what the hell? What damage has this done being silent? How many ulcers do I have? How many opportunities have I lost?... Regretfully, you get to a point in your life when you're older when you just say [what's important]? (Legrand, 2005, p. 87)

This quote beautifully illustrates the career continuum from her early 1970s career beginning when she had seen police raids of gay dances, to an emerging sense of a need for that identity, even as, in the early 2000s a bit of public discourse (and nearing retirement) allowed her to carefully embrace her social movement. For most educators, security, acceptance, and paycheck were real needs but so was their sense of authentic identity, their need to integrate who they were as educators, as people, and as citizens.

Of particular note, chapter 3's women saw less interest and capacity in line administrative positions but they did seek central office kinds of job as specialists. Perhaps this was their way of avoiding the positions where they would be forced to answer queries about the professional and personal dilemmas, so staff positions were more comfortable. Comfort, identity with one's cause and movement, and career position, then, led activists to certain career choices, sometimes suppressing identity and activism. Another insight emerged regarding the assistant principalship, with several participants reflecting that being so involved in day-to-day issues it was nigh impossible to look at policy and the big picture. It appears that educators' positions with visible, accountable, immediate, constant, and intensive demands (such as assistant principals and principals) do not allow space for talk and reflection about societal and educational purposes and social justice.

Perceptions of risk motivated activists to assess risks and potential losses. They often went through inner battles over conflicts between social justice ideals and their sense of self, as well as the need to maintain status and succeed in the career and the community. The career continuum does not perfectly place all activists. Nevertheless it is useful for asking questions about how our participants weighed their activist involvement as they made career choices, given the context and risks they perceived. It should be useful too, to readers who wish to think through their past, present, and future social justice activism and career choices.

Moral Triage: Weighing Identity vs. Risk vs. Making a Difference

People can stand only so much risk. Participants spoke of ulcer avoidance. Suppressing one's activism when the risk is too high can be a trade-off with losing pride and sense of identity with the activist movement. Throughout the research we heard variations on this theme. The previous section described the interplay of position, career stage and age affecting one's action in specific situations. Chapter 2's Keisha would speak up when she was one of two or three in a group of 15, and Edward avoided the events where people still wanted to discuss the issues, saving himself for those ready for getting things accomplished. Yet he reflected that there are "some fights that are not worth being involved in." Remember Cheryl being an advocate yet avoiding the visibility of NAACP involvement and parades. The pro-choice activists, more than others, felt these dilemmas and their own loss of identity. The floundering for identity is poignant in this quote from Ashton who questioned the activist label even though she supports national abortion rights organizations:

> Can I really even consider myself an activist for choice?... I'm definitely a believer in a woman's right to choose. But an activist? In my mind that means I do something. I'm not sure what I've actually done lately...there would have to be a community of choice activists I could feel a part of, and I'm not sure that community exists here. And I'd have to have the sense that I was doing something important as a part of this community. Not always storming the capitol, but passing around petitions at [the grocery store], wearing a T-shirt or something that announces my politics...something. (personal communication, April 2007)

Such self-doubt, search for social network amidst clear signals that one's realistic and practical activism opportunities were negligible represents the extreme of loss of social movement and activist identity among our participants. Many spoke of or acted in ways that pushed aside aspects of their activist identity. Some spoke of the lack of time, and lack of creative control in administering the curriculum. Sara had rationalized and also rationed her risk, recalling efforts to help the frustrated, troubled students who were mistreated at school and home while hiding other aspects of her identity saying, "I can give them advice without telling them I am a lesbian" (see chapter 5). But, reflecting and with deep introspection, she left teaching for graduate school to find space to work through the conflict. Schools, with tightened accountability and decreased professional autonomy, provide no growth and reflection time.

For some involved in GLBT issues, identity, risk, and activist stances were full of evolving dilemmas, and spoke about needing to maintain participation in the mainstream. Recall Fred, knowing of his homosexuality since third grade, but, "making the choice not to be 'out' per se, it's been difficult because I want to fight so hard. I want to be out there, but it's my personal [decision], and that's why I'm not quite the activist where I need to be yet...making that personal sacrifice to where I am out there being seen, because I love my job (Legrand, 2005, p. 85). George spoke to the dilemmas and triage when he spoke of Black folks having "divided souls," which he related to his divisions of sexuality, activism, and wanting to be accepted by other educators and community members.

As he slowly and cautiously revealed more of his identity, he said, "the benefit is I can go home and feel comfortable" (Legrand, 2005, p. 85). Listening to his story, one wonders and hopes that, as he progresses into higher positions and security, he will feel more "at home" in his professional world and that other activists will too.

Denial and Suppression

The participants recognized that the assumptive world's rules against defying dominant values sometimes meant denial and suppression. To take a stand, "out" oneself as identified with a cause, was too risky. Remember in chapter 4 Kim suppressed the urge to speak to the administration at her school about the sexual harassment law, and remember Sarah and Kim suppressing the urge expressed when Kim told us what she *wanted* to say was: "I think that you handled [the interpretation of sexual harassment law] very flippantly and that's why it's so pervasive in society." But, she said, "I wouldn't go to the administration because I would feel backlash."

Raven rationalized hiding her GLBT activism, saying that her job was to teach kids, to teach music, so she did not think it proper to display her "political concerns and my passions, but I refused to let things go by that I thought were unfair or unjust or mean or harsh" (Legrand, 2005, pp. 53–54). Similarly, Fred would get people to rethink when there were derogatory stereotypes about lesbian, gay, bisexual, or transgendered people. Using logics and appealing to people's sense of rights as African Americans, he'd argue, "You've got to protect all people's rights" (Legrand, 2005, p. 77). Feeling a need for suppression and disguise, activists aligned with more acceptable, dominant professional values and rationales.

Denial and suppression was revealed most in chapter 3, accompanied by an unwillingness to make connections to the wider feminist movement. Conservative upbringing and fear of loss of a sense of privilege prevailed. These women were intelligent achievers, and their professional training gave them a sense that empowering girls was right, but wider activism was not. Professional educator training had not been connected to any feminist philosophy. Recall Carol, saying "I honestly don't pay nor have I ever paid attention to those movements, simply because I felt I could do whatever I wanted based on my own capabilities." This denial of a need for the feminist movement may be part and parcel of an avoidance of personal and professional risk, a language of denial. Maria, when asked about the women's movement, stated, "I just observed it on the periphery, and just found it interesting, but…some of the women that were leading that movement were just too radical." Finding rationales for disassociation became a comfortable way for educators to maintain their status within a profession that provided them with no knowledge or support if they raised a ruckus.

Deny or Quit? At times the suppression of identity, idealism, and the lack of opportunities for activism are so constraining and so powerful that one denies identity, as shown above, denies participation in the social movement, as shown by some (especially in chapter 3), finding the safer, less visible positions in school districts. Some, like Sara and Mike, even quit their school-based positions. While our data show numerous examples of restraints, retreats, and suppressions, only George left but he actually found a position above and free from school district career realities where he could be much more effective as a trainer of educators, and in a position where it was less essential that he hide his sexual orientation.

Creative Strategies for Activism

What strategies do activists who continue their careers and, at the same time, retain identification with a social justice cause use?

Curricular Activism

Just by being educators, Ginsburg (1995) argued, one is acting politically. Cleverly, many activists "activised" (Jones, 2005). They embedded their activism in their jobs. Within their sites, working behind the scenes mostly, they created pedagogical opportunities for activism about the issue (e.g., confronting harassment, -isms). Educators discussed the use of curricula to disseminate information and create spaces for discourse about sexual harassment, sexuality, gender roles, and related topics within their workspaces—classrooms, offices, hallways, and other arenas within the school building. Such microactivism through pedagogical strategies was common among all participants (except those in chapter 6). Recall, chapter 2 activists encouraging Black students; registering them for the honors or the AP classes, and placing minority students on the advanced track, and Janet, who is introduced in chapter 5, using an opening in American literature class to help students understand how gay bashing was harmful. Recall George in chapter 5, reviewing library books to weed out those that presented misinformation, bringing in presenters, and "having conversations…creating safe spaces for kids," and Mary, in her classroom, always intervening to stop the homophobic remark.

Some used reading and character education to teach about what is appropriate and to find the teachable moment, as did chapter 3's Sarah, using literature that has strong female protagonists and, on a broader scale, Jill's empowering school-wide forum for her middle school, provided math, science, and technology information as well as female community leaders. In contrast, pro-choice activists, except for the biology teacher who "gives factual information—I won't lie about the biology of reproduction," none described creative strategies for working pro-choice activism into her daily job.

Positioning Activism

Activists find stances or ways of framing their activism so that they can make a small difference without making obvious challenges to the status quo. Listen to Joseph as he calculates his positioning: "I know that sometimes I have to pull back from what I would like to do in order to maintain participation in the mainstream" (Legrand, 2005, p. 83).

A pattern that emerged from activists' words was their finding ways to position their social movement cause as part of dominant cultural and professional values. Listen to chapter 2's Cheryl (quoted in Hood, 2005), recognizing the shifting cultural support for civil rights to a new acceptable framing:

> You know what it is that has made it easier to talk about it?... We know we no longer have to talk much about the Black kids, because everybody's sick of hearing about the Black kids. That's why the Supreme Court's going the way it's going. But now we can talk about the free and reduced, the poor children. And in doing so, who's the greatest percentage of poor children? Black kids. That's something everyone can talk about.... So now, everyone wants to join the conversation. Through that avenue, by broadening it so everyone can understand it and buy into it, the work that we need to do is easier for people to swallow, for everyone to join into.... So you speak to issues of all children...it's easier to get your ultimate goal accomplished and not make it an "us versus them." (Hood, 2005, p. 78)

Similarly, Diane worked with the multicultural committee in her district to make sure issues for Black children were addressed while incorporating it into conversation about "all students." All educators know that the I-do-this-for-the-good-of-all-students is the revered mantra of all educators, used to gain acceptance of a wide range of actions in and around schooling.

Still, arguments about discrimination and the protection of rights could be used to legitimize more marginalized movements. Recall Joseph, in chapter 5, was positioning his GLBT activism in any discussion about gays and lesbians, challenging students' fears and stereotypes "on an intellectual level," demanding students come up with rationales to exclude these people (Joseph, quoted in Legrand, 2005, p. 80). Similarly, Fred, while remaining "in the closet" would tell people to rethink their assumptions by relating GLBT rights to everyone's rights, especially those of African Americans and other minorities, reminding people of race discrimination, the civil rights struggle, and asking "how would you feel?... It's the same." So, the rights, fairness, and decency rationales and the historically embedded civil rights movement, and perhaps even the sense of rights ingrained from studying the Declaration of Independence could be hauled out to create an acceptable positioning of social justice activism.

Sly, Underground, Undercover Activism

The most widely used strategy was, "keeping it on the down-low," that describes Rhonda's method of tackling issues (see chapter 2)—referring to "keeping one's behavior secret, usually to avoid negative consequences" (Hood, 2005, p. 91). Our educators' seemed to know the hidden rules of the profession. They took small initiatives when there was high likelihood of success. Along with picking their battles and choosing the situations where they could make a difference, they also devised clever strategies to enact activism quietly, just like the street level bureaucrats who, facing unmanageable demands, find work-throughs (Weatherly & Lipsky, 1977). One educator activist's words represent one of the various ways of explaining this: "I think activists can take a much quieter role…I think I probably lead by example more that anything else" (Legrand, 2005, p. 55) always avoiding the limelight, the marches, bullhorns, and signs. Fred explained, "I make people think, so I say 'closeted activist' in a sense that…. I'm the one behind the scenes fighting for it." He wrote regularly to politicians to protest their votes or their use of language that he found derogatory (Legrand, 2005, p. 56).

But even quiet activism is not an option when no community or peer support is apparent. Think of the chapter 6 teacher who could not name another pro-choice educator at her school, and knew not to talk about choice in that setting even though holding the opposite position was possible (if only through passive bumper sticker displays). Interestingly, Raven's career reflects an evolution to emerging acceptance of her role as an LGBT activist (chapter 5).

Summarizing Risk and Responses

Thus, the choices regarding educator activism for social justice entail balancing acts. Educators who speak out take the brunt of risks and losses and sometimes suffer personally and professionally. Sometimes they move to alternative career spaces where activism is less risky. More often, they find ways to remain loyal to their education profession (and to cultural conservative values). They still find ways to be activist, but within and around schools; these are carefully constructed strategies. Table 7.1 below applies our findings, using the framing (mentioned in chapter 1) that, when faced with workplace and professional dilemmas, people choose to find some way to speak out (expressing voice), or they express loyalty (by finding ways to stay without causing disruption), or they exit, suppressing part of their identity or literally leaving for a different job or line of work. The table should help readers reflect upon career and life choices for educators and for other activists.

Spaces for Activism

In chapter 1 we reviewed critical race, critical pedagogy, and feminist theories, identity theory, and social movement theory. The review sensitized our questions

Table 7.1 Responses to Risk: Exit, or Voice and Loyalty

Mode	Enactments	Choices and Consequences
Exit	Change oneself or one's situation	• Leave district level education. • Change districts. • Suppress parts of one's identity. • Take it out of town. Join, lobby and protest in national groups and in far-away counties.
Voice	Take a stance, and live with discomfort	• Losing friendships, time and relationship with children and spouses.
	Use voice and activism for/from school	• Isolation • Ulcers • Sarcasm, innuendo, and labels
Loyalty	Risk and Choose	• Find safe tasks • Activism "on the Down-Low" • "Tempered Choices" • Calculate place on the career continuum and wait for safer status.
	Pick safe career spaces	• Create curricular strategies • Create and shape jobs that encompass the cause • Let go of aspirations for highly visible positions • Find like-minded collaborators • Find local professional groups
	Find and use legitimators/sponsors	• Superintendent support • Laws and policies like Title IX, the Achievement Gap and NCLB
	Denying and silencing	• Demonstrate agreement that "there's no real issue" (while taking small actions for social justice).

and analysis, asking about the public and private spheres as locations for identity development and civic engagement, about movement networks, shared values and collaboration, and about the ways in which activists were attuned to each others' efforts and to the wider national/international movements. We also framed the research using insights from literatures asserting that education is about empowerment and, thus, *is* social and political activism. We also presented literatures on the professional culture and confounding factors of Southern conservatism. So, now we search for patterns about how educators do find ways to maneuver past conservative messages, find spaces to enact their "personal" politics in their public profession. What are the locations for activism? Can activists engage in their local communities and districts as public citizens?

We have seen, above, that microlevel and creative activism make spaces in school sites. We have seen the creative quiet activism, "on the down-low," and the positioning of activism. We admired the individual actions in schools and, a few, locally, outside of schools (e.g., starting GSAs, memberships outside schools).

However, from among 52 participants, just one unabashedly claimed being a leader while staying in his own community, calling himself a "pitbull" (chapter

2). This very seasoned high level educator, especially in terms of rights of African Americans, found spaces both locally and on wider stages. Educators only maintain such high status by making choices about how/where to act, and along their career continuum, by choosing not to be visibly active in some situations. For most others, the minimal support for their activism allowed the minimal space in the micropolitics of classroom and curriculum. Even job descriptions and mandates were inadequate supports, in many instances, for making space, in schools, in districts, and in community life, for openly activist interventions. Thus, space for being public in the local context is tightly bound.

Community Values and Expectations Affecting Participation

Community and professional cultural conservatism not only affected individuals' identities, it also defined the strong and limiting boundaries of the spaces for activism. Recall the risks and the labeling, being seen as a nut, fear of the Religious Right. Carl knew that bringing in a GLBT cause speaker to his class would "really…blow the roof off this place" (Legrand, 2005, p. 83).

So, where are the spaces that provide support and the possibility of collaborating? Is there a national context supporting their activism? Do activists access larger movements? What are the points of contact? How do movement identities and language reach activists and thus shape identities?

Supports and Safe Spaces

Finding ways to express dilemmas and ideals, and finding others with shared values is a benefit gleaned from participants in social movements. Some of our activist participants did find and create space on the job when there were community values and when their activities were sanctioned and even mandated space/requirements for intervention, as shown, to some extent, in chapters 2, 3, and 4. Even those in chapter 5 were increasingly finding GLBT protections written into some school policies—the wished-for support most often mentioned to make their activism possible. "Specific language about harassment, bullying, and…gender identification and sexual identity and orientation [indicates that it's] not tolerated…but it's a responsibility to take action about it (Legrand, 2005, p 94). Other needed supports were ally participation, LGBT educators "coming out," and organizational support from professional and school systems.

Collaborations Outlets included informal groups and collaborations. Chapter 2's Ernest had his Saturday group for "talk with the guys about what we needed to do" (Hood, 2004, personal communication) and chapter 3's Anna spoke of her comfortable and candid group where "we talk about these [women's issues]." And Kimberly, introduced in chapter 5, spoke about socializing with people that most straight people don't get to "…a broader, more interesting group" (Legrand, 2005, p. 70).

Activist educators' sense of risk and loss was lessened when supported by the establishment of networks on a microlevel. This was most evident in networks established based on the shared goal to raise awareness about student-to-student sexual harassment. This notion that shared beliefs are at the center of social networks is supported in the literature (Diani & Eyerman, 1992). The following examples illustrate this construction of social networks and the arenas in which they functioned. In addition to Sara's classroom activism, some of her activism was school wide for Women's Month: "we would organize a bunch of different activities…I would set up one committee…and the students would, too, collaborating …for sexual violence, one might be for sexual harassment" (Jones, 2005, p. 99). Notice she spoke of "we," not lone ventures and that Women's Month made the space in their site. Randy, too, spoke of activist work "right at my school where me and administration and some of the other counselors would come together and devise a plan." Note the phrase: "come together." Tim, the elementary school principal, created an approach and rationale for collaborating with parents to discuss curriculum for children going through puberty.

Most collaboration took place on school sites: teachers would collaborate with the counselor; the counselor would enlist the help of the school resource officer; the administrator would utilize materials and workspace of staff, and the principal would facilitate school community meetings.

Still, in chapters 2, 3, and 5, we saw some activists joining groups like the local professional organization for African American educators, a sorority, a group for women educational leaders, and GLSEN and BGLAD affiliations (Legrand, 2005), thus finding niches where their activism was embraced in professional ways by peers so, while remaining in their educator identity, their efforts were part of the larger social movement. In contrast, for Mike and Sara (chapter 4), the two educators who left their site positions, their sense was that school site collaboration was on too small a scale to make a dent. This led them to activism in arenas outside of school. Still, among our participants, the dominant pattern of participation was at the site level. Only four (Ernest "the pitbull," Richard and Edward in chapter 2, and chapter 4's Mike) worked openly and actively at the state level. A few found safe comfortable spaces locally, with outside groups. Safe spaces at the district level were rare.

Supports: Job Descriptions and Policies The structure and legitimacy from laws and district policies created spaces for social justice activism. Title IX and the court cases, regulations, and program that ensued were huge supports for the activists in chapters 3, 4, and 5. Recall Jill's response (chapter 3) to Title IX: "Title IX does mean something. And I mean when that came out, I was singing Hallelujah for us, you know. And I used that a few times [when talking with fellow coaches about female students' athletic programs]." Such federal law created obligations for educators, which were used, especially by some in chapter 4, to be assertive about intervening to stop sexual harassment, saying "It's the law."

Strong activist administrators used legal precedents and their job roles as the rationale for interventions. Administrators, speaking about sexual harassment, described speaking in faculty meetings and one-on-one with students. Several spoke of women's studies groups, district-wide counseling and guidance programs, community groups, and zero tolerance policies as ways to bring along the community support needed to take sexual harassment seriously.

Activists mentioned in chapter 2 felt that the federal No Child Left Behind (NCLB) policy indirectly supported their interventions on behalf of African American students, for example, leading Andrea to give talks to university students and community groups (Hood, 2005). But, as we saw in chapter 6, policy serves as a deterrent to the extent that abstinence-only sex education took hold.

Site, and even local community level activism, gains tremendous momentum when the activist stance is embedded in jobs. Activists could say, "It's my job" as the basic justification and then embrace the social movement sentiments and needs. Lorraine's words are representative of such educators: "My membership in the social movement regarding sexual harassment is directly from my job, which is as an assistant principal and administrator of a school through Title IX and the sexual harassment policy that is from a federal mandate. This is mandated through the federal government under Title IX policy. So that's how I participate." Mary (chapter 5) described the significance of specificity in her district's nondiscrimination policy as covering harassment, bullying, speaking to gender identification and sexual orientation, thus demanding that educators take action for stopping harassment.

Locally Fragmented Activism

Activists for different social justice causes did not create and share spaces, either within or outside school or district boundaries. Although they were socialized and licensed into the same profession, and their activism's goals and dilemmas have much in common, there was little crossover or common knowledge among the educators' movements. For the most part, activists in chapter 4 didn't know or participate in the causes and dilemmas of those in chapter 2, or chapter 3 and they didn't work in coalition. The exceptions, such as chapter 4's Sara and chapter 5's Kimberly were those seeking to understand and find space in their identities and in their professional and personal communities where they could integrate their general urge to create tolerance and equity for all. The other interesting exception is in the creative strategies whereby activists used a more valued and understood equity issue (e.g., civil rights history and laws) to help stop intolerant speech and action of resisters and bring them along to see, for example, the parallels with the hatred, discrimination, and harassment from homophobia.

Without professional cultural support, the activist educator felt alone and even mistrustful. Poignant experiences of feeling isolated were revealed. Representative of this was Kerry's expressing her sense that her own ethics guided her, and trusting a colleague was iffy. Throughout our data, participants reflected the need to pick and choose who you talk with and a feeling of isolation and marginalization by colleagues. Remember Maria in chapter 3 who felt the physical separation from the other administrators in the building was their way of silencing her? Much power and sustenance is lost in the fragmentation. It also shows that their activism really is closeted, and is not introduced or sanctioned in their professional preparation. We are left with this question: If they had openly displayed their activist ideals in their teacher training, would they have been able to get and keep jobs? Does education lose powerful potential leaders who see the conservatism and the disempowerment and choose other professions?

Meager Supports from National Movements Social movement theory suggests that activism is buttressed by locals' knowledge of and participation in their national movement. Also, there should be a sense of support from a "conscience constituency" (Tarrow, 1998); that is, support of those who take little action but who give nods of approval, pay dues to organizations, and find ways to connect to others with shared values. Our activists did not emphasize having access to the larger network and activities of their movement. A small portion of chapter 2's participants joined the national organizations and sororities as well as local professional associations and one seasoned and retired activist's career featured working with churches, community groups, fraternities and sororities. So how did our participants connect to larger social and political world?

Macrolevel Spaces

Our participants' activism was mostly micropolitical, mostly at sites. Did they participate nationally working at the macrolevel for policy change? What value do they perceive coming from national social movement activity?

Connections to the National Movement

Involvement with one or more political organizations having the agency to address student-to-student sexual harassment in some capacity was meaningful for five participants in chapter 4. Memberships in teacher and administrator organizations, NOW, NARAL, and Planned Parenthood, Gay Straight Alliance (GSA), Gay Lesbian Straight Educators Network (GLSEN), Human Rights Campaign (HRC), and Parents, Family and Friends of Lesbians and Gays (PFLAG), often connecting via the Internet and sometimes participating in letter writing campaigns, through web alerts and through newsletters—all were examples from our research of connections to national movements. Some in chapters 2 and 6 mention taking part in large-scale marches in the 1970s or 1980s for civil rights and women's rights. In chapter 6 three educators referenced taking part in large-scale Washington, DC events for abortion rights (seen as safe because they were removed from the schoolhouse). National participation, then, is possible but isolated. For many of our educator activists, it is a personal connection, a part of their personal politics.

Aversion to the National Rhetoric The theories, assumptions, rhetoric, and the ways the media frame a social movement greatly affected our activists. From the national to the community to the site, the cultural chatter affected whether or not educator activists could find ways to integrate their educator identities with the movement. Recall the perception of risk and the worry about language and labels recounted throughout the chapters. Particularly recall how this was revealed when some of the women in chapter 3 viewed the national feminist movement activities so negatively that they denied the actions they took, themselves, for women and girls in schooling. On the other hand, some saw the real "politicking for women's issues" happening at a national level and, although they were not averse to the goals, felt disconnected from that politicking. Still, all felt comfortable with any framing that encompassed equal rights and equal employment laws useful for legitimating their microwork, as did those who intervened against sexual harassment. This focus from chapter 3 provides insight for all social justice movement leaders. Controlling and positioning the rhetoric so that the movement's values, leaders, and symbols make the connection with the realities of the daily lives of educators can unleash a widened power base.

The National Movement as History That the national movement had played out its usefulness was a strong theme, especially in chapters 2 and 3. Cultural compliance with landmarks in attaining some civil rights and women's rights achieved, on paper, took the edge off activists' involvement. In chapter 2, some participants remembered their civil rights activism, enjoying the benefits of increased equality in schooling while still working for more equality. The former group worried about the strength and capacities of the latter group to see the continuing need for the fight, for example, against resegregation. In chapter 3, most activists' careers developed when schools had to show at least minimal compliance with Title IX and equal employment laws. However, a few with more knowledge of the struggle for enforcement, the continuing deeper issues about self esteem, women in leadership, and so on, as well as the significance of the failed movement for an Equal Rights Amendment, spoke of concern about younger women understanding the need for vigilance and persistent activism.

Activism against sexual harassment, with relatively recent Supreme Court rulings (as cited in chapter 4 and expanded on in Jones, 2005) is still filtering down to educators. It has had more space and support from the national movement, which has provided well-known strategies and programs.

From our analysis of all our cases, we see that activists' identification with movements does need continuous reconnection and reassessment. The proud and heroic acts of past activists and the achievements in legislation are too easily forgotten. They are too easily belittled and distorted in the powerful backlash.

They are too easily undermined as dominant political and cultural values dictate new legislation and budgets that emphasize efficiency and accountability over social justice agendas.

Taking It Out of Town

Although a great deal of micropolitical activism was enacted quietly by our activists, educators could shed their educator identities in more macrolevel spaces by getting out of town. The difficulty in finding space in one's own county or district could be neutralized by participating outside the district. This decreased the worry about getting one's picture in the paper.

Recall Mike in chapter 4, who could not be "out" so he quit the local level of the education profession. In chapter 6 none of the choice activists were "out" at school, nor would they consider being "active" where they live, while in the career. Chapter 6's research process might be indicative that the difficulty of finding pro-choice activist educators means not only are they so hidden, but like Mike, they may have left teaching or sought higher level activism.

In all of the social justice causes, though, taking it out of town was a safer way to be with others (sometimes noneducators) whose activism played out in more public and militant actions. For activists for women's rights to choose taking it out of town was *the* safe space. When they marched, signed petitions, and collaborated with like minded activists, it was almost always by going where their faces would not be recognized, and by their contributing to state and national movement actions. Finding this pattern makes us question whether educators give up their citizenship rights as they learn the norms of their profession and sense their vulnerabilities to community judgments, hearkening back to times of requirements that teacher attend church, avoid hair dye and immodest dress, and sleep eight hours per night!

Seeking Wider Spaces When older or in higher ranks, a few educators felt more emboldened to look at policy issues and see needs for political action as making a difference. So, taking it out of town was, in part, about seeking wider and greater impact. Recall chapter 4's Lorraine visualizing herself lobbying the state senate (especially "after I left the field of education"). And Pat in chapter 3 recognized that her presenting at state conferences and being a search consultant for superintendencies were methods for widening her activism for women. Taking it out of town was a risk-reduction strategy but also a means to widen their activist work, as with Mike and Sara (chapter 4).

Thus, for effective and safe activism, our educators felt they could work carefully and creatively at their local sites, some found support from national laws and movements, some participated carefully in national movements that were framed in ways that they identified with, and a very few stayed in education but found more macrolevel spaces where they could be themselves and enact activism in more all-encompassing and political ways.

Figure 7.2 below, portrays the spaces for activism. The figure is both a summary and a commentary. It shows that, within schools, the spaces are those given legitimacy by laws and job descriptions. Moreover, spaces for activism within and close to schools can include creative activising "on the down-low" and the sharing in rare groups of like-minded educators. On the other hand, in rare circumstances, individuals stay in education and create roles for themselves beyond the school district, as leaders and trainers, but only by making major career shifts or by having security from high community and career status, gained over decades. This is activism contained in spaces interwoven with educators' professional roles. More of activists' identities have no space in their educator roles. They either suppress, self-censor, or deny their social justice activism or they monitor their identities so that their activism can be seen only outside of their roles, out of town, in letter-writing, and the like. Readers who are educators, and readers who are activists, may reflect on Figure 7.2 to consider where they can find and expand spaces and potential collaborations in the pursuit of social justice through education careers. If that exercise is depressing, remember that

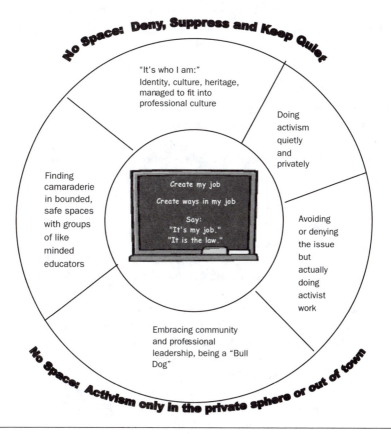

Figure 7.2 Where are educational space for activism?

social movements' possibilities can shift, with reduced risk and increased support as Raven, mentioned in chapter 5, spoke of her earliest teaching years in a context where vice squads raided gay dances, then seeing a widened acceptance as she saw Ellen Degeneres and "Queer Eye for the Straight Guy" on television. She said, "It's…just so talked about. And I came up in a time when it was so silent" (Legrand, 2005, p. 66). Not only does societal context change, identities shift too. Raven and others' stories illustrate ongoing and fluid construction of identity. Still, the overarching theme is the search for congruence of professional and personal values and choices in a profession that seldom encourages their overt participation in political challenges to oppression.

Expansions to Theory and Literature

We have presented a portrait of educators' professionalism as encompassing the desire to intervene for social justice but having to be oh so careful! The themes and patterns elaborated above provide significant findings, fascinating in their strength across the cases but also in variations among cases (e.g., among the movements, among the participants' career status). We now push our analysis to identify contributions to literatures and theory-building, asking, what are the surprises, challenges, and expansions?

The Interdisciplinary Expansion

Analyses of education careers and policies rely, often, on assumptions developed for business (e.g., organization and leadership theory) and psychology. Feminist critiques demonstrate that leadership theory was developed from studies and stories of White heterosexual males' careers, especially those running countries, corporations, and wars (Blount, 1998; Marshall, 1995; Young & Skrla, 2003). Narrow lenses for understanding and theorizing work in education prevent complex and contextualized analyses, and over time have led to the perpetuation of oppressive professional cultures. We provide broader analysis, benefiting from diverse and interdisciplinary frameworks.

This research demonstrates the benefits of using literatures on education careers, expanded by sociological insights framed by social movement and identity theory, to understand the actions and lives of educators. As presented in chapter 1 and demonstrated in chapters 2 through 6, this expansion framed patterns of behavior, activity, and sentiment that encompassed educators' determinations to keep schools contributing to empowerment and social justice—as places where societal, cultural, economic, and political failures and wrongs should be righted. As a result, this work buttresses emerging literatures on teacher leadership, on schooling as liberatory democratic practice, and on the values bases of educators' career commitments. Our research also points to expansions necessary to identity theory and social movement theory.

Expanding Identity: Education Careers and Social Justice Leadership Potential

Identity theory, used to amplify questions regarding educator professional identity and career choices, provided terms, assumptions, and questions about how our activists' development intertwined with their fluid and evolving attitudes, commitments, beliefs, and behaviors. From this literature, we knew that individuals undergo ongoing identity construction, affected by a host of factors including personal and professional contexts and experiences. Our findings show that sociopolitical control of teacher identity, limited opportunities for nontraditional leaders, narrow definitions of teacher leadership, an absence of history and theory in educator preparation and in-service education, and limited opportunities for the expression of moral and empowerment identities challenge extant identity theory when considering the lives of educator activists.

Sociopolitical Controls over Professional Identities Our research expands identity theory by adding to the growing literature on adult identity development in a neglected profession. It illustrates how a conservative sociopolitical and professional culture works to focus and limit identity in spite of an individual's interests, especially when those interests are progressive. As elaborated in chapter 1, previous literatures define the scope of this issue. On the one hand, Casey's (1993) narratives described heroic teachers connected to radical social movements and social justice; Ginsburg et al. (1995) outlined the various political powers of educators, at both the micro- and macropolitical levels. But other authors focus more on the political controls over educators' choices. Speaking from the British context, Lawn (1995) said, "both the Left and the Right may view teachers as possible agents in the creation of a new society:…this means that certain groups of teachers were favored while others were expelled" (p. 118), pointing to educators' vulnerability to their cultural-political contexts. Our analysis demonstrates both: educators' heroics *and* the power of social and political controls. Heroics in this case, however, are best understood in the context of Ginsburg et al.'s (1995) frame, as the empowerment work of education writ large, based in educators' ethos to work on behalf of kids no matter what. The power of the word *professional* and the worries of our activists about protecting their professional status, along with concerns that other socially and politically tainted labels would be deployed as threats, highlight the limitations of identity theory for adults whose professions are, in actuality, controlled by state and local agents. Etzioni (1961) posited that teachers are semiprofessionals since they have so little power control over their work. Our research shows it isn't that simple.

Identity Development of Nontraditional Leaders Because leadership is understood in rather narrow frames, expansion of leadership literatures must emerge from research on undesignated, unsanctioned, and nontraditional quiet leaders. Our research contributes to this expansion.

By traditional assessments, few of our activists would be designated as leaders. Instead, their leaderlike behaviors are nontraditional and unsanctioned. (Actually, as they took on sanctioned and visible leadership positions, their activist behaviors were all the more risky.) Our research displays leaders who, incorporating the realities of educator identities, still take on social justice causes, making choices for their lives, and their career directions. Doing so meant confronting their profession's institutionalized protection of the status quo while, at the same time, showing loyalty to their profession—quite a balancing act! Leadership then meant sly diplomacy, compromise, but also living with stressful incongruities, including staying loyal to status quo expectations of the education profession even as they caught glimpses of and worked to challenge embedded institutional racism, sexism, and homophobia. In this scenario, however, the patriarchal cultural assumptions that protect top male leadership, and associated outcomes in student bullying and harassment, and that also forbid free exchange of information to give women and girls choices about childbearing can go unchallenged. Thus, loyalty to norms of the profession at times overshadowed educators' choices and covert activism, inhibiting their freedom to take greater, more visible leadership in defying schooling's subtle status quo protections. Thus Black activists quietly channeled kids out of special education and into gifted classes, but often avoided visible leadership and strident demands for systemic changes to avoid "acting too Black." Although frustrated by the need for sly as opposed to open activism, by acting on the down-low, educators' remained loyal and retained their respected educator status.

Thus, education stifles the identities of leaders who have the insights and potential to open the discourse and offer critiques of the racism and sexism embedded in the historical structuring of education careers. The resulting silences contribute, in spite of affirmative action and diversity trainings, to a continuation of White male dominance in school leadership positions. We present quiet activism, circumscribed by fears that assertive activism risks looking too Black, too obsessed about sex, too feminist, too queer, too outside mainstream Christian culture, even as we wail about achievement gaps and bullying endemic to patriarchal systems. So, education systems function to socialize all children into White dominated society, as Shujaa (1994) posited in *Too Much Schooling*. Even while policy makers are declaring that women's career barriers have been dissolved, that race isn't really about race but rather about economic disparities, and that we have laws in place to protect students against harassment, educator identities are molded within embedded school practices that soften the enforcement of equity policies. Activists also know that equity policies were constructed without plans and funds for monitoring and enforcement. So, again, monitoring and enforcement can be positioned as being "too"—"too radical," "too feminist," "too controversial." It is the affront of putting your personal issues into a political arena. But the political arena is only an understanding, not an actual, visible arena. Thus, you can't really argue it—no one called a meeting time or location for the argument.

In the past, radical nontraditional leaders (e.g., Martin Luther King, Margaret Sanger, Mahatma Gandhi, W.E.B. Du Bois, Mao, Lenin, Castro, Martin Luther King, Jr.) came from middle-class backgrounds. They found or created positions which gave them the independence, credentials, money, and status that supported their identity development as leaders of social movements (although expatriation and assassination were sometimes the eventual consequences). Educators, too, either come from or attain at least lower middle-class status. Still, their vulnerability (e.g., needing that paycheck and needing community approval) and their professional cultures greatly undermine the independence to develop identities as leaders in social movements. Educators risk spoiled identity when they engage in antimainstream causes in assertive ways. The simplest thing—being called a feminist, a lesbian, too Black, obsessed with sex, out of the Christian mainstream—undermines their hard-won legitimacy as respected and respectable middle-class community members and professionals, as is most poignantly illustrated by chapter 3's women, but really by all of our loyal, sly, activists. The result: educator activists tiptoeing around other educators who still disregard sexual harassment, for example, and teachers and students who shy away from developing to their full potentials because formal and informal curricula in schools teach the limitations on the Black, gay, and female parts of their identities.

Teacher Leadership New literatures are capturing the reality that teacher leadership, leadership from among the ranks, is powerful for curricular change (Cochran-Smith, 1991; Fullan, 1993). We expand further.

We identified activist leadership that is quiet and sly, where educators, not seeking promotions, not seeking credit and visibility, are manipulating the system to get something done, to fix something, for kids. Creating mentoring for women in leadership, bringing in programs for sexual harassment awareness, challenging a sex education curriculum, working to change discrimination policies to include sexual orientation—these are grassroots leadership acts in the service of getting a job done.

This is educator leadership in spite of policies, structures, and appointed and institutionalized leaders who fail to intervene, or who work to prevent social justice action. Again, it is careful and sly, but a comfortable settlement of identity conflicts can be found when activists can speak of their activism as part of their job and part of caring for and protecting children, even though they might disavow change-the-world politicking and picketing.

Which part of educators' identities derived from class and cultural consciousness, race, sex, and professional training *do* have space and comfortable location for expression. Our participants often relied on the professional ethic of "just do what's best for the children." This mantra can be a useful cover for activists since it cannot be attacked. Factors impacting the development of activist identities varied, as did the expressions of those identities. The educators' identities were arrayed along a continuum benchmarked by caution, capacity, and challenge.

Where's the History and Theory? This study also reveals educator activist identity as personal political contestation, wherein individuals' stances, voices, and interventions often require taking personal risks, with little or no preparation or support from their professional or community culture. When forgotten and pushed aside or silenced, issues of equity, racism, sexism, and homophobia never go away, they just wait for champions to emerge again, take up the fight again. Educators have little or limited sense of the history and theory that create contemporary contexts, especially as coursework in education foundations or contexts gets diminished in the pressure for practical methods and for accountability. Educators identify with activism, but they have little sense that others are writing about it. Educators have limited exposure to feminist, critical race, and emancipatory literatures or traditions, for example, and so seldom have preparation that gives them knowledge of the history of their profession, never mind the sense of connection between education and social movements.

Moral Identities and Empowerment Our research refutes stereotypes about obsessed-about-salary and go-home-at-three teachers. These activists entered education careers believing that schooling helps children and changes society. Holding on to these beliefs meant coping with shock when they see how poorly schools are equipped to intervene for advances in social justice. Few of our educators knew of the literatures that frame emancipatory pedagogy, critical race theory, feminist theory, or queer theory. Few were tied in with the larger social movements (e.g., women's movement, gay rights movement) that could provide historical perspective, political goals, and lobbying, and a sense of being part of a larger social movement. Further, few were able to identify themselves as leaders who have compatriots working on a range of social justice issues, and who are finding ways to challenge the conservative dominant discourse and practices that perpetuate inequality.

The mantra of caring for kids is sacred, but passionate outrage or spiritually driven mission are banned behaviors, at least when they are associated with more progressive causes. Passion and spirituality are disallowed and seen as unprofessional in the education professional culture. The term *professional* implies an identity guided by a set of particular skills, a generic code of ethics, and an adherence to stated rules of behavior. Our findings point to the identity conflicts caused by the education profession. Educators' sense of "what's good for kids" and the societal deficiencies that schooling needs to tackle, create dilemmas for activists when their job descriptions, their colleagues, mentors, sponsors, and personnel systems suppress these interests in the maintenance of the status quo. By exploring these dilemmas, we expand the newly developing literatures that explore educators' emotions and spirituality. Our findings demonstrate ways in which activists were inspired by a sense of moral obligation. For most, this came from their upbringing but these issues are undertheorized in the intersection of identity and leadership theories.

Values and Passions Organizational structures and leadership definitions are structured as if educators were apolitical and dispassionate. These presumptions mask a cultural norm espoused in schooling, born of the middle-class, Christian aspirations of mainstream U.S. society. Values-teaching (e.g., in "character education") in the curriculum is couched in behavioral, not moral, terms. Yet all educators understand the hidden curriculum that delineates acceptable and unacceptable identities in this so-called values-free apolitical schooling.

This study reveals the educator, who knows she or he is a public servant, struggling to repress the values that undergird the spiritual and moral inspiration that brought that person to an education career. Thus, the energy and joy in joining this helping profession is shunted and stifled. What if, instead of stifling, we tapped into that energy that emanates from educators' moral and spiritual sense of purpose? This does open up cans of worms: Which religion's morality is being promoted? What about church-state separation? "I don't want teachers' imposition of their values on my kid." But pushing the moral inspiration of educators under the rug doesn't totally make it go away. It may, however, make some of our most energetic and equity-oriented teachers and leaders go away, to other careers. Pushing the moral inspiration of educators for progressive causes under the rug also ignores the very real and very powerful moral forces that buttress conservative practices of schooling.

Summary: Activist Identities in Constrained Conservative Cultures

We know that identities are shaped in the interweaving of contexts like family and community and religion. It was surprising, however, how those forces so dominated the work lives of professional educators when exacerbated by conservative Southern cultures. Too often, the cultural geography of the South, entwined with Bible Belt injunctions, bound those who otherwise felt affinity with social justice values and causes that defy the status quo. The careful self-presentation and avoidance of controversial labels were demonstrated in Casey's (1993) narratives of activist teachers as well: in their conversations with Casey, activists resisted labels such as "socialist," or "communist," preferring to allow their actions to define what they believed and who they were.

Recall that most of our participants chose a quiet way of exercising their voice and their loyalty (building upon exit, voice, or loyalty options mentioned in chapter 1, and earlier in this chapter). Exiting, quitting the career, usually meant giving up the best opportunity for social justice interventions for children.[3] Even those whose activism had to be hidden (e.g., the proponents for women's right to choose) wanted to stay in schooling, finding any opportunity to use their insights and values to open social justice discourse. Indeed, as we anticipated (see chapter 1 p. 16) they did "tactically take up submerged and lesser discourses...mobilizing other aspects of their nonunitary self" (Thomson, 2001, p. 7), presenting a degree of compliance with dominant values while conducting "secret business"

(Thomson, p. 7). No matter what path brought them to the point of defining themselves as activist educators, all participants saw themselves as committed to liberating students through learning, what hooks (1994) describes as "education as the practice of freedom" (p. 6). Almost all participants responded affirmatively when asked if they were activists. The lone educator to eschew the label described his commitment to uplifting others in a manner consistent with the definition of activism used in this study. The activist identities of the educators fit Castells's (1997) focus on the relationship between identity and meaning. He suggested that identity organizes the purpose of a person's behavior within a particular context. Defining themselves as activists challenged the educators to act and guided their choices of action in their respective work environments.

So, as identity and social movement participation activities coexist, what is gleaned from our use of social movement theory?

What Social Movement Theory Predicts and Overlooks

Audre Lorde (quoted in Maggio, 1980) reminds us that if we wait until we are not afraid, we will be speaking from our graves. Traditionally conceived, activists will not let fear silence them, but instead join forces with influential citizens to confront elites, authorities, and opponents. Such union and subsequent action is considered "contentious politics" (Tarrow, 1998). When social networks back contentious politics, social movements are born. Within social movement theory, random mobilization theorists view social movements as extensions of institutionalized actions. They focus on movements of institutional change that attempt to alter elements of social structure, organize previously unorganized groups, and represent interests of groups excluded from popular culture (Jenkins, 1983). This institutional and macroperspective was useful for our research insofar as it helped us ask, and then find little evidence, of such networks or connections to institutional movements and to note how educators *avoided* contentious politics.

Still, using social movement theory to focus on educators enabled us to ask what social movement activism looks like in this conservative profession. By focusing on a profession rather than a movement, we demonstrate a missed angle of inquiry. From our research in social movement theory, we knew to listen for choices that participants made about activism and their levels of participation, social networks, and how shared values glued grassroots and national organizational activities together. But is social movement theory adequately flexible to frame our findings, such as activising, activism that is on the down-low, which is quiet and personal and at the street level?

Educators in this study learned closeted activism. The angle of focus on education, and on the South, yielded complicated but useful new themes. Rather than looking like participation in large-scale collective protests and banners, activism can look like simple and quiet contributions. Action for social justice occurs even when some educators deny involvement in activism.

The theme of constrained participation prevailed across all the movements and all the participants. Age, generation, career longevity, region, and other characteristics affected educators' perception of the risks of activism, given the conservative political context of education. However, there did not appear to be a relationship between any particular trait and the educators' beliefs about the constraints of the political context of public education. Across varied ages, regions, and career positions, all sensed that they were expected to appear apolitical in their professional roles. They met this expectation by positioning themselves as public servants. We did find the increased level of risk in midcareer, coinciding with increased investment and increased visibility, as shown in Figure 7.1 above. We did find that the more professionally validated movement in this group (i.e., for race equity) allowed, for very secure and mature educators, greater comfort with bull-dog type activism and proud, open participation in social movement leadership and networking. So societal discourse on racism, for example, had provided some legitimacy for "bulldog" behavior. Where there is minimal societal discourse the sly, minimized "it's-my-job" activism, and the take-it-out-of-town activism, with little or no professional or community support for their movement participation prevailed.

When Ginsburg (1995) theorized educators as political actors, he did not anticipate the hostility to activism experienced by our participants. As they implemented activism within the constraints of their positions, schools, and systems, "keeping it on the down-low" to avoid negative consequences and to avoid attention, theirs was a politically astute but contortedly constrained political participation. This was particularly so at the microlevel, although sometimes they found flexible spaces within their professional responsibilities where they could activise to pursue their objectives. They were least constrained when they connected their actions to broadly accepted agendas and networked behind the scenes to get others to promote their aims.

The word *politics* has negative connotations for educators. Perhaps *activism*, too, is a negative term for well-socialized educators.

Intensity of the Discourse and Backlash It would be easy—too easy—to simply say that these educators were not really activists since their participation in their social movements was so constrained and unconnected. However, by eliciting educators' meaning-making, and hearing our participants' careful calculations of risk and potential loss and their subsequent and evolving choices about exit, voice, and loyalty, we show a nuanced and reality-based expansion to social movement theory. We heard their perceptions of risk, loss, and isolation, and, in their sense of the power of the conservative culture, their activism was all the more remarkable. Cooper (1997) described the power and tactics of the Christian Right backlash, making those risk-perceptions into reality. Fear of this backlash would be intensified in Bible Belt contexts.

Fragmented, Isolated, Lonely Untheorized Activism As noted in chapter 1, social movements have structuring organizations, whether through informal networks, clubs, or gatherings where connections are made and where goals to make change in political or social institutions are identified. Social movements, then, collectively name beliefs about what needs to be done and how to challenge opponents. However, in our research, we found meager evidence of educators' connections with larger social movements' activities and the rationales used to formulate goals. Those most closely connected to larger movements were educators in the most legitimated social movement (i.e., for minority opportunities) and the least legitimated (i.e., for sex education and women's right to choice). There were exceptions to the isolation and disconnection. Activists for GLBTQ and pro-choice rights were more aware of and involved in the larger social movement, finding regional allies and literatures that helped them know of the state and national movement successes and struggles. This may result from national organizations' ongoing efforts to protect and develop tenuous legal protections regarding sexual orientation and reproductive choice. Educators who grew up with desegregation and the civil rights movement were raised with knowledge of that social movement. For some, identity was maintained through professional organizations for African Americans, and attuned to the institutionalized barriers faced by African Americans in current schooling practices. However, for the most part, the social movement organizations and networks have not penetrated or made connections to those who control the education profession.

Although they were socialized and licensed into the same profession, and their social justice activism's goals and dilemmas have much in common, we saw little evidence of crossover or common knowledge among the educators about others' activism. It indicates that their activism is closeted and silenced from their very early training and induction where they learn, together, what is and is not sanctioned in their professional preparation. Activists in chapter 3 did not speak about any connections to activist causes discussed in chapters 4, 5, or 6, for example, although their issues regarding gender and sexuality and rights do overlap and they sacrifice the chance to work in coalition. (This may have been a function of the research process.) The greatest overlap in understanding among the causes and dilemmas emerged from the few who spoke of the wider societal intolerances; for example, activists in chapters 4 and 5, along with those in chapter 6 were sensitive to the nuances of feminist activism. In addition, as was suggested by the timeline in chapter 1, the civil rights movement hovered in the background of all activists, not just those involved in the movement. Nevertheless, absent opportunities for collaboration, networking, and mutual support of shared values, much power and sustenance is lost.

Some activist educators had little knowledge of the larger social movement whose values they were enacting. Most of our activists had a sense of movements regarding civil rights, but they made little or no mention of gaining historical or philosophical perspective from their professional preparation to see education as empowerment, for example, nor did they have special training on Title IX, on sexual orientation, or how to prevent sexual harassment. For the educators described in chapters 3 through 5, theirs was a liberal feminist framing—concerned with protecting rights and opportunities—but they did not speak of feminist literatures that expand our understandings of the intertwining hierarchies of power and domination and oppression that use sexuality as a power tool. For most, their engagement with the cause came more from their upbringing and their professional ethic than from any professional knowledge or formal training of the responsibility of educators to uncover and intervene against oppressive and limiting structures in society. Their knowledge of a movement's lobbying activity for legislation and court rulings at the state and national level, for example, was minimal. Educators used the letter of the law to reinforce their activism against sexual harassment (chapter 4), but often their fellow professionals were proceeding as if MacKinnon's (1989) and others' scholarly critiques of patriarchal legal and institutional assumptions had never been written. For many professionals, Equal Employment Opportunity guidelines, Title IV, Title IX, and major court decisions were not overarching guides to their professional work. For some, the Bible (with community support and encouragement) was their guide.

As part of their professional pre- and in-service training, educators have limited access to critical race, feminist, or queer theories, never mind to heroes and role models who might shape their attachments to the movement's activities and its leaders. Thus, activism is closeted and isolated, even seen as subversive in their own profession! In their professional training and licensure programs, and in professional development, there is no promise of microlevel support and very little opportunity to envision the connection between curricula and daily workings of schooling and the macrolevel picture of education as empowerment and citizen-community-building.

Missed Opportunities While working to monitor national legislation and budgets, social movement organizations have left behind, isolated, and left unsupported the educators who could and would do more, if they had the language and the connections. So, movements lose potential collaborators.

Professors who could present the critical social justice, emancipatory, social movement language, connections, frameworks, and literatures to educators' professional socialization are often marginalized in schools of education. Such professors create cognitive dissonance, requiring educator-students to think of the big picture. Often, received framings from social movement literatures, theories, icons, and symbols (and unflattering media representations) exaggerate the dissonance. But these professors in schools of education, as activist intellectuals, are increasingly marginalized. They give up course requirements and readings that could provide the alternative languages and connections. They are complying with state and national boards' licensure and credentialing demands that teachers and administrators have the preparation *these credentialing agencies* see as vital compromises in the teaching of expansive discourses. Such professors also challenge colleagues whose training and scholarship is rooted in positivistic research traditions that disparage diverse interpretations. The more practice-oriented professors are more likely to present literatures and frameworks that ease and promote educator-students' career mobility. Thus, the presentation of social movement values offers little attraction and comfort to educator-students. So, social justice movement-oriented professors lose their oomph.

As a result, potential recruits into education, whose values and ideals about helping children and changing society are ripe for development, are lost. Recruitment opportunities are lost when the professional preparation and the social movement leaders do not help young idealists to view education careers as spaces for societal change. Public school students also lose when educator activists tiptoe around other educators who still disregard sexual harassment, for example; and teachers and students who shy away from developing to their full potentials because formal and informal curricula in schools teach the limitations on the Black, gay, and female parts of their identities.

Summary: Acknowledging the Realities of Closeted, Sly, Direct, Hands-on Activism

As we have shown, social movement theory does not adequately encompass the activism of our educators. When they simply *did* things, without making protests and without reference to a social movement's values, slogans, and leaders, their activism was brave and independent but lonely. When they smoothly and diplomatically presented the needs and values of their movement, avoiding parades and haranguing, they found ways to grab onto the coattails of more dominant, prioritized, and supported values and needs.

Isolated and insulated in their conservative profession, with little or no specialized literatures and training and with limited exposure to leaders, literatures, and activities of the social movement, these educator activists devised their own versions of how and why they worked for their social justice cause. Social movement theory misses these unsung self-led social justice workers. When they created programs, intervened to help with or remedy a situation, they were not thinking of social movement leaders or slogans but more about how to make a small change, one step at a time, without calling attention. As often as not, they were thinking about a particular kid rather than about how their action would improve society and education.

Our research presents a challenge to social movement theory. Activising for social justice, often unconnected to the movement, inspired by family background more than by literatures and networks and leaders—such activism needs to be incorporated in social movement theory. No doubt this occurs in other professions!

What Educators, Policy Makers, and Citizens Should Learn from Our Research

Legislators, district human resources managers, school boards and professional associations, licensure boards, professors of school administration and teacher educators, and administrators (hereinafter called policy makers)—all should see implications and uses for this research. We now show ways these policy makers can reframe the worlds of educators as they design and supervise educators' work, status, and expectations, create the requirements for job applicants, develop curriculum for preservice and in-service training, and consider the powerful messages deployed in the informal systems of assumptive worlds rules (see chapter 1). We also show how social movement leaders can expand their base in communities and among education professionals with social justice intentions.

When Policy Makers and Practitioners Design Educators' Work

This research offers significant insights for aspiring teachers (and their supervisors) who need to search to make education and social justice activism compatible. What can be done with our findings that the impetus and support for activism came less from codes of ethics, supports, policies, laws, texts, training, directives, and models and more from values, ideals, and relationships? Or that our cross-case comparison portrays educators gingerly and cautiously working as professionals and as citizens for social justice? These educators are constructing politically astute strategies for protecting their professional status, particularly given the political nature of the education career (described in the review of the literature reviewed in chapter 1 (e.g., Casey, 1993; Dillard, 1995; Ginsburg et al., 1995; Ladson-Billings, 1994). Given our portrayal of social justice-inclined educators having to tailor activism into the margins of their jobs—what should be changed in the profession, and how?

Policy makers can start by considering social movement and identity theories whose emphasized phraseology includes: shared emotions and values; intersectionality; integrating the personal and the political; human development; empowerment; joy; sustenance; nurturance and caring; networks; grassroots; collectivity; social capital; and joint action. These phrases are in sharp contrast to concepts that frame educators' professional socialization experiences such as: administrative hierarchy, standardization, certification, dispassionate, apolitical and value neutral, measurable tasks and goals. Rethinking the job and the career around the former set of phrases might allow policy makers to reframe and thereby to honor educators' commitments to children and to equity. The importance of certification and the need for some measures of accountability can then be organized around principles embraced by social movement literatures. We might then begin to set up better approaches to teacher recruitment and training.

Change does not happen by introducing and giving short shrift to some new program that faces the barriers of existing programs, habits, norms, needs, and structures. Policy makers must identify and eliminate the forces within the institutional structures of schooling that are barriers to change (Coughlan, 1994) such that educators can embrace their social justice commitments. As noted above, this might include rethinking educator preparation programs and redesigning in-service opportunities for educators.

Rethinking Training, Recruitment, Retention, Promotion, and Job Security

Consider: if educators openly showed their activist ideals as novices, would they be able to get and keep their jobs? Young people bring ideals to their consideration of education careers; they want to make a difference in the world—they want to help children. Yet most of our activists avoided any risks and labels in their first years as teachers, fearing poor evaluations and tenure denial if their passion and their activism, even if done on the down-low, were viewed by supervisors as unprofessional. Then, once they move up the ladder, educators are more accountable and have more career investment to lose. Recall Figures 7.1 and 7.2 above, and how the few educators who could be "bulldogs" were so senior, so secure, and so fully backed by antiracism rhetoric and sentiments in the profession, as well as by antidiscrimination laws, that they could be protected from sanction. Teaching in nonunion states and denying administrators tenure creates additional constraints for all whose activism does not have such contextual support.

Policy makers who are pondering recommendations for educator recruitment and retention can glean insights from our study, perhaps focusing on Figures 7.1 and 7.2 and on chapter 2's activist job continuum. Educators limit their aspirations to positions that allow them flexibility or to job descriptions of low visibility as they pursue their activist identity, searching for a sense of congruence between their work and their values. Many may simply avoid education careers altogether; others may drop out, citing "stressful demands" in the profession, thus using an acceptable phrase to encompass the insecurity born of frustration from the perceived need to stifle their activist interventionist idealism once they encounter, full time, the conservative professional community that makes them vulnerable.

Think of the waste! Energies are wasted suppressing and being sly and diplomatic and suppressing selves. The potential of widened views of leadership and priorities are lost when educators choose the relative invisibility of teaching and relatively invisible central staff positions rather than encounter the losses and labels risked by exercising their voices.

Educator Recruitment and Preparation As Lofland (1996) said, "the way educators earn their livelihood encourages them to be…sensitive to ideas and ideals… to conceptions of…how the world might and should be changed" (p. 134). If their early and their continuous professional socialization tapped into the idealism of teachers (be they 22-year-olds, lateral entry, Teacher Corps), then cohorts of educators with shared social justice values could sustain themselves in their beliefs that teaching is emancipatory practice and that schools are locations for collaborative engagement with the societal challenges of democracy. Professors and supervisors and staff development decision makers have many opportunities to promote a model of education as social justice activism to new education professionals. Professors and policy makers need to reframe activism as part of professional work rather than an act of subversion or political contestation.

A caution, though: Oliva and Anderson (2006) found that education leaders, even with cohort-based social justice-driven curricula, left their doctoral training and found themselves adhering to more traditional and conservative values in the communities that hired them! Most educators have heard that race and gender matter but have no exposure to critical race, feminist, never mind queer theories. So a bit of training for a select few and several add-on readings will not transform education into emancipatory practice. Band-Aids such as one-shot diversity training will not suffice.

Professional associations, unions, and policy makers are missing a major piece of the educator recruitment, promotion, and retention puzzle by not engaging in the change-the-world, care-about-children, and social justice idealism that inspires educators. These interests are maintained among educators yet only operate micropolitically. It is the energies and passions of educators as participants and as levers to broader structural change that are lost.

More than Policies Our research shows that laws and even professional standards and principles are not enough. Antidiscrimination laws, Title IX, prohibitions against sexual harassment in Title IX and in employment laws, and the various statements of professional associations were not enough to adequately penetrate the conservative cautions that educators sense in their communities and their schools. Even for those mentioned in chapter 4, educators knew little of the landmark *Franklin v. Gwinnett County* Supreme Court ruling (1992) on districts' responsibilities to prevent sexual harassment. The letter of the law printed on mission statements means little if the spirit of the laws and policies are not embedded in the community and professional values. Remember, those educator activists discussed in chapters 5 and 6, were not protected by laws when enacting their identities or their beliefs. Even in the few districts with antidiscrimination policies that included them, LGBT activists still felt vulnerable as they carefully embedded some BGLAD activities and incorporated gay role models in their schools' curricula. Our activists for the right to abortions as part and parcel of girls' and women's empowerment and for health education and comprehensive sex education as elements of equal opportunity though knew better than to enact their beliefs as citizens in their communities.

Activism as the Job Description When educators are creating pedagogical opportunities for activism or engaging in political movements in the community, they need to believe that this activity blends well with their job descriptions. "Realized activism" (Jones, 2005, p. 123) created tensions and fears that directly affected educators' personal and professional lives. But with recruitment processes, job descriptions, tenure policies, and evaluation and promotion systems redesigned to accommodate activists, the education profession would recruit and retain young people who are ready, willing and able to put the best of themselves into making schools and curricula empowering for all children.

How ridiculous it is that, given decades-old civil rights and Title IX legislation and recent NCLB legislation, educators still feel a need to hide their values, their intentions, and their actions and must invent ways to actually implement those laws! How ridiculous it is that educators know so little of the social justice activism history of their profession and have to search to find policy statements or actions by their own professional associations that would support their values! How ridiculous it is that activist educators must pay their own way out of town to find the sustenance of groups with shared values and strategies for enacting social justice interventions!

Policy and mission statements must be written and *backed up* with specific demonstrations such as active recruitment into activist networks, travel grants to activist conferences, professional days for activists participating in social justice political action to improve education, and professional development workshops focusing on effective activism strategies within and beyond school sites and districts. Why not create high level central office, regional, or state positions to support educators' social justice activism, as exemplified in a recent job advertisement for a California School district, for "Justice Matters Campaign Coordinators" to research and develop policy ideas, increase public awareness, and campaign from grassroots to national levels to build coalitions for social justice? With such structures, activists would have "go-to" persons and the potential for coordinating their professional development in networks with other social justice activists.

Honoring Activism as Part of the Job

So many in our study were activists *in spite of* their jobs, sensing the looming delimiters of organizational, regional, and professional assumptions, even when the laws (e.g., Title IX) supported them. When policies prohibit (e.g., abstinence-only sex education) and when job descriptions and personnel evaluation systems inhibit, then activism threatens the idealist educator's career commitment and potential. Policy makers must foster social justice interventions, not just as a possibility, but as a responsibility for educators. Social justice activism must be structured and rewarded as part and parcel of the moves to further professionalize education.

Awards, Supports, and Role Models Societal honoring of the traditions of social justice activist educators will motivate young adults teetering on the edge of choosing education careers. Examples of educator activists should inspire policies on education recruitment and retention. For example, from the stories of educators in chapter 2 we saw the significance of Blacks' sense of social debt to their race and community (Dawson, 1994; Higginbotham & Weber, 1992). That sense of responsibility, that determination to speak up for the oppressed, in spite of the professional and personal risks, should have rewards and honors— imagine education Nobels.

Why not honor the icons, role models, and spokespeople and make visible tangible and symbolic awards to groups and individuals whose work demonstrates that the education professionals are transforming society to be inclusive of all people? Teachers and Superintendents of the Year and honored professors should be those who have taken brave stands in leading others to work for progressive social causes. (Too often such people are labeled as weird while the awards go to those who are simply popular for their outgoing personalities, their social network, their ability to get along with and compromise within the dominant ways of thinking and acting.) Instead of popularity contests, criteria statements and procedures for nominating and selecting for awards and recognition should explicitly solicit the kinds of interventionist and creative work-expansion actions exhibited by the activist educators who promote progressive causes both within and beyond school walls.

Unions, professional associations, and foundations' efforts to promote the quality, working conditions, supply, and effectiveness of educators can rethink, using our research, to construct ways to honor and support activism. For example, foundations appropriate money to improve school leadership and effectiveness but they need to see, from our study, that beyond pay raises and work hours, educators' working conditions can be measured by whether or not they incur risks when they participate in social movements. For example, the National Association of Secondary School Principals, working to ensure that principals and assistant principals have the best information available to be more successful with the children who "fall through the cracks," needs to see how educator activists crave the strategies and support of networks with those who share their social justice values. The School Boards Association and the American Association of School Administrators, as well as the teachers' associations, have the money, the publication outlets, and a major role in interpreting the laws and codes of ethics that govern school lives. Using this clout for honoring activism in education and for opening spaces for community conversations about schools and social justice would be courageous, visible, and inspiring acts of leadership—by the people we designate as our leaders!

Those who worry that this will encourage out-of-control politicizing can rest assured. Educators' primary motivations are to help children learn (not to run for political positions). As long as they find ways to use their voice, loyally, within the context of their jobs, theirs will be, at best a careful, with-the-system "tempered radicalism" (Ngunjiri, 2007). But think of the possibilities if they were unleashed as citizens with ideals and passions centered on reducing oppressions, using schooling as their best space for enacting those ideals!

Opened Spaces and Professional and Community Conversations

Educators have so little space for expressing the emotion, the frustrated caring, and the idealism that so many felt when choosing their careers. Extensive literatures describe the isolation many educators experience once in the profession. Encouraging educators' collaboration and expanding those spaces where educators can enact their commitments will excite new recruits to education and will provide places for activists to be inspiring, energetic role models and fully engaged citizens. Positioning educator activists as role models would be *so* different from the traditional socialization by well-intentioned mentors who try to protect recruits into teaching and administration by telling them how to fit in, encouraging their obedience to assumptive world rules! Although it is more comfortable to assume social justice issues are being managed by policy statements and licensure standards, in reality these statements are vague, inadequate, and seldom discussed and reevaluated. Chapters 2 through 6 should be used as grist for frank conversations among school staff and community members to bring to the surface the pushed-under-the-rug issues and the conflicting values that infiltrate education's best intentions.

Enlarging and Multiplying Existing Spaces Outlets exist already for educators wanting support in their quest for more socially just schools. Professional Learning Communities (PLCs) are communities of educators "with an explicit focus on student learning" (York-Barr, Sommers, Ghere, & Montie, 2006, p. 148). The goal is to minimize barriers that interfere with students' ability to learn. Another existing strategy is Critical Friends Groups, which emerge as collaborations from members' shared values which can lead to shared activism (see http://www.nsrfharmony.org/faq.html#1). CFGs come together voluntarily, collaborate across disciplines, reflect on their work, confront assumptions, and problem solve while they avoid blaming students. As such, CFGs could prove vital structures to facilitate educators' justice and activism work. In addition, the Education for Liberation Network (http://www.edliberation.org.resources) provides resources and connections that are emancipatory and equity-oriented and directly related to educators' work.

Among professors of educational administration and teacher education, several special interest groups combine their scholarship, teaching, and research in ways that will embed social justice in curricular and in licensure policies (e.g., the camaraderie and shared contributions of leadership professors, demonstrated in the chapters of *Leadership for Social Justice*; Marshall & Oliva, 2006). Educators can subscribe to *Rethinking Schools* and know that they have peers throughout the country working for school reform.

Educators in social justice causes with greater societal support (e.g., race and cultural diversity, the environment) can embrace and support the right to be activist and provide role models for others. Educators cannot be compelled to support all causes of their educator activist colleagues (e.g., antiwar/peace, abortion rights, and gay marriage activism fall outside the domain of some citizens' beliefs). However, developing connections, collegiality, and networking among educator activists can alleviate the numbing and dispiriting loneliness, fear, and isolation poignantly illustrated by some of our activists. One result will be increased power for social justice causes broadly conceived instead of the loss of power that resulted from fragmented efforts of the past.

Educators can learn the activist techniques of co-opting dominant or mainstream discourses and values, deployed so successfully by conservative causes. For example, we saw our educators using civil rights to illustrate and demand gay rights, a common technique of taking the visibility and legitimacy of more politically viable causes to illustrate the value of more marginalized social justice causes. When legislatures and school board members are paying attention to obesity, for example, activists can move that attention to embrace children's body image as it connects to issues of gender, sexuality, and bullying and harassment. Instead of allowing dominant culture values to name important issues and ignore more controversial stances, activists can work to expand the circle and bring issues from the margins to the center (Marshall & Gerstl-Pepin, 2005).

Ongoing Community and Staff Development Perhaps our most appalling finding is that activists are working with colleagues and superiors who do not know the laws that address social justice issues in some cases. Beyond laws, research, and policies, educators must be made aware of how subtle and yet disempowering racist, sexist, harassing, and homophobic remarks work to marginalize educators and students. Required training is the logical structure. Most districts use staff development and in-service training for a potpourri of state- and district-priorities, often focused on implementing accountability measures. Instead, staff development participants could hear that attending to messages and beliefs of activist causes are essential steps for providing safe and empowering spaces for all children.

Ideally, the training would not be simply a course and simply for the educators. Training that enables students, family members, and the community to understand the harm and exclusion of discriminatory practices, as well as the resulting loss of social and human potential, would move participants past their naysayer stances. Such an approach would (1) encourage expression of values- and needs-conflicts through social justice lenses; (2) support activist expressions of basic ideals (e.g., democracy, community, do-unto-others); (3) identify coalitions of people who express similar degrees of, or types of social justice activism to which they commit; and (4) demonstrate district support for principled opposition to forms of oppression that limit children and educators.

Quite possibly such training could be regional, so costs could be shared and coalitions could draw from beyond a school or district. It would be rough and tumble, with rural school board members, students, parents, administrators' association executives, taxpayers association, the American Civil Liberties Union and organizations espousing comprehensive sex education, and exasperated but idealistic young teachers expressing themselves. But the real possibilities of making schools instruments for democracy and social justice can be started from such conversations.

Conversations among Educators and Community Members Policy makers must proclaim that, in a democracy, schooling must, first and foremost, provide sheltered, protected, and nurtured access to the education that will enable young people to develop their best potential as citizens—in the polity and the markets, as well as in homes and communities. At the same time, education must be about engaging students and educators with real world experiences, including controversial issues and their consequences. Not all educators, community members, and policy makers will agree that it is the job of educators to take a stand against racism, sexism, classism, religious intolerance, and homophobia. Naysayers will argue that the job of education is to teach traditional knowledge skills that prepare students for jobs, with standardized tests as our best measure of that preparation. Naysayers will say that educators have enough to do without taking on the deep problems created in society and in social policy. However, without that first step, without framing and making explicit education's social justice purposes, any next steps will be weakened. Adopting clear, direct policy statements that define proactive social justice action and interventions as the job of educators should be a first step for policy makers.

Still, one cannot simply assert that policy makers should allow educators to bring their ideals to work. Structures and rules are needed to tap energies and create community connections and collegial professional development. For example, rules must prohibit public school educators from using their workplaces to promote religious practices, and must deny groups and causes that would undermine efforts for social justice. In some instances, such as disallowing use of schools for Boy Scouts groups (which exclude gays), courts have set limits. Professional associations' codes of ethics and educator training and licensure, too, establish minimum expectations. But these statements are so vague as to leave educators who contemplate taking a stand dangling and wondering. For example, North Carolina's and some other states' licensure policies require demonstration of educators' competencies for promoting cultural diversity. But the activist still does not know whether they will be reprimanded if they make a scene tearing down the sexist posters in the teacher's lounge or whether "promoting cultural diversity" means visibly joining the community protest for immigration reform.

Rules and guidelines are helpful. Setting up a Social Justice Advocacy Organizer or a Justice Matters Coordinator could be a symbolic *and* instrumental step for making rhetoric reality. Resources for initiatives and for educators' conversations and community conversations could be facilitated instead of stifled. Too often, educators (and all of society) have no training on how to handle tough conversations around conflicting values and no preparation to help them judge, for example, what constitutes sexual harassment and what intervention is appropriate. Cultures of fear and silence stifle passions and growth, as shown in our research. Avoiding conversation(s) is not the solution. Conversations on social justice issues open difficult discourses.

Teacher/administrator education courses can be good training grounds for such discourses. But, along with the course professors, superintendents, board members, union leaders, human resource directors, and site administrators need skills in facilitating difficult discourses so that constructive and community-building strategies result. Otherwise opened wounds will be left festering and educators will have new reasons to stay silent while the unresolved social justice issues are swept back under the rug.

Ending the silences in schools, communities, and educator preparation, requires structures. Faculty meetings could begin with discussions of the implications of the chapters in this book, for example, as educators see and locate themselves and locate the spaces available (or not) for their taking social justice stands. Daily Dilemmas Dialogues (Marshall & Hooley, 2006), PLCs, CFGs, and collaborative, face-to-face, ongoing professional development can be built into the work spaces of educators. To qualify as opened spaces, these structures must be part of the paid-for work of educators, subsidized by districts and state funds, with top school and community leaders participating in order to demonstrate commitment to educators' roles as social justice actors. No, it should not be web-training, subject to flattened conversations and masked affect. What if hugs are needed? No, it should not be an add-on to work days and work years as new and tested, but not supported requirements, adding new stressors to already full lives.

Funding Links to Community Groups School board members, superintendents, and site supervisors can demonstrate their valuing of the progressive and social justice work of activist educators by funding task forces or committees whose needs might be refreshments for reading groups, film rentals, twice-yearly speakers or consultants, or bus trips to lobby at the state capital. Committees of community volunteers and educators could collaborate in constructing appropriate local ways of meeting the needs. Such a step could turn a negative—namely the fears and frustrations of educator activists—into positive social capital! It could help educators believe that their district and their profession and their community is *the* place to be. It could provide leadership opportunities for educators who do not really want to be administrators but who do want to have chances, beyond their classrooms, to make a difference. Who better to take the lead on the causes than the educators who have seen, up close and personal, the needs of middle school girls thinking they need to look skinny and dumb, or the Black boys whose acting out is not a special education issue, or the adolescents whose parents and churches are never going to tell them "the facts of life?"

With district funds for reading groups, led by teacher/parent/business community/church representatives, school and community sites could become venues for opening dialogues. By viewing the movie or play version of the community reaction to the murder of Matthew Shepherd, or the Public Broadcasting Studio video of conversations between the Civil Rights activists and the ex-Ku Klux Klan members from Durham, North Carolina, by discussing the chapters in this book, or books like Casey's *I Answer With My Life* (1993), by discussing Sadker and Sadker's (1994) analysis of schools' failure at empowering girls, conversations will create spaces for activist educators. Citizens could join—could come out of their gated communities and come out of their ethnic isolations as well, to create allies and form coalitions and consider how to support school boards and educators wanting help in their social justice interventions.

Spaces can be opened with very practical books and tasks too. Specific strategies on specific topics can be found in books like *Sexual Harassment and Sexual Abuse: A Handbook for Teachers and Administrators* (Cohan, Hergenrother, Johnson, Mandel, & Sawyer, 1996). Educators who just can't dig into critical theory can, instead, try *Critical Pedagogy: Notes from the Real World* (Wink, 2000). Deep understandings, along with specific exercises can be found in books like *Teaching for Social Justice* (Ayers, Hunt, & Quinn, 1998), and *Teaching for Diversity and Social Justice: A Sourcebook* (Adams, Bell, & Griffin, 1997). Or, going deeper, books like *Ethical Educational Leadership in Turbulent Times* (Shapiro & Gross, 2008), or *Who's Afraid of Feminism* (Oakley & Mitchell, 1997) or *Disputing the Subject of Sex* (Mayo, 2004) would be great as starters for Professional Learning Community projects.

Going deeper, Labaree's (1997) provocative article could task educators and community leaders to consider ways in which American schools and society perpetuate the individualistic, meritocratic myths that laud pioneers and capitalists who tamed and claimed frontiers and iron ore deposits. He (see also Kahne, 1996; Noddings, 1992, 2002) offers alternative visions and values that, if embedded in schooling and our cultural assumptions, would support educators and children in valuing collaboration, caring, relationship-building, and equality, peace, community, and tolerance. School communities that create such grassroots conversations and collaborative work would go far toward opening spaces for making educators feeling comfortable enacting their social justice activism with pride and hope.

Reinforcing Educator's Rights as Citizens A century ago educators had to swear oaths regarding their dating behavior and Sunday school attendance. Although we may look back on such practices and laugh, remnants of those social controls permeate our data in educators' sense of risk and backlash. Conservative community members, parents, and colleagues will phone and protest, and even call for the firing of activist educators whose social justice activism angers them. Conservative values are entrenched in practices of schooling; most recently these values have enjoyed federal support through policies of the Bush administration, and are unlikely to be relinquished without a struggle. Their values and methods may not be as extreme as the Ku Klux Klan, but boards and supervisors must be ready to assertively articulate the right, the duty, and the pride they take in social justice work and the activist educators at the fore of that work.

Buffering and protection of activist educators must be provided by school board members, superintendents, unions, professional associations, and site supervisors. Their repertoire of leadership skills must include an ability to articulate the value of this work in promoting democracy, diversity, and in meeting children's needs.

School leaders must, therefore, not only defend activist educators and stand up against conservative forces. They must also find ways to explain and bring into the fold those people who create barriers to social justice activism. Educator activism will continue as muted and cautious without such political backing, without leaders' buffering, and without professional association leaders fighting for educators' citizenship rights. We acknowledge that this requires significant changes to current practices of schooling, yet offer the experiences of these educator activists as evidence that the work is ongoing. Leaders must reiterate, in all venues, both the rhetoric of social justice and the specific ways such activism is part of what it means to be an education professional and advocate for children.

Wonderings, Reflections, and Thoughts for Future Studies

By using comparative case studies and by using theoretical frameworks from sociology as well as from education, the significance of our research was greatly enhanced. Still, we are left with a few wonderings. (Wonderings means "implications for further research" and "limitations of the study" in more traditional formats.) Wonderings include:

- Our participants were working for progressive, liberal causes—what would activism be like for those engaging in activism for more conservative ones? This approach to research could be used to identify patterns of risk, activism, and spaces for those in anti-abortion, anti-immigration, anti-desegregation and affirmative action, for example. What would the differences reveal about education's values? Its culture? Its powerbrokers?
- Our participants were mostly Southern. How would activism be different in other regions? How much does location (e.g., urban to rural) matter? How does region and political culture matter? How does unions' strength matter?

- How many educators are driven out of the profession because of conflicts between educator and activist identities? What activists from history started their careers as educators and moved away to spaces, professions, organizations, or political careers? Were they forced out of education or simply seeking a larger stage?
- What research design could be useful to follow up on the patterns generated by our study?
- How can future teachers, policy makers, and the public appreciate the dilemma-laden poignancy, the quiet creativity, and courage of activist educators so that social justice activism is seen as positive and possible, and our recommendations are seen as a valuable beginning to the validation of educators working for social justice causes?
- How can we get human resource managers and superintendents to recruit and retain energetic and idealistic educators—to structure supports so that they and their districts receive the multiplying benefits from employing these valuable educators?

Finally, we wish to end our cross-case analysis with the following reflections of hope and inspiration drawn from our work:

1. Even the little actions matter—even small supports and sly actions affect/effect educator activism. When educators are doing something for social justice, it matters and it inspires others to see that doing more is possible. Fear and silence limit opportunities for growth. Avoiding conversation(s) is not the solution.
2. People can maintain an activist identity even in culturally conservative communities or climates. It is not career suicide and one *can* find allies.
3. Faces of activism are as varied and individual as are individuals.
4. For educators the job does have a higher purpose beyond getting the paycheck.
5. As long as we have educators willing to keep social justice issues at the forefront, there is the promise that these things will not be simply written off as "fixed" or "finished."

Notes

1. This chapter reflects the contents of chapters 1 through 6 but also uses more, and deeper insights and data that can be found in much fuller display in the following dissertations: Hood (2005), Walters (2004), Jones (2005), and Legrand (2005). Please take a look at the dissertations for this expanded presentation of each specific group of activists. Also note that Annice Hood is now Annice H. Williams: she is the author of chapter 2 and Hood (2005).
2. Though clear boundaries for the Bible Belt do not exist, the region extends to include Texas to the west, Kansas to the north, Virginia to the east, Florida to the south, and the states located within this area. The term refers to the large groups of fundamentalist Christians residing in the area. Bible Belt Christians have very conservative religious and political practices (Dorough, 1974).
3. It must be noted that our research sampling technique allowed only a peek at those who exited.

8
Doing Collaborative Research

AMY L. ANDERSON AND CATHERINE MARSHALL

This book is the culmination of seven years' work among six women. Over the course of our years together, we discovered how working together provided deeper insights into the phenomena related to educators' activist interests. Picking up where the brief introduction of methodology in chapter 1 ends, this chapter details our methodological processes, designed to be useful for articulating the benefits of collaborative qualitative inquiry. This chapter elaborates how this book is derived from systematic, in-depth, exploratory research, demonstrating that there are ways to manage the ambitious and at times overwhelming adventure of multiresearcher, multicase inquiry.

Interspersed throughout the chapter are first-person reflections of members of this group about critical events and processes that guided our work together. These reflections are intended to amplify the significance of the group's work to our individual projects, at the same time elaborating lessons learned in our individual studies for the larger project. Also included in this chapter are documents that guided our process, from the invitation to participate, to research guidelines, to the interview protocol and sample analysis documents. As such, this chapter is an archive of our collaborative group work offered as model other groups can consult for similar endeavors.

We define our work as collaborative, drawing strength from our commitments to the work, to our participants, and to each other.

Collaborative Research

In *Collaborative Inquiry in Practice: Action, Reflection, and Making Meaning,* Bray, Lee, Smith, and Yorks (2000) describe collaborative inquiry as a vehicle both for adult learning and for research. They name several characteristics of this research, which include:

1. The collective construction through lived experience of a new understanding and meaning of the world.
2. It makes systematic human inquiry accessible to people in a participatory and democratic way.
3. It produces meaningful knowledge for the public arena: constructing knowledge and theory for public discourse.

Collaborative inquiry is typically defined as research in which researcher and researched collaborate in meaning-making (Bray et al., 2000; Creswell, 1998; Stake, 1995). What we describe in this chapter, however, is a seven-year, six-researcher project characterized by deliberate and ongoing collaboration between researchers who were trying to understand various expressions of activism among educators. In this respect, we come closer to what Stake (1994) called collective case study, in which "researchers may study a number of cases jointly in order to inquire into a phenomenon, population, or general condition" (p. 237). Reason (1994) offered this description of collaborative inquiry that named our process: "Collaborative inquiry involves the individual practitioner in continually reflecting on his or her own behavior-in-action while simultaneously behaving in a fashion that invites other members of the community to do the same" (p. 331).

Bray et al. (2000) indicated that "Effective collaborative inquiry demystifies research and treats it as a form of learning that should be accessible by everyone interested in gaining a better understanding of his or her world" (p. 3). Supporting this goal of gaining better understanding, our methods were clearly qualitative, befitting a project focused on understanding the experiences and dilemmas of educator activists. Miles and Huberman (1994) elaborated the strengths of qualitative inquiry:

> Qualitative data...are a source of well-grounded rich descriptions and explanations of processes in identifiable local contexts.... Good qualitative data are more likely to lead to serendipitous findings, and to new integrations; they help researchers to get beyond initial conceptions and to generate or revise conceptual frameworks. (p. 1)

Qualitative research methods were appropriate to this work because it required the researchers to hear and work to understand the complexities of others' stories. We not only wanted to know *that* educators were activists, but *how and why* they were activists. As Denzin and Lincoln (1994) indicated, qualitative inquiry involves "an interpretive, naturalistic approach to...subject matter" (p. 2). The primary research text we consulted to help us think about conducting qualitative research as a group was Miles and Huberman's (1994) *Qualitative Data Analysis*. They pointed to recurring features of qualitative research that define its strengths, including:

- Qualitative research is conducted through an intense and/or prolonged contact with a "field" or life situation.
- The researcher's role is to gain "holistic" overview of the context under study: its logic, its arrangements, its explicit and implicit rules.
- The researcher attempts to capture data on the perceptions of local actors "from the inside" through a process of deep attentiveness, empathetic understanding, and suspending...preconceptions.
- A main task is to explicate the ways people in particular settings come to understand, account for, take action, and otherwise manage their day-to-day situation.
- Most analysis is done with words. The words can be assembled, subclustered, broken into semiotic segments. They can be organized to permit the researcher to contrast, compare, analyze, and bestow patterns upon them. (pp. 6–7)

Each of these features was significant to our process as we joined this project.

How It All Began: A Brief History of the Educator Activists Research Project

Gloria Jones

Educator activists? ? Sounds provocative, risky even.... As I reflect back to the invitation to join the Educator Activist project, these were my first thoughts.... I questioned whether my participation would be professionally impairing.... I was out of my comfort zone.... My initial reservations grew out of my myopic and somewhat antiquated views of the concept of educators as activists. It seemed quite the oxymoron.... The role of an educator was to educate not eradicate.... It was out of character for educators to be political agents, carrying flags, banners, symbols, chanting.... Based on my "old school" teaching experiences, educators avoided being labeled as militant and would tread carefully if they engaged in behavior that could potentially illuminate problems of the profession.... This was even supported by Marshall and Kasten's research (1994) which warned, "Those who respond by bringing attention to the problems are viewed as disloyal, troublemakers, or poor team players (pp. 14–15).... We knew the potential repercussions could be insurmountable.... In hindsight, my initial thinking would foreshadow what would be disclosed in conversations with participants in my study.

The Invitation

The Educator Activists research group formed in May of 2000 at the invitation and under the leadership of Dr. Catherine Marshall, professor of Educational

Administration at the University of North Carolina at Chapel Hill. Marshall issued a call to graduate students targeted at those who might be interested in studying the lived experiences of educator activists, including their practices and challenges.

The Invitation

Catherine Marshall

I have conceptualized a research project, "Activist Educators," in which you might wish to participate. While there is no funding for the project, your expenses could be minimal (audio tapes, tape recorder, some phone bills, and manageable travel). Although, ultimately, the overarching project is mine, you would have guidance, collaborators, and potentially, dissertations and/or presentations and publications.

I've drafted some procedures and expectations to be fleshed out over time. However, I wish to convene a meeting soon. If you are interested, please let me know and tell me which of these meeting times will work for you: May 31, June 1, 2, 5, 6, 7, 8, or 9 from 4 – 6 p.m. If you are not interested in participating, please notify me of that as well.

Thank you, Dr. Catherine Marshall

Nine graduate students and an alumna of the UNC-Chapel Hill EdD program indicated initial interest and began naming potential research topics: sexual harassment in schools, the Algebra project, lives of women administrators, sexual harassment in schools, the lives of gay and lesbian educators, Latino/a educators, educator unions in the south, and the role of progressive nonprofit education organizations (e.g., Rethinking Schools, Coalition of Essential Schools). As this text indicates, five members persisted and along with Dr. Marshall comprised this research group. Chapters 2 through 6 explore the issues that were chosen by ongoing members.

The invitation issued and the ground for the work articulated, it was time to begin.

Group Meetings

Beginning in the summer of 2000, the Educator Activist research group began meeting for several hours on Saturday mornings every six to eight weeks. Marshall provided initial procedures for the group, including minimal participation requirements.

How To Create Meaningful Dissertation Research

Catherine Marshall

It was a quiet disaster-in-making. In my tiny Educational Leadership Program, we had lists, in 2000, with 50 to 60 Ed.D. students needing dissertation chairs and topics. Our Program, by focusing more on supplying the state with licensed administrators, hadn't done enough to prepare students to conceptualize theoretical framing, compile relevant studies, and design their own research project. I was facing piled-on hours of reading and refining far too many, far too drafty proposals and I could predict that the resulting dissertations would be lonely and painful and, in some cases, failing, or at least compromised dissertation experiences. Plus, my time would be eaten up so I could not pursue scholarly agendas myself.

Inviting students to join a research project was, therefore, a worthwhile risk. If I could create enough structure, facilitate group camaraderie, and, thus maintain the group as research partners, if I could set up shared literatures, procedures to ensure comparability of data collection procedures, and pauses for comparative data analysis, then I could deliver on my promise of significant, supported dissertations and publications.

The choice of topic came from my own frustrations and dissonance with:
(1) being an idealist/progressive educator, and (2) 35 years of being immersed in the realities of education politics, especially in preparing school administrators and having colleagues stress how we must help our students get and keep jobs and thus not open up cans of worms that would lead to me wanting to just quit…. All of this was accentuated by realizing that, when I taught Politics of Education courses, I could see my students' idealism horribly jarred by seeing the realities of the politics highlighted for them, for example, in my own literatures on assumptive worlds, and Gary Anderson's (1990) areas of silence, etc. etc. But I re-discovered the literature on street level bureaucrats, grass roots politics, Kathleen Casey, my own research on gender equity activists in the United States and Australia…, and my research in the 1990s on Caring as Career, on assistant principals. Around the same time (2000) I conspired with Gary Anderson and a bunch of other education administration scholars to create Leadership for Social Justice, which for me became an avenue for becoming more activist myself, defying scholarly norms. I came up with the idea of reframing (which led to my Re-Framing Educational Politics text) which helped me to ask, "What are the exceptions, who are the people in education who take on causes in spite of the messages to cover up dilemmas?" Thus the project.

Now, my little heart bursts with pride as I look at four completed Ed.D.s, as I review the years of Saturday morning meetings, and marvel how, now, we still like each other, we are still meeting, mining the juicy data for main findings from the five different, but parallel studies!

Goals and Expectations of the Project

While the deeper theoretical and practical goals are something we will write about, discuss, and keep files on, the more concrete goals may include: a book prospectus to be written by Dr. Catherine Marshall with potential chapters to include subprojects around specific topics (e.g., feminist activists; minority rights; abortion rights; promoting "fringe" political party candidates; environmental justice; gay/lesbian/bisexual issues); potential dissertations; potential conference presentations; potential smaller publications.

You can be a part of the project regardless of whether you prefer to finish quickly or finish over a longer period of time. An estimated timeline for book publication is three to five years. There is no guarantee of inclusion in a potential book; a decision will be made by Dr. Marshall considering fit and quality. Potential independent publications must be discussed with Dr. Marshall. Independent studies can be arranged when mutually beneficial.

This research will challenge knowledge and stereotypes about educators, and it will offer a significant contribution to aspiring teachers (and their supervisors) who need to know that education and social justice activism can be compatible.

Minimal Participation Requirements

- There will be project meetings approximately every other month to compare notes and comparative data analysis.
- There should be at least 15 individual interviews with respondents in your chosen subject area—at least three should be in a "relatively supportive" context and three in a "not very supportive context"; at least three and preferably five should be in a state with conditions similar to North Carolina.
- You will be expected to provide a literature review of pertinent research in your subject area.
- You will need to complete a qualitative research methods course or equivalent (or see Dr. Marshall).
- Cooperation is essential to ensure geographic spread.

Structure

Susan Walters

When I met with Dr. Marshall to ask for her assistance with my dissertation, she described this project and her ideas of how it would work. She invited me to join the group, and that invitation began a journey of friendships, collaboration, support, and learning.

The group began as a group of women educators in various stages of their formal education and professional careers with Dr. Marshall acting as facilitator. Early in the first year, two of the women dropped out, and the remaining five members have remained committed to the completion of the project. I had completed the coursework for my Ed.D. in 1996 and was fast becoming one of the ABD's (all but dissertation) that I said I would not become. I thought that the structure of this project would give me the support that I needed to move to successful dissertation completion. The opportunity to research and explore activism in education from different perspectives engaged and excited me. The group began by meeting once a month on Saturday mornings in Chapel Hill. As we became more sure of what we were doing and the shape of each member's contribution to the larger project, we met less frequently; however, we continued to communicate our progress, share interesting literature, and generally offered support to each other as we moved seriously into our individual areas of research. The structure was loose enough to allow for individual needs as well as tight enough to offer the necessary group collaboration support to keep the project members moving forward.

Upon reflection of how our group project worked, I could see similarities between our structure and social movement group structures that worked to keep members engaged and committed to their activist causes. There was definitely a sense of belonging to something bigger than the individual's agenda, and each of us felt a sense of letting others down if we did not hold up our end of the project. The group offered an outlet for frustration and celebration as we worked through our individual pieces and a sense that one person's achievement was achievement for all of us. As with any activist movement, we also had that one person in Dr. Marshall who had the vision from the beginning and kept the vision alive throughout the project by sharing, supporting, and facilitating our work. Each member moved in and out of the support network depending upon individual need and obligations and the perceived group needs and obligations.

As Susan indicates, being a part of a group moved individuals *and* the group forward. In Susan's case, it moved her from ABD to Dr. Walters.

Being a part of the group helped build confidence as we tackled the tougher theoretical leaps in social movement and identity theory, and spent hours talking about others' research and its relevance to our group work. Although we were pursuing individual interests in terms of activism, at all times we knew we were working toward a collective project to which we all felt responsibility.

Critical Moments

Gloria Jones

Imagine preparing an onion, tearing away at the rough outer layers to get to the crisp freshest layers, dicing or chopping to add flavor to the recipe. Metaphorically, my initial reaction to our meetings can be likened to peeling an onion, for this process can lead to tears. I found the concept of a group of individuals collaborating toward a common goal to be ideal. Nevertheless, it would be several meetings before I could truly appreciate the importance of meeting so frequently, so intensely. Initially, I felt that I could move at my own pace—and a much faster one—working independently. It was when we began sharing perspectives and insights on theory and how to best parlay theory into practice that I first realized: I needed these meetings, these women, and the support. There would be many more times when gratitude and thankfulness for the group would overwhelm me. To borrow a phrase, this was collective improvisation at its best. Although each of us, Amy, Annice, Susan, Wanda, Dr. Marshall, and I worked diligently toward a common goal, we each approached the project with our distinct personalities, interests, preparedness, spontaneity, and creativity. Our collective fortitude enabled us to move through each stage of the process fashioning, refashioning, framing, defining, and fleshing out, thus bringing clarity to our vision, and us a step closer to the goal. Along the way extraordinary things happened at these meetings…critical moments.

The majority of the meetings were held in a large sparsely furnished conference room in Peabody Hall. We also changed venue on occasion, meeting in Amy's kitchen, Dr. Marshall's new house, Susan's dining room, the Chapel Hill Public Library, my school, and the graduate students' lounge and computer lab in the School of Education. I describe our initial meeting as a "seek first to understand" meeting. I remember vividly all of us sitting scattered around an enormous table listening and taking notes as Dr. Marshall shared with us the idea for the Activist Educators project along with related goals and expectations for participation, reading, and research requirements. We all signed on with hidden fervor, still really not knowing the full extent of the project. Full conceptualization of the project was a distant blur. With each monthly meeting, we formed additional lenses, gaining greater insight, meaning, and clarity.

Initial readings on social movement theory, identity theory, activism, and qualitative data analysis were integral to our work together. Our ability to engage in informed discourse on these topics and how they related to the larger project and our independent research was significant.

Meeting in the computer laboratory to gain an understanding of QSR Nvivo, the software program that would serve as a supplemental tool for facilitating much of our qualitative data analysis was one of the most critical moments of our meetings. Wow! Annice emerged from that meeting as the Nvivo guru and was a tremendous support to us all for understanding how to input and scaffold our codes, nodes, and trees, and run reports with common themes.

As Gloria suggests, success depended on several key factors: regular, ongoing meetings; willingness to share and learn among participants; "seeking first to understand" as we pursued the dilemmas of educator activists; reading literatures in common; developing appreciation of each other's skills; and gaining faith that the work would lead us to something of value. A breakthrough event was the Saturday Annice passed around a copy of a short survey from a dissertation from another EdD program and pronounced: "Look at this thing!" Our joint recognition that in comparison our work was more complex and interesting helped solidify the hope that our Saturdays would pay off.

The Research

The collection and analysis of data for individual projects occurred over a four-year period, culminating in dissertations for four of the five members of this group (chapters in this text are distillations of interesting findings from the dissertation research). Initial meetings were devoted to elaborating group procedures and discussing readings set out as central to framing our work, so that a lot of things were happening at the same time. One focal area was researching key literatures; the second was research procedures.

Researching Key Literatures

Initial meetings of our group were devoted to identifying literatures we thought would be significant to the study of educator activists. Conceptual texts we read in common included Kathleen Casey's (1993) *I Answer with My Life: Life Histories of Women Teachers Working for Social Change*, and chapters from Ginsburg's (1995) *The Politics of Educators' Work and Lives*. As discussed in chapter 1, our beginning research into the lives of educator activists led us to three areas: theories of identity, social movements, and education careers.

Our work at this time was intense and ongoing, seemingly endless, and took place over a three-year period. It should be understood that this pace was in part dictated by the dissertation proposal writing and approval process, in part by our shared sense that full-time educators in graduate school need not, and perhaps could not, work at a faster pace, especially given the group context. This highlights, however, that being part of a group one may necessarily sacrifice speed to the process.

Individually, members gathered titles in each area and brought them to the group table, at which point we divided the readings up based on interest (or quota if necessary) and left to do reading. When next we met, we presented reviews of readings and began to keep lists of interesting themes. Individual chapters in this text highlight works that were significant to and influential in our individual research interests. Some texts were particularly central to the group endeavor, and although the list is not exhaustive, include: Calhoun (1994), Darnovksy, Epstein, and Flack (1995), Holland, Lachicotte, Skinner and Cain (1998), hooks (1994), on identity, including educator identity; Castells (1997), Darnovsky, Epstein, and Flack (1995), Epstein (1990), and Oberschall (1993), on social movements; Connell (1995), Crocco, Munro, and Weiler (1999), Dove (1995), Friere (1990), Ginsburg et al. (1995), and Urban (1989) on educator activism; and Casey (1993), Marshall (1993a, 1993b), Marshall and Mitchell (1991), Ortiz (1982), and Weiler (1988), on education careers.

Common Literatures

Gloria Jones

Out of these discussions emerged four terms defined by the group common to the larger project: educator, activism, social movement, and identity theory as well as common codes and themes— semantically whittling away at global definitions until their meanings were specific to our cause. These were meaningful, crucial outcomes of the meetings—critical moments.

As the research progressed and this text came together, we expanded the literatures to include feminist theory, queer theory, critical race theory, and literatures on the culture(s) of the U.S. South as elaborated in chapter 1, but that happened much later.

Over this three-year period of researching literatures, we generated extensive lists of interesting themes and categories that might be useful when working to understand the lives of educator activists. These lists were also used to develop and refine the interview protocol that was the basis of our individual interviews.

Establishing Research Procedures

At the same time we were researching key literatures, we were also establishing research procedures. As named above, as a group we consulted Miles and Huberman (1994) in regards to research processes; each researcher also supplemented this text with other qualitative methodology references. In our individual chapters, and in the cross-case analysis of this work, features of qualitative research guided our work. We also received training in the use of NVivo qualitative software to facilitate individual as well as cross-case data analysis (see data analysis, below).

At the outset, we established guidelines for insuring the quality of data collection. As novice researchers, these guidelines established practices that facilitated our entry "in the field." As will be discussed below, common processes also facilitated the cross-case analysis work of the larger project. Reminded that qualitative data are seductively rich and "have a lot of spring," we knew to take design decisions seriously.

Data Collection and Data Quality:

- We will have sessions to practice the interview protocol, including entry procedures and issues of role, reciprocity, and rapport.
- We assume that researchers will try very hard to have audiotape recorded interviews; we will practice managing the audio tape recorder and issues of audio quality.
- We will practice back-up note-taking and field notes issues.
- We will discuss transcription procedures (e.g., format, resources).
- Everyone will transcribe his/her interviews using pseudonyms for name and place.
- We will discuss being sure to allocate time and space for immediate methodological notes after each interview.
- Phone interviews work only if you have a personal relationship and/or special status on the issue or with the individual.

The interview protocol (see appendix A, "Activist Educators Interview Protocol") was comprised of a comprehensive collection of inquiries standardized for the larger project, yet offering the flexibility to probe further and sustain questioning as the interview evolved. This type of exploration allowed participants to share anecdotes, perspectives, suspicions, feelings, and additional insights that produced rich descriptions and narratives. Gloria continues her reflection of critical moments in the life of our research group, detailing the importance of the shared interview protocol. The Saturday we practiced the protocol by interviewing each other was another breakthrough, and Gloria highlights its importance in the scope of the larger project:

Critical Moments (continued)

Gloria Jones

We must have said a hundred times, the research needs the freedom to evoke reflections, perspectives, and knowledge driving educators' activist choices. Such latitude required a standardized but open-ended and comprehensive interview instrument. The interview protocol was treated as a living, breathing document that underwent many refinements until we were satisfied with the common language and understanding pertaining to its inquiries. We role-played the interview protocol, assuming the role of interviewer, then interviewee, and then going back to the group table to share insights.

One of the questions on our interview protocol asked participants to talk about "defining moments"—those experiences that made them realize something about themselves through their work in social movements—and I asked that question of myself as a researcher. One of the most powerful defining moments was when I began interviewing participants, and these respondents began sharing their life experiences that brought life to my research, to the project, validating the worthiness, timeliness, and necessity of both—powerful!

Finally, initial meetings served as brainstorming sessions for choosing individual areas of research. Ours was a collaborative and dialogic process. We learned from each other, challenged each other, disagreed with each other, and encouraged each other. After a year or more of literature research and planning for the collective project, we began to focus on our individual projects, all the while continuing the Saturday meetings focused on troubleshooting issues and moving the group forward into data collection.

Data Collection: Into the Field

Data collection for individual projects began in the summer and fall of 2003, three years after our first meetings together. The qualitative research methods selected for this study were appropriate to explaining and understanding the lived experiences of educator activists in the context of their professional and private lives. Glesne and Peshkin (1992) emphasize the researcher's position as learner when collecting qualitative data:

> It is important to have this sense of self from the beginning. The learner's perspective will…set you up for a particular kind of interaction with your others. As a researcher, you are a curious student who comes to learn from and with research participants. You do not come as an expert or authority…. As a learner, you are expected to listen; as an expert or authority

you are expected to talk. The differences between those two roles are enormous. (p. 36)

Given that we were asking participants to reveal choices they made and dilemmas they confronted, it was especially important that we begin our work with a learner's perspective. Data were collected using formal interviews, observations, and collection and interpretation of artifacts. Interviews ranging from one to two hours were tape-recorded, hand-noted, and transcribed verbatim.

A combination of snowball, opportunistic, and convenience sampling was employed to obtain a purposive sample for each of our respective interests (Marshall & Rossman, 1999; Miles & Huberman, 1994). Snowball sampling provided a viable means of making initial contacts with potential research participants, while convenience sampling provided opportunities to select participants based on convenience and contributed to cost effectiveness and time efficiency. Finally, opportunistic sampling was advantageous for accessing new leads. Significantly, however, our Institutional Review Board (IRB) mandated that we avoid jeopardizing our participants, so we could not contact them at their school or work site.

Data collected in this study were gathered from participants who were interested in the research topic and willing to participate, but the search for key participants willing to share their experiences was deliberate. Our initial goals stipulated that each researcher's sample include 15 educators who were currently working or had held professional positions in the public K-12 setting;[2] practitioners from the Southeastern regions of the United States were recruited, primarily North Carolina, Texas, Virginia, and Georgia. Authors of chapters 2 through 6 include tables that provide geographic and demographic data for participants. Typically, recruitment was initiated by contacting a key informant at a major area university to identify potential participants. Once the first interviewee was identified, that respondent disclosed names of other individuals who then recommended additional participants who knew of activist educators they believed would be interested in the study and could share a wealth of experiences. The sampling plan facilitated efficient and effective entry into the busy schedules of K-12 educators.

In 2004 and 2005, Activist Educator group members were in the thick of individual data collection and were beginning to draft dissertations. Susan, first to collect data, told tales that made the process seem less scary, and even fun. Annice's first transcribed interview provided another breakthrough moment. One Saturday, for example, we all used her interview to practice data analysis and to hear her initial reactions (e.g., having to patiently listen to long stories) and initial worries (e.g., all of her early sample were men). The group continued to meet on a regular—if somewhat less frequent—basis to continue to support each other and also to report out about interesting insights along the way. Wanda Legrand (chapter 5) explores the benefits of the group to her dissertation work:

Seniors in High School

Wanda Legrand

I have spent most of my time in public education working in high schools. I taught high school math for seven years, worked as a high school assistant principal for two years, and a high school principal for 5½ years. During this time, there was one phenomenon I never understood until I finished my doctoral coursework and was nearing the completion of my dissertation. The phenomenon I could not explain was seniors who dropped out of high school during their senior year, when all they had to do was complete the courses they were in. Why would they give up and drop out of school when they were so close to the finish line? Working on my doctorate while being a middle school, then high school principal was the most difficult task I ever accomplished. I was so close to the finish line while working on my dissertation, but it was just so tough to balance the demands of work and graduate school. I often wondered why I was putting myself through the torture when I was already successful in my career.

The monthly Saturdays in Chapel Hill with my fellow researchers provided me with the strength and motivation I needed to continue with my doctoral work. The sharing of ideas, literature, and assignments inspired me to hang in there and keeping working toward graduation. Each work session was like a booster shot that propelled me forward to our next meeting. Even though the meetings were incredible, the power of the collaborative experience went beyond what occurred when we got together on those Saturdays. Prior to each of our meetings, I would work to complete my assigned tasks because there was no way I could let the others down. The completion of my assignments was not just for me but for others who relied on me to assist them with reaching their goals. Because of this collective dependence, I would work on our assignments despite the fact that my job as a high school principal required approximately 70 to 80 hours a week to accomplish. No matter what, I could not let my partners down or have them fail to reach their goals because of me.

I was fortunate to have partners when developing the literature review for my dissertation, practicing interviewing, learning to use NVivo, and sharing dissertation chapter drafts, while most doctoral students work on these tasks alone. Because of our dedication to each other and to the work, I knew I had partners and support throughout the journey.

As a group, we shared the hardships of finding participants and brainstormed recruitment strategies; we talked about how we were applying research on identity, social movements, and educator identity to our individual topics; we shared initial analysis of individual projects; and we began to develop preliminary themes that might inform the cross-case analysis work.

Data Analysis: Individualized, and For the Good of the Group

Data analysis proceeded at two levels. As interviews concluded, researchers began data analysis to write individual dissertations. Although this work largely took place at the individual level, ongoing meetings of the research group allowed us to share insights from individual work and consider the implications for the larger project. At this juncture in our group's timeline, our symposium proposal to the 2005 annual conference of the American Educational Researchers Association (AERA) was accepted, giving us another boost, along with the opportunity and motivation to begin organizing our research in order to present it to the educational community.

As dissertations came together, ongoing group meetings were devoted to fleshing out themes to shape our cross-case data analysis (see Appendix B, "Preliminary Themes"). Miles and Huberman (1994) named the benefits of cross-case analysis:

> to reassure yourself that the events and processes in one well-described setting are not wholly idiosyncratic. At a deeper level, the aim is to see processes and outcomes across many cases, to understand how they are qualified by local conditions, and thus to develop more sophisticated descriptions and more powerful explanations. (p. 172)

As elaborated in the themes list, we began by looking at participants' reflections on personal background and professional career; ways educators talked about dilemmas they encountered in relation to perceived or real constraints and choices they made; and insights shared about identity and connections to social movements. Annice H. Williams (chapter 2) describes the impact of efforts multiplied among the group.

Multiplier Effect

Annice H. Williams

The experience of working in the educator activist group has had a "multiplier effect" on the outcomes of our individual work as we collaborated to do research and construct knowledge. The graduate students of the educator activist group arrived with varying levels of authentic research experience. Most of us had only been involved in small research assignments required in specific classes. Throughout the project, we spent time practicing and making real the concepts we had studied in our coursework. As we each gathered data for our individual projects, having the opportunity to share our progress (or lack thereof), and get feedback from multiple perspectives significantly enhanced our effectiveness and success as researchers. Having a shared vision for the larger project gave each of us a more refined context for our individual work, which forced each of us to extend our conceptualization of our own work.

Another benefit of having several peers who were familiar with our research ideas, processes, and progress was that we were each able to get needed support to expand our proficiency as researchers without the "competing intellectual directives" sometimes given to doctoral candidates who only have the support of their committee members available to them. As we came together to discuss our individual findings and conclusions, hearing the ideas of our colleagues based on their research gave us additional directions and perspectives to consider, which made the individual projects stronger. Group members challenged each other's thinking, shared additional resources, and offered emotional support, which may be an undervalued aspect of the research process.

As Annice indicates, when researchers completed their individual work, they began to share insights useful for the good of the group. For example, when discussing her data analysis, Annice described how she conceived of the activist job continuum to reflect on levels of congruence between participants' job assignments and their activist interests or behaviors. Some of her respondents had positions in the student services realm that were directly focused on addressing issues of Black students' success in school, so she coded statements that reflected that as "high congruence." Other times, folks made statements that referred to current or past positions providing limited or no opportunities to effect change in this area, so she would code that as "low congruence." These types of statements seemed to come out most in talk about career conflicts and dilemmas.

As a group we were trained in the use of NVivo software for the analysis of qualitative data. Annice, Gloria, and Wanda each used the software when completing their dissertation work. Although we intended to use NVivo to facilitate our cross-case work, over the course of our years together, the software outpaced our work such that versions bought in 2003 were virtually obsolete by the time cross-case work began. As a result we relied on a combination of NVivo analysis and tried-and-true paper techniques to complete cross-case analysis.

As is to be expected, engaging with and analyzing data challenged and changed our initial understanding of factors that shape educators' activism. Gloria Jones, for example, revised the conceptual framework that guided her initial understanding of activists working to interrupt student-to-student sexual harassment. In her words,

> the [original] conceptual framework was constructed from theoretical perspectives drawn from identity theory, social movement theory, and related educator activist literatures. The historical significance of sexual harassment was also examined…. I expected to find that both personal and professional resources and factors frame how educators identified with the issue of student-to-student sexual harassment (i.e., time, money, energy, talents, skills, goals, values, profession, family, career mobility), and that identity factors drove their activism to intervene and stop sexual harassment.

Yet data collection and analysis led Jones to revise her conceptual framework. The conceptual framework (Figure 8.1) was refined based on additional personal and professional impacts unique to the activism of the educators in her study to include two significant influences beyond Jones's expectations. Data collection and analysis illustrated the importance of educators' knowledge of Title IX and sexual harassment law, so these were incorporated into the framework, for this knowledge impacted how educators identified student-to-student sexual harassment and how they deployed their activism. For example, awareness of the laws governing sexual harassment in schools did not automatically influence educators' behavior, for the research showed a range of practice, from disregarding what laws stipulate, to relying on the victim's interpretation to define harassment, to enforcing the policy to the letter of the law. Data analysis also revealed the importance of residing in the Bible Belt as regards the educators' activism, an influence Gloria depicted by situating her model within the circle of the Bible Belt.

As dissertations were completed, group members committed to read each others' work with an eye to beginning our cross-case work. Emerging from our individual interview and analysis experiences, and our list of preliminary themes,

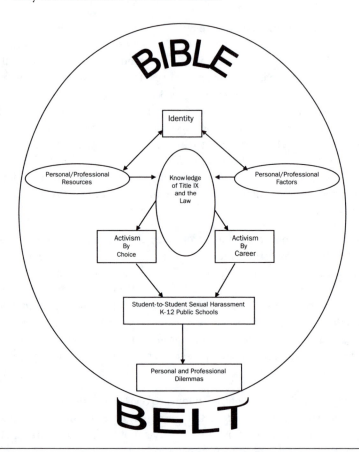

Figure 8.1 Gloria Jones' reconstructed conceptual framework.

we began to develop questions to ask of the data to begin to consider implications of educator activists' work writ large (see Appendix C, "Questioning Our Data for Cross-Case Analysis"). Applying these questions to everyone's data, we had additional process insights, including the need to clarify the meanings of words or concepts we were using; for example, *conservative*, *Bible Belt*, and even *activism*. We began to notice instances of similarity and difference among educators working in different activist arenas; for example, how some educators worked to embed activism in their job, how others saw the work as part of their job, and how still others indicated that activism was too risky while in the career.

More than the Sum of Our Parts

Amy Anderson

I admire the women in this group and have learned so much from each of them. From Catherine, skills in navigating research literatures, and persistence in writing your way into a paper or a chapter. From Annice, the importance of leaders and role models in any group as she set the pace and standard for the rest of us. From Susan, the importance of maintaining strong family commitments outside career and study, yet not subsuming personal interests to those commitments. From Gloria, I learned the importance of maintaining a healthy sense of humor, and taking on challenges outside the comfort zone. And from Wanda, the importance of taking professional and educational risks by taking on challenging career opportunities, and learning about and advocating for marginalized issues.

In addition, all of these women provided meaningful connections to life in schools. I was a full full-time graduate student for most of our time together, lost in the halls of the School of Education and the stacks of the graduate library. Each Saturday with my co-laborers (as Annice would say), returned me to life in schools, a reminder of why we're in this work. I tried to support this work by acting as record-keeper for the group, trying to relieve them of some of the organizational details.

The beauty of this experience is seeing these talents come together in this book. Our work can stand alone, but it stands beautifully together.

In addition, our cross-case analysis unveiled our group recognition of the power of professional socialization in educators' careers, conveying the message that the spiritual and emotional is presumed to belong to the private sphere and thus remain illegitimate for professionals' work, likely to undermine their credibility. This realization first came from Annice's data (chapter 2), but also appears in Susan's work (chapter 3) as participants discussed the jeopardy of focusing on the domestic sphere to their credibility as educational administrators.

> **The Multiplier Effect**
>
> *Annice H. Williams*
>
> The overarching project has in some ways, allowed each of our projects to be "born again." We each developed conclusions about the findings of our research, culminating in dissertations for most of us. As we continued to meet and co-labor on the larger project, analysis of our work around specific themes and threads yielded many new insights, and cast different perspectives on our individual work. Reviewing our results through lenses that may have had little or no presence in our original work allowed us to mine even deeper into our data when it became part of a much larger sample. Trends that were not apparent to us individually tended emerge as group members connected the dots across projects.

As the cross-case work developed (and with the book prospectus reviewers' encouragement), we recognized that our initial literature reviews were an adequate starting point, but inadequate for a more complex theoretical understanding of activist educators' work. We expanded our lenses and turned explicitly to feminist, critical race, and queer theories to consider alternate interpretations. This in turn caused us to consider the place of theory in teachers' and administrators' professional preparation programs. These issues are taken up in greater depth in chapter 7, but the importance of our ongoing group work around a succession of conference and kitchen tables cannot be overstated.

Methodological Advances and Lessons Learned

This text and this chapter demonstrate the power of collaborative group research, for the researchers and for the topic as well. Reason's (1994) explication of Torbert's (1987) characterization of collaborative inquiry is useful for understanding this work:

> For the organization or community, collaborative inquiry involves explicit shared reflection about the collective dream and mission, open rather than masked interpersonal relations, systematic evaluation and feedback of collective and individual performance, and direct facing and creative resolution of those paradoxes that otherwise become polarized conflicts. (Torbert, 1987, p. 128, cited in Reason, 1994, p. 331)

This chapter is offered as one model of a collaborative research endeavor, a model others may adapt to their own collective process.

The Power of Our Group Work, the Power of Persistence

Gloria Jones

I had used the term *group* loosely, but the day we photographed ourselves, this assemblage of dynamic women, it was etched in my mind that we were united, not just in presence, but also in our commitment, priceless. Our solidarity strengthened the significance of our 2½-hour gatherings. The meetings brought the group together and were the thread that bonded us, the oxygen that kept us breathing life into the larger project and our independent studies. Although we communicated our own life experiences (i.e., deaths, marriages, illness, promotions, new homes, etc.) through the listserv, it was at the meetings that we were able to see each other, share with one another, lean on the other, and know that we were all okay, still committed to the cause.

Our final chapter portrays shared values and supported, collaborative, and structured work. Our hope is that all educator activists find similar experiences in their work for social justice.

Notes

1. Ultimately the project also led to Dr. Williams, Dr. Jones, and Dr. Legrand!
2. Fifteen participants per researcher was the initial target, although that number was scaled down to 10 as fewer participants were recruited for some issues as described in chapters 2 through 6.

Activists Interview Protocol

Interview Protocol for Activists

The interview will begin with a brief restatement of the focus of the research.

1. **General information about self as a warm-up:**
   - How long have you been an educator?
   - What different positions and locations have you held in education?
   - There are lots of ways of taking a stand and/or getting involved in what you care about politically. In what ways do you do this?
2. **Membership in social movement/activism: (reference activism that brought us to them)**
   - How did you first get involved in this area?
   - Is there an organization, movement, or group?
   - What do you know about its organization and history? Is this a local group? National? International?
3. **Coping**
   - What are ways you've devised to manage being an X activist and being an educator? Has your participation with X created any conflicts with being an educator? In what ways?
   - Are there ways you can be an activist *within* the system, as an educator?
   - Are there ways you are an activist within the classroom?
4. **Defining Moments**
   - Sometimes people experience "defining moments" when they realize something about themselves through their work in social movements like X. Can you talk about any such moments? What did that do for you? Did you make new choices?
   - What kinds of things have you done/activities have you participated in while working with X?
5. **Context and Contacts**
   - What are factors in your community and school site/district that make it harder or easier to engage in activism for you (and discuss contexts in other jobs you've had in education)?

- Can you speculate on kinds of things that would make it easier (unions, liberal community, colleagues who were more brave, different teacher training…)?
- What sorts of rhetoric and strategies does your movement use? (e.g., are there slogans, marches, demonstrations, tactics, that your movement is known for?)
- Have there been times when the rhetoric or strategies caused you problems with your educator role?
- How have you and others like you managed such problems?
- How do you define activism?
- Do you consider yourself an activist?

6. **Choices**
   - Could you talk about the kinds of choices you have made in deciding to participate in this kind of activism? This kind of movement? This movement given that you're an educator?
   - Choices you have made about the kinds of activities you will do?
   - For example, have you been a one-time volunteer to sustained, in-depth participant? Have you/will you assume leadership? What choices have you made about costs vs. benefits of participation with X?

7. **Conflicts**
   - Sometimes people involved in social movements like X find that their involvement creates strains and tensions and dilemmas. Has your X activism aroused conflicts with:
   - family/lifestyle
   - career
   - other goals (money, fun, security, status?)
   - health

8. **Community**
   - What do you get from being with the people in X? What are they like?
   - Were there aspects of your family background that affected your involvement?
   - Elements of your education affecting your involvement?
   - Your friendships?
   - Elements of who you are personally?
   - Elements of who you are as an educator?
   - Are there ways that being involved in X have shaped who you are?
   - What kinds of realizations about yourself have you had while working with X?
   - What talents and skills do you bring to X?
   - What talents and skills have you learned while working with X?
   - Are there ways these talents and skills transfer to your educator role? To the classroom?
   - What spirit and values do you bring to X?

- How has involvement with X shaped/changed your values?
- What are limitations to your involvement with X?
- Can you suggest others I should contact who are activists? (Get names, phone numbers, addresses—get them for your activist issue but also for others in the project).

9. **Ending and Background**

Do you have any mementos or example of what you've done in this movement that I could see? A scrapbook, pamphlets, photos? I appreciate your willingness to be part of this study and share your experiences.

Educator Activists, Preliminary Themes

Educator Activists: June 28, 2004

Themes

Background
- Geographic: Area of country; urban, rural, suburban; school/career sites; size of district
- Length of career as educator
- Aha moment
- Family background: Class; race; age ranges

Career
- Being silenced and ignored
- Legal and contractual constraints
- Education/credentials
- Experience
- Desire for advancement
- Self-efficacy

Dilemmas

Constraints
- Legal and contractual
- Resources
- Tokenism

Choices
- Silence/voice
- Closet vs. public activism
- Staging of activism
- Coming out
- Denial
- Owning the movement
- Coping
- Safe/contentious
- Personal/political
- Whether/how you connect it in your work: Curriculum
- Power over/power with

Risk
- Contradictions
- Backlash

Identity
- Social level of identity
- Political power of identity
- Identity competition/Identity correspondence
- "Fit"—between category and situation
- Socialization factors influencing identity
- Racial identity
- Acculturation and identification from interactions with heritage and host cultures
- Ethnic enclosure—identity influenced by similar features, close contact
- Risk
- Gender identity
- Personal relationships/identification
- Maintenance of identity
- Professional identity
- Life experience with activism (e.g., family tradition)
- Level of identification with movement
- Class
- Education & family background
- Collective action/solidarity

Social Movement
- Social networks
- Adversary: Confronting elites
- Powerful opponents
- Contentious politics
- Identity, vision, or goal: Common purpose
- Collective action, social solidarity
- Sustained interaction, mobilization
- Organization: hierarchical; organized at the point of contact with its adversaries; connective structures
- Solidarity
- Emotion as motivation for action
- Strategies, slogans, music, symbols, dress
- Critical events and catalysts
- Form of involvement, level of involvement
- Tokenism?
- Recruitment into movement/time of entry: Personal/professional
- Current political climate
- Legal and contractual concerns

Educator Activists, Questions for the Data

Educator Activists: Questioning Our Data in Cross-Case Analysis

1. What are the (conservative) messages in education around this issue? What gets folks past conservative messages/messages of conservatism in education?
2. What are examples of microinteractions (participants and one other; "looks," e-mails) around activism?
   a. How are these influenced by macrointeractions (e.g., conference participation)?
3. What are the larger groups affiliated around this issue?
   a. What do these groups say about the issue?
4. What defines acting "too x" (e.g., too Black, too radical, too queer...) what is the line in the sand? How did you learn that?
5. What are the pedagogical opportunities for activism about the issue? (e.g., confronting harassment, -isms)?
   a. What are system mandates about the issue? (e.g., confronting harassment, -isms)
6. What are the driving regional and/or cultural supports or limitations for activism?
   a. Do community expectations affect participation?
7. What is the relationship between perceived level of risk and levels of activism? Does fear around activism match reality of reprisals?
8. What is the relationship between perceived level of risk and perceptions of job security (credibility, security, mobility)?
9. How does perceived level of risk change over the course of a career?
10. How/where does the issue of collaboration appear in your data?
    a. How is collaboration—in the experiences of your participants—like and not like our original conception of social networks?
    b. Are they working in collaboration with others in their activism?
    c. Does their activism isolate them?
11. What is the intensity of the public discourse on this movement? When did it peak? How has intensity of public discourse affected participants' careers? Their activism? Their perception that it's okay to be an activist? That their activism is viable? Their perception that it's a problem?

12. What is the role of conscience constituency? Those that give nods to and pay dues in the issue, but not much else?

13. Is activist participation individual or group? Private or public? (check to see if this is the same as questions 2 and 3?)

14. Social movement theory: Does it encompass women, private, down-low, quiet activism which is personal and the street level?

15. Education itself is activism—but the profession is hostile to activism. So how is that reconciled? When do participants see that activism is a part of (not apart from) education? How does fairness play a role in activism?

16. Which issues "cause a ruckus" and which are labeled or considered "fixed?" How has that developed historically? What is the timeline of involvement? (Progressive bell curves) (may be related to question 11)

17. What is backlash in re: our topics?

18. What is the influence of emotion, caring, spirituality?

References

Adams, M., Bell, L.A., & Griffin, P. (1997). *Teaching for diversity and social justice.* New York: Routledge.

Alan Guttmacher Institute. (2007a). Sexuality education. Retrieved August 25, 2007 from http://www.guttmacher.org.

Alan Guttmacher Institute. (2007b). State policies in brief as of October 1, 2007: Sex and STI/HIV education. Retrieved October 12, 2007 from http://www.guttmacher.org.

Allen, J. (Ed.). (1999). *Class actions: Teaching for social justice in elementary and middle school.* New York: Teachers College Press.

American Association of University Women Educational Foundation. (1993). *Hostile hallways: The AAUW survey on sexual harassment in America's schools.* Washington, D.C.: Author.

American Association of University Women Educational Foundation. (2001) *Hostile hallways: Bullying, teasing, and sexual harassment in school.* AAUW Education Foundation. Washington, D.C.: Author.

Anderson, G.L. (1990). Toward a critical constructivist approach to school administration: Invisibility, legitimation, and the study of non-events. *Educational Administration Quarterly, 26*(1), 38–59.

Anderson, G.L. (2001). Disciplining leaders: A critical discourse analysis of the ISLLC National Examination and Performance Standards in educational administration. *International Journal of Leadership in Education, 4*(3), 199–216.

Armstrong, E. (2002). *Forging gay identities: Organizing sexuality in San Francisco, 1950–1994.* Chicago: University of Chicago Press.

Ashton (2007) Personal communication with Amy Anderson, April 3, 2007.

Atwood, M. (1998). *The handmaid's tale.* New York: Anchor Books.

Ayers, W., Hunt, J.A., & Quinn, T. (1998). *Teaching for social justice.* New York: Teachers College Press.

Beane, J., & Apple, M. (1995). The case for democratic schools. In M. Apple & J. Beane (Eds.), *Democratic schools* (pp. 1–30). Alexandria, VA: ASCD.

Bell, C., & Chase, S. (1993). The underrepresentation of women in school leadership. In C. Marshall (Ed.), *The new politics of race and gender* (pp. 141–154). Washington, D.C.: The Falmer Press.

Berlin, L. (1996). *Peer to peer sexual harassment: Emerging law as it applies to school building administrators' legal responsibility for prevention and response.* Blacksburg, VA: Virginia Polytechnic Institute and State University.

Besner, H.F. & Spungin, C.I. (1995). *Gay and lesbian students.* Washington, DC: Taylor & Francis.

Billington, M.L. (Ed.). (1969). *The South: A central theme?* New York: Holt, Rinehart & Winston.

Blount, J.M. (1998). *Destined to rule the school: Women and the superintendency, 1873–1995.* Albany, NY: State University of New York Press.

Bray, J.N., Lee, J.A., Smith, L.L., & Yorks, L. (2000). *Collaborative inquiry in practice: Action, reflection, and meaning making.* Thousand Oaks, CA: Sage.

Brisbane, R.H. (1974). *Black activism: Racial revolution in the United States, 1954–1970.* Valley Forge, PA: Judson Press.

Britzman, D. (2000). "The question of belief": Writing poststructural ethnography. In E.A. St. Pierre & W.S. Pillow (Eds.), *Working the ruins: Feminist poststructural theory and methods in education* (pp. 27–40). New York: Routledge.

Broman, C., Neighbors, H., & Jackson, J. (1988). Racial group identification among Black adults. *Social Forces, 67*(1), 146–158.

Brown, R.K., & Brown, R.E. (2003). Faith and works: Church-based social capital resources and African American political activism. *Social Forces, 82*(2), 617–641.

Buechler, S.M. (1990). *Women's movement in the United States.* New Brunswick, NJ: Rutgers University Press.

Buechler S. M. (2000). *Social movements in advanced capitalism: The political economy and cultural construction of social activism.* New York: Oxford University Press.

Burstyn, J.N., Bender, G., Casella, R., Gordon, H.W., Guerra, D.P., Luschen, K.V. et al. (2001). *Preventing violence in schools: A challenge to American democracy.* Mahwah, NJ: Erlbaum.

Cahill, M. (2001). *The social construction of sexual harassment law: The role of the national, organizational and individual context.* Burlington, VT: Ashgate.

Calhoun, C. (1994). *Social theory and the politics of identity.* Oxford: Blackwell.

Cammack, J.C., & Phillips, D.K. (2002). Discourses and subjectivities of the gendered teacher. *Gender & Education, 14*(2), 123–133.

Cannon, K. (1988). *Black womanist ethics.* Atlanta, GA: Scholars Press.

Casey, K. (1993). *I answer with my life: Life histories of women teachers working for social change.* New York: Routledge.

Cass, V.C. (1979). Homosexual identity formation: A theoretical model. *Journal of Homosexuality, 4*(3), 219–235.

Castells, M. (1997). *The power of identity.* Malden, MA: Blackwell.

Clifford, G.J. (1987). Gender expectations and American teachers. *Teacher Education Quarterly, 14*(2), 6–16.

Cochran-Smith, M. (1991). Learning to teach against the grain. *Harvard Educational Review, 61*(3), 279–310.

Cohan, A., Hergenrother, M.A., Johnson, Y.M., Mandel, L.S., Sawyer, J. (1996). *Sexual harassment and sexual abuse: A handbook for teachers and administrators.* Thousand Oaks, CA: Corwin Press.

Collins, P.H. (1991). *Black feminist thought: Knowledge, consciousness, and the politics of empowerment.* New York: Routledge.

Connell, R.W. (1987). *Gender and power.* Cambridge, UK: Polity Press.

Connell, R.W. (1995). *Masculinities.* Berkeley, CA: University of California Press.

Cooper, D. (1997). At the expense of Christianity: Backlash discourse and moral panic. In L. Roman & L. Eyre (Eds.), *Dangerous territories: Struggles for difference and equality in education* (pp. 43–62). New York: Routledge.

Coughlan, D. (1994). Change as re-education: Lewin revisited. *Organizational Development Journal, 12*(4), 1–8.

Creswell, J.W. (1998). *Qualitative inquiry and research design: Choosing among five traditions.* Thousand Oaks, CA: Sage.

Crisci, G.S. (1999). When no means no: Recognizing and preventing sexual harassment in your schools. *The American School Board Journal, 186*(6), 25–29.

Crocco, M.S., Munro, P., & Weiler, K. (1999). *Pedagogies of resistance: Women educator activists 1880–1960.* New York: Teachers College Press.

Dantley, M.E. (2005). African American spirituality and Cornel West's notions of prophetic pragmatism: Restructuring educational leadership in American urban schools. *Education Administration Quarterly, 41*(4), 651–675.

Darnovsky, M., Epstein, B., & Flacks, R. (Eds.) (1995). *Cultural politics and social movements.* Philadelphia: Temple University Press.

Davis, A.Y. (1989). *Women, culture, and politics.* New York: Random House.

Dawson, M.C. (1994). *Behind the mule: Race and class in African-American politics.* Princeton, NJ: Princeton University Press.

De Hart, J.S. (1997). Second wave feminism(s) and the South: The difference that differences make. In C. Franham (Ed.), *Women of the American South* (pp. 276–301). New York: New York University Press.

Delmar, R. (1986). What is feminism? In A. Oakley & J. Mitchell (Eds.), *What is feminism? Seeing through the backlash?* (pp. 8–33). New York: Pantheon Books.

della Porta, D. & Diani, M. (1999). *Social movements: An introduction.* Oxford: Blackwell.

Demo, D., & Hughes, M. (1990). Socialization and racial identity among Black Americans. *Social Psychology Quarterly, 53*(4), 364–374.

Denzin, N., & Lincoln, Y. (1994). Entering the field of qualitative research. In N. Denzin & Y. Lincoln (Eds.), *Handbook of qualitative research* (pp. 1–17). Thousand Oaks, CA: Sage.

Diani, M., & Eyerman, R. (1992). *Studying collective action.* Newbury Park, CA: Sage.

Dillard, C.B., (1995). Leading with her life: An African American feminist (re)interpretation of leadership for an urban high school principal. *Educational Administration Quarterly, 31*(4), 539–563.

Donovan, P. (1988). School-based sexuality education: The issues and challenges. *Family Planning Perspectives, 30*(4), 188–193.

Dorough, C.D. (1974). *The Bible belt mystique*. Philadelphia: Westminster Press.

Dove, L.A. (1995). The work of schoolteachers as political actors in developing countries. In M.B. Ginsburg (Ed.), *The politics of educators work and lives* (pp. 169–205). New York: Garland.

Elliott, P. (1997). Denial and disclosure: An analysis of selective reality in the feminist classroom. In L. Roman & L. Fry (Eds.), *Dangerous territories: Struggles for difference and equality in education* (pp. 143–158). New York: Routledge

Epstein, B. (1990). Rethinking social movement theory. *Socialist Review, 20*, 33–56.

Ernest (2003). Personal communication with Annice Hood, September 6, 2003.

Etzioni, A. (1961). *Complex organizations: A sociological reader*. New York: Holt, Rinehart & Winston.

Falwell, J. (1979). *America can be saved*. Murfreesboro, TN: Sword of the Lord Publishers.

Ferree, M. (1992). The political context of rationality: Rational choice theory and resource mobilization. In A. Morris & C. Mueller (Eds.), *Frontiers in social movement theory* (pp. 29–52). New Haven, CT: Yale University Press.

Fineran, S. (2002). Sexual harassment between same-sex peers: Intersection of mental health, homophobia, and sexual violence in schools. *Social Work, 47*(1), 65–79.

Fineran, S., & Bennett, L. (1998). Teenage peer sexual harassment: Implications for social work practice in education. *Social Work, 43*(1), 55–64.

Fleer, J.D. (1994). *North Carolina government & politics*. Lincoln, NE: University of Nebraska Press.

Francis, L. P. (2001). *Sexual harassment as an ethical issue in academic life*. Lanham, MD: Rowman & Littlefield.

Franklin v. Gwinnett County Public Schools, 503 US 60 (US Court of Appeals for the 11th Circuit) (1972).

Freire, P. (1990). *Pedagogy of the oppressed*. New York: Continuum.

Friedan, B. (1963). *The feminine mystique*. New York: Dell.

Friedman, D., & McAdams, D. (1992). Collective identity and activism: Networks, choices, and the life of a social movement. In A.D. Morris & C.M. Mueller (Eds.), *Frontiers in social movement theory* (pp. 156–173). New Haven, CT: Yale University Press.

Friend, R. (1993). Choices, not closets: Heterosexism and homophobia in schools. In L. Weis & M. Fine (Eds.), *Beyond silenced voices: Class, race, and gender in United States schools* (pp. 209–235). New York: State University of New York Press.

Fullan, M. (1993). *Change forces: Probing the depths of educational reform*. London: Falmer Press.

Gallas, K. (1998). *"Sometimes I can be anything:" Power gender and identity in a primary classroom*. New York: Teachers College Press.

Gamson, W.A., (1990). *The strategy of social protest* (2nd ed.). Belmont, CA: Wadsworth.

Gilkes, C.T., (1980). Holding back the ocean with a broom: Black women and community work. In L. Rodgers-Rose (Ed.), *The black woman* (pp. 217–232). Beverly Hills, CA: Sage.

Gilkes, C.T. (1983). Going up for the oppressed: The career mobility of black women community workers. *The Journal of Sociology, 39*(3), 115–139.

Gilroy, P. (1993). *The black Atlantic: Modernity and double consciousness*. Cambridge, MA: Harvard University Press.

Ginsburg, M.B. (Ed.). (1995). *The politics of educators' work and lives*. New York: Garland.

Ginsburg, M., Kamat, S., Raghu, R., & Weaver, J. (1995) Educators and politics: Interpretations, involvement, and implications. In M. Ginsburg (Ed.), *The politics of educators' work and lives* (pp. 3–54). New York: Garland.

Ginwright, S.A. (2002). Classed out: The challenges of social class in Black community change. *Social Problems. 49*(4), 544–562.

Goodman, G., Lackey, G., Lashof, J., & Thorne, E. (1983). *No turning back: Lesbian and gay liberation for the 80s*. Philadelphia: New Society.

Grumet, M. (1988). *Bitter milk: Women and teaching*. Amherst, MA: University of Massachusetts Press.

Gurin, P., Miller, A., & Gurin, G. (1980). Stratum identification and consciousness. *Social Psychology Quarterly, 43*(1), 30–37.

Hall, S. (1996). Minimal selves. In H.A. Baker, M. Diawara, & R.H. Lindeborg (Eds.), *Black British cultural studies: A reader* (pp. 114–119). Chicago: University of Chicago Press.

Hankins, K.H. (2003). *Teaching through the storm: A journal of hope*. New York: Teachers College Press.

Hansot, E., & Tyack, D. (1981). *The dream deferred: A golden age for women school administrators* (Policy Paper No. 81-C2). Stanford, CA: Stanford University Institute for Research on Educational Finance and Government.

Harbeck, K.M. (1997). *Gay and lesbian educators: Personal freedoms, public constraints*. Malden, MA: Amethyst.

Hartzell, G.N., Williams, R.C., & Nelson, K.T. (1995). *New voices in the field: The work lives of first-year assistant principals*. Thousand Oaks, CA: Corwin.

Helms, J.E. (Ed.). (1990). *Black and white racial identity: Theory, research, and practice*. Westport, CT: Greenwood.

Higginbotham, E., & Weber, L. (1992). Moving up with kin and community: Upward social mobility for Black and White women. *Gender & Society, 6*(3), 416–440.

Hilliard, A. (1991). Do we have the will to educate all children? *Educational Leadership, 49*(1), 31–36.

Hirschman, A.O. (1970) *Exit, voice and loyalty: Response to decline in organizations and states.* Cambridge, MA: Harvard University Press.

Hodgkinson, H., & Montenegro, X. (1999). *The U.S. school superintendent: The invisible CEO*. Washington, D.C.: Institute for Instructional Leadership.

Hogg, M.A., & Terry, D.J. (Eds.). (2001). *Social identity processes in organizational contexts*. Philadelphia: Psychology Press.

Holland, D., Lachicotte, Jr., W., Skinner, D., & Cain, C. (1998). *Identity and agency in cultural worlds.* Cambridge, MA: Harvard University Press.

Hood, A.F. (2005). *Impact of involvement in race-related activism on the careers of Black educators.* (Doctoral dissertation, University of North Carolina, 2005). UMI No. 3170587.

hooks, b. (1994). *Teaching to transgress: Education as the practice of freedom.* New York: Routledge.

Hotelling, K. (1991). Special feature: Sexual harassment. *Journal of Counseling & Development, 69*(6), 495–496.

Human Rights Watch (2001). *Hatred in the hallways.* Retrieved January 5, 2006 from http://www.hrw.org/reports/2001/uslgbt/Final-06a.html.

Jay, M.H. (2006). *Race in education, anti-racist activism and the role of white colleagues: Listening to the voices of African American educators.* (Doctoral dissertation, University of North Carolina, Chapel Hill). UMI No. 3219468.

Jenkins, C.J. (1983). Resource mobilization theory and the study of social movements. *Annual Review of Sociology, 9*, 527–553.

Johnston, R.C., & Viadero, D (2000). Unmet promise: Raising minority achievement. *Education Week, 19*(27), Retrieved August 20, 2004, from http://www.edweek.org/ew/ewstory.cfm?slug=27gapintro.h19

Jones, G.H. (2005). *Site-based voices: Dilemmas of educators who engage in activism against student-to-student sexual harassment.* (Doctoral dissertation, University of North Carolina, Chapel Hill). UMI No. 3170588.

Jones, R. (1999, November). Your legal duty to protect gay kids from harassment. *American School Board Journal,* 27–31.

Jones, E., & Montenegro, X. (1983). Factors predicting women's upward career mobility in school administration. *Journal of Educational Equality and Leadership, 3*(3), 231–241.

Kahne, J. (1996). *Reframing educational policy: Democracy, community, and the individual.* New York: Teacher's College Press.

Keisha (2003). Personal communication with Annice Hood, November 29, 2003.

Keith, J. (2002). *The South: A concise history.* Upper Saddle River, NJ: Prentice Hall.

Kisen, R.M. (1993). *Voices from the glass closet: Lesbian and gay teachers talk about their lives* (report No. S0023-493). Atlanta GA: American Educational Research Association. (EDRS Document Reproduction Service No. 363-556)

Knight, Michelle G. (2000). Ethics in qualitative research: multicultural feminist activist research. *Theory into Practice, 39*(3), 170–176.

Labaree, D.F. (1997). Public goods, private goods: The American struggle over educational goals. *American Educational Research Journal, 34*(1), 39–81.

Ladson-Billings, G. (1994). *The dreamkeepers: Successful teachers of African American children.* San Francisco: Jossey-Bass.

Ladson-Billings, G. (1995). Toward a theory of culturally relevant pedagogy. *American Educational Research Journal, 32*(3), 465–491.

Laible, J. (1997). Feminist analysis of sexual harassment policy: A critique of the ideal of community. In C. Marshall (Ed.), *Feminist critical policy analysis—A perspective from primary and secondary schooling,* (Vol. 1, pp. 201–215). London: Falmer Press.

Landry, B. (1987). *The new Black middle class.* Berkeley: University of California Press.

Lather, P. (2000). Drawing the line at angels: Working the ruins of feminist ethnography. In E.A. St.

Pierre & W.S. Pillow (Eds.), *Working the ruins: Feminist poststructural theory and methods in education* (pp. 284–311). New York: Routledge.

Lawn, M. (1995). The political nature of teaching: Arguments around schoolwork. In M. Ginsburg (Ed.), *The politics of educators' work and lives* (pp.115–132). New York: Garland.

Lawson, B. (1992). Uplifting the race: Middle-class Blacks and the truly disadvantaged. In B. Lawson (Ed.), *The underclass question* (pp. 90–103). Philadelphia: Temple University Press.

Leck, G.M. (1990). Examining gender as a foundation within foundational studies. *Teachers College Record, 91*(3), 382–395.

Leck, G.M. (2000). Heterosexual or homosexual? Reconsidering binary narratives on sexual identities in urban schools. *Education and Urban Society, 32*(3), 324–348.

Legrand, W. (2005). *Activism for LGBT rights: How participation affects the lives of activist educators.* (Doctoral dissertation, University of North Carolina, Chapel Hill). UMI No. 3190482.

Lofland, J. (1996). *Social movement organizations: Guide to research on insurgent realities.* New York: Aldine De Gruyter.

Lopez, G.R. (2003). Parent involvement as racialized performance. In L. Parker & G. Lopez (Eds.), *Interrogating racism in qualitative research methodology* (pp. 71–98). New York: Peter Lang.

Luebke, P. (1990) *Tar Heel politics: Myths and realities.* Chapel Hill, NC: University of North Carolina Press.

Lugg, C.A. (2003). Our straitlaced administrators: The law, lesbian, gay, bisexual, and transgendered educational administrators, and the assimilationist imperative. *Journal of School Leadership, 13*(1), 51–85.

Lumsden, L.S. (1992). *Getting serious about sexual harassment.* (Report No. EDO-EA-92-8). Washington, D.C.: Office of Educational Research and Improvement. (ERIC Document Reproduction Service No. ED347699)

Macgillivray, I. K. (2004). *Sexual orientation and school policy.* Boulder, CO: Rowan & Littlefield.

Macgillivray, I.K., & Kozik-Rosabal, G. (2000). Introduction. *Education and Urban Society, 32*(3), 287–302.

MacKinnon, C.A. (1989). *Toward a feminist theory of the state.* Cambridge, MA: Harvard University Press.

Maggio, R. (Ed.). (1996). *The new Beacon book of quotations by women.* Boston: Beacon Press.

Marsh, C. (2005). *The beloved community: How faith shapes social justice, from the civil rights movement to today.* New York: Basic Books.

Marshall, C. (1993a). *The unsung role of the career assistant principal.* Reston, VA: National Association of Secondary School Principals.

Marshall, C. (1993b). Politics of denial: Gender and race issues in administration. In C. Marshall (Ed.), *The new politics of race and gender* (pp. 168–182). London: Falmer.

Marshall, C. (1995) Imagining leadership. *Educational Administration Quarterly, 31*(3) 484–492.

Marshall, C. (Ed.). (1997). *Feminist critical policy analysis: A perspective from primary and secondary schooling.* Washington, D.C.: Falmer Press.

Marshall, C. (2002). Teacher unions and gender equity policy for education. *Educational Policy, 16*(5), 707–730.

Marshall, C., & Gerstl-Pepin, C. (2005). *Re-framing educational politics for social justice.* Boston: Allyn & Bacon.

Marshall, C., & Hooley, R.M. (2006). *The assistant principal: Leadership choices and challenges.* Thousand Oaks, CA: Corwin.

Marshall, C., & Kasten, K.L. (1994). *The administrative career.* Thousands Oaks, CA: Corwin.

Marshall, C., & Mitchell, B. (1991). The assumptive worlds of fledgling administrators. *Education and Urban Society, 23*(4), 396–415.

Marshall, C., & Oliva, M. (2006). *Leadership for social justice: Making revolutions in education.* Boston: Allyn & Bacon.

Marshall, C., & Rossman, G. (1999). *Designing qualitative research* (3rd ed.). Thousand Oaks, CA: Sage.

Marshall, C., Taylor, S., & Gaskell, J. (2001). *Teacher unions and gender equity policy: Building social capital in three countries.* Unpublished manuscript.

Marshall, C., & Ward, M. (2004, September). "Yes, but…": Education leaders discuss social justice. *Journal of School Leadership, 14*(5), 531–563.

Mayo, C. (2004). *Disputing the subject of sex: Sexuality and public school controversies.* Lanham, MD: Rowan & Littlefield.

McAdam, D., & Snow, D. (1997). *Social movements: Readings on their emergence, mobilization, and dynamics.* Los Angeles: Roxbury.

McCarn S.R., & Fassinger R.E. (1996). Revisioning sexual minority identity formation: A new model of lesbian identity and its implications for counseling and research. *The Counseling Psychologist, 24*(3), 508–534.

McDonald, K.B. (1997). Black activist mothering: A historical intersection of race, gender, and class. *Gender & Society, 11*(6), 773–795.

McFadden, A.H., & Smith, P. (2004). *The social construction of educational leadership – Southern Appalachian ceilings.* New York: Peter Lang.

McRobbie, A. (2007). Top girls? *Cultural Studies, 21*(4/5), 718–737.

Melucci, A. (1989). *Nomads of the present: Social movements and individual needs in contemporary society.* London: Hutchinson Radius.

Michie, G. (2005). *See you when we get there: Teaching for change in urban schools.* New York: Teachers College Press.

Miles, M., & Huberman, A.M. (1994). *Qualitative data analysis.* Thousand Oaks, CA: Sage.

Mitchell, J. (1986). Reflections on twenty years of feminism. In A. Oakley & J. Mitchell (Eds.), *What is feminism? Seeing through the backlash* (pp. 34–48). New York: Pantheon Books.

Moore, M.J., & Rienzo, B.A. (1998). Sexual harassment policies in Florida school districts. *Journal of School Health, 68*(6), 237–242.

Morris, A.D. (1984). *The origins of the Civil Rights Movement: Black communities organizing for change.* New York: Free Press.

Morris, A., & Mueller, C. (1992). *Frontiers in social movement theory.* New Haven, CT: Yale University Press.

Munro, P. (1995). Educators as activists: Five women from Chicago. *Social Education, 59*(5), 274–278.

Naples, N.A. (1992). Activist mothering: Cross-generational continuity in the community work of women from low-income urban neighborhoods. *Gender & Society, 6*(3), 441–463.

National Abortion Federation. (2007). *History of abortion.* Retrieved July 17, 2007, from http://www.prochoice.org/about_abortion/history_abortion.html

National Academy of Sciences. (2001). *No time to lose: Getting more from HIV prevention.* Washington, D.C.: Author.

National Campaign to Prevent Teen and Unwanted Pregnancy. (2001). *Halfway there: A prescription for continued progress in preventing teen pregnancy.* Washington, D.C.: Author.

National Coalition for Women and Girls in Education. (1997). *Title IX at 25: Report card on gender equity.* Washington, D.C.: Author.

Nesbitt, P.D. (Ed.).(2001). *Religion and social policy.* Walnut Creek, CA: AltaMira.

Ngunjiri, F.W. (Fall 2007). Rocking the boat without falling out: Spirited tempered radicals as agents of community transformation. *UCEA Review, 46*(3), 1–4.

Noddings, N. (1992). *The challenge to care in schools: An alternative approach to education.* New York: Teachers College Press.

Noddings, N. (2002). *Starting at home: Caring and social policy.* Berkeley: University of California Press.

Oakley, A., & Mitchell, J. (Eds.) (1986). *What is feminism? Seeing through the backlash.* New York: Pantheon Books.

Oakley, A., & Mitchell, J. (1997). Introduction. In A. Oakley & J. Mitchell (Eds.), *Who's afraid of feminism?* (pp. xix–xxxv). New York: New Press.

Oberschall, A. (1993*). Social movement: Ideologies, interests, and identities.* New Brunswick, NJ: Transaction.

Oliva, M., & Anderson, G.L. (2006). Dilemmas and lessons: The continuing leadership challenge for social justice. In C. Marshall & M. Oliva (Eds.), *Leadership for social justice: Making revolutions in education* (pp. 279–306). Boston: Allyn & Bacon.

Ortiz, F.I. (1982). *Career patterns in education: Women, men and minorities in public school administration.* New York: Praeger.

Owens, R.G. (2001). *Organizational behavior in education: Instructional leadership and school reform* (7th ed.). Needham Heights, MA: Allyn & Bacon.

Paludi , M.A., & Barickman, R. B. (1998). *Sexual harassment, work, and education* (2nd ed.). Albany, NY: State University of New York Press.

Paul, J.L., & Smith, T.J. (Eds.). (2000). *Stories out of school.* Stamford, CT: Ablex.

Pearce, K.D. (1995). *Women's rugby participation in a leisure context: A site for feminist resistance.* Unpublished master's thesis, University of North Carolina, Chapel Hill.

Permanent Commission (CT) on the Status of Women. (1995). *In our own backyard: Sexual harassment in Connecticut's public high schools.* Hartford, CT: Author.

Perry, M. (2000). *Walking the color line: The art & practice of anti-racist teaching.* New York: Teachers College Press.

Peterson, E.A. (1992). *African-American women: A study of will and success.* Jefferson, NC: McFarland.

Pinar, W.F. (1998). *Queer theory in education.* Mahwah, NJ: Erlbaum.

Pipes, W.H. (1997). Old-time religion: Benches can't say "Amen". In H.P. McAdoo (Ed.), *Black families* (3rd ed., pp. 41–66). Thousand Oaks, CA: Sage.

Ramsey, R.D. (1994). *Administrator's complete school discipline guide: Techniques & materials for creating an environment where kids can learn.* Englewood Cliffs, NJ: Prentice Hall.

Reason, P. (1994). Three approaches to participative inquiry. In N. Denzin & Y. Lincoln (Eds.), *Handbook of qualitative research* (pp. 324–339). Thousand Oaks, CA: Sage.

Reed, J.S. (1993). *My tears spoiled my aim and other reflections on Southern culture.* Columbia, MO: University of Missouri Press.

Roe v. Wade, 410 U.S. 113 (1973)

Rothenberg, P.S. (Ed.). (2001). *Race, class, and gender in the United States: An integrated study.* New York: Worth.

Rowell, L.L., & McBride, M.C. (1996). The role of the school counselor in confronting peer sexual harassment. *School Counselor, 43*(3), 196–208.

Sachs, J. (2000). The activist professional. *Journal of Educational Change, 1,* 77–95.

Sachs, J. (2001). Documents and debates: Teacher professional identity: Competing discourses, competing outcomes. *Journal of Education Policy, 16*(2), 149–161.

Sadker, M., & Sadker, D. (1994). *Failing at fairness: How America's schools cheat girls.* New York: Scribners.

Sattler, C.L. (1997). *Talking about a revolution: The politics and practice of feminist teaching.* Cresskill, NJ: Hampton.

Schmuck, P. (1975). Deterrents to women's careers in school management. *Sex Roles, 1*(4), 339–353.

Schmuck, P. (1995). Advocacy organizations for women school administrators. In D. Dunlap & P. Schmuck (Eds.), Women leading in education (pp. 199–224). Albany, NY: State University of New York Press.

Schmuck, P.A., & Schubert, J. (1995). Woman principals' views on sex equity: Exploring issues of integration and information. In D.M. Dunlap & P.A. Schmuck (Eds.), *Women leading in education* (pp. 274–287). Albany, NY: State University of New York Press.

Schwartz, W. (2000). *Preventing student sexual harassment.* (Report No. EDO-UD-00-9). Washington, D.C.: Office of Educational Research and Improvement. (ERIC #: ED448248).

Selden, D. (1985). *The teacher rebellion.* Washington, D.C.: Howard University Press.

Sexual Information and Education Council of the United States. (2005). *No more money for abstinence-only-until-marriage programs.* Retrieved August 12, 2007, from http://www.nomoremoney.org/history.html

Shakeshaft, C. (1989). *Women in educational administration.* Newbury Park, CA: Sage.

Shapiro, J.P., & Gross, S.J. (2008). *Ethical educational leadership in turbulent times—(Re)solving moral dilemmas.* New York: Routledge.

Shujaa, M.J. (Ed.). (1994) *Too much schooling, too little education: A paradox of Black life in White societies.* Trenton, NJ: Africa World Press.

Shuttleworth, D.E. (2003). *School management in transition.* New York: RoutledgeFalmer.

Singham, M. (1998). The canary in the mine: The achievement gap between Black and white students. *Phi Delta Kappan, 80*(1), 9–15.

Sjoberg, G. (1999). Some observations on bureaucratic capitalism: Knowledge about what and why? In J. Abu-Lughod (Ed.), *Sociology for the twenty-first century: Continuities and cutting edges* (pp. 43–64). Chicago: University of Chicago Press.

Solórzano, D. (1998). Critical race theory, racial and gender microaggressions, and the experiences of Chicana and Chicano scholars. *International Journal of Qualitative Studies in Education, 11,* 121–136.

Southern Education Foundation. (2007). *A new majority: Low income students in the South's public schools.* Retrieved November 2, 2007, from: http://www.sefatl.org/pdf/A%20New%20Majority%20Report-Final.pdf

Stacey, J. (1986). Are feminists afraid to leave home?: The challenge of conservative pro-family feminism. In A. Oakley & J. Mitchell (Eds.), *What is feminism? Seeing through the backlash* (pp. 8–33). New York: Pantheon Books.

Stake, R. (1994). Case studies. In N. Denzin & Y. Lincoln (Eds.), *Handbook of qualitative research* (pp. 236–247). Thousand Oaks, CA: Sage.

Stake, R.E. (1995). *The art of case study research.* Thousand Oaks, CA: Sage.

Stein, N. (1993a, January). Sexual harassment in schools: Administrators must break the casual approach to objectionable behavior. *The School Administrator, 50*(1), 14–21.

Stein, N. (1993b). *Secrets in public: Sexual harassment in public (and private) schools.* Working paper series No. 256. Wellesley, MA: Center for Research on Women.

Stein, N. (1999). *Classrooms and courtrooms: Facing sexual harassment in K-12 schools.* New York: Teachers College Press.

Strober, M., & Tyack, D. (1980). Why do women teach and men manage? *Signs, 5*(3), 494–503.

Stott, J.R.W. (1999). *Human rights and wrongs.* Grand Rapids, MI: Baker.

Stromquist, N.P. (1997). Gender policies in American education: Reflections on federal legislation and action. In C. Marshall (Ed.), *Feminist critical policy analysis: A perspective from primary and secondary schooling* (Vol. 1, pp. 54–72). London: Falmer.

Stryker, S. (2000). Identity competition: Key to differential social movement participation? In S. Stryker, T.J. Owens, & R. White (Eds.), *Self, identity, and social movements* (pp. 21–40). Minneapolis, MN: University of Minnesota Press.

Stryker, S., Owens, T., & White, R. (Eds.). (2000). *Self, identity, and social movements.* Minneapolis, MN: University of Minnesota Press.

Sudarkasa, N. (1997) African American families and family values. In H.P. McAdoo, (Ed.), *Black Families* (3rd ed., pp. 9–40). Thousand Oaks, CA: Sage.

Tarrow, S. (1998). *Power in movement: Social movements and contentious politics.* New York: Cambridge University Press.

Taylor, V., & Whittier, N. (1992). Collective identity in social movement communities: Lesbian feminist mobilization. In A. Morris & C. Mueller (Eds.), *Frontiers in social movement theory* (pp. 104–130). New Haven, CT: Yale University Press.

Tatum, B.D. (1997). *Why are all the Black kids sitting together in the cafeteria?* New York: Basic Books.

Thomson, P. (2001, April). *Ambiguous practice: The professional education of public sector leaders.* Paper presented at the annual conference of the American Education Research Association, Seattle, WA.

Timar, T., & Tyack, D. (1999). *The invisible hand of ideology: Perspectives from the history of school governance.* Denver, CO: Education Commission of the States.

Titus, J.J. (2000). Engaging student resistance to feminism: "How is this stuff going to make us better teachers?" *Gender and Education, 12*(1), 21–37.

Torbert, W.R. (1987). *Managing the corporate dream: Restructuring for long-term success.* Homewood, IL: Dow Jones-Irwin.

Touraine, A. (1995). *Critique of modernity* (David Macey, Trans.). Oxford: Blackwell.

Turcotte, L. (1996). Queer theory: Transgression and/or regression? *Canadian Woman's Studies, 16*(2), 118–121.

Umoja, A.O. (1999). The ballot and the bullet: A comparative analysis of armed resistance in the Civil Rights Movement. *Journal of Black Studies, 29*(4), 558–578.

Urban, W.J. (1982). *Why teachers organized.* Detroit, IL: Wayne State University Press.

Urban, W.J. (2000). *Gender, race, and the National Education Association: Professionalism and its limitation.* New York: RoutledgeFalmer.

Urban, W.J. (1989). Teacher activism. In D. Warren (Ed.), *American teachers: Histories of a profession at work* (pp. 190–210). New York: Macmillan.

U.S. House of Representatives Committee on Government Reform—Minority Staff Special Investigations Division. *The Content of Federally Funded Abstinence-Only Education Programs,* prepared for Rep. Henry A. Waxman. December 2004. Retrieved August 21, 2007, from http://oversight. house.gov/Documents/20041201102153-50247.pdf

Valverde, L., & Brown, F. (1988). Influences on leadership development among racial and ethnic minorities. In N. Boyan (Ed.), *Handbook of research on educational administration* (pp. 143–158). New York: Longman Press.

Ventura, S.J., Mosher, W.D., Curtin, S.C., Abma, J.C., & Henshaw, S. (2001). Trends in pregnancy rates for the United States, 1976–97: An update. *National Vital Statistics Reports, 49*(4). Retrieved August 22, 2007, from http://www.cdc.gov/nchs/data/nvsr/nvsr49/nvsr49_04.pdf

Walters, S. (2003). *Quiet activists: Women in educational leadership* (Doctoral dissertation, University of North Carolina, Chapel Hill). UMI No. 3112102.

Weatherly, R., & Lipsky, M. (1977). Street-level bureaucrats and institutional innovation: Implementing special-education reform. *Harvard Educational Review, 47*(2), 171–197.

Weiler, K. (1988). *Women teaching for change: Gender, class, and power.* South Hadley, MA: Bergin & Garvey.

West, A.M. (1980). *The National Education Association: The power base for education.* New York: Free Press

Wetzel, R., & Brown, N. W. (2000). *Student-generated sexual harassment in secondary schools.* Westport, CT: Bergin & Garvey.

Willett, C. (2002). Parenting and other human casualties in the pursuit of academic excellence. In A. Superson & A. Cudd (Eds.), *Theorizing blacklash: Philosophical reflections on the resistance to feminism* (pp. 119–131). New York: Rowman & Littlefield.

Williams, J. (1987). *Eyes on the prize: America's civil rights years, 1954–1965.* New York: Viking Penguin.

Wilson, W.J. (1980). *The truly disadvantaged: The inner city, the underclass, and public policy.* Chicago: University of Chicago Press.

Wink, J. (2000). *Critical pedagogy: Notes from the real world.* New York: Longman.

Winn, P. (2005, December 14). Sex? Systems vary on what to say—or not say. *Raleigh News & Observer,* B1.

Wolfe, M.R. (1995). *Daughters of Canaan: A saga of Southern women.* Lexington: University Press of Kentucky.

Yaffe, E. (1995, November). Expensive, illegal, and wrong: Sexual harassment in our schools (Kappan special report). *Phi Delta Kappan, 77*(3), K1–K16.

York-Barr, J., Sommers, W.A., Ghere, G., & Montie, J. (2006). *Reflective practice to improve schools: An action guide for educators* (2nd ed.). Thousand Oaks, CA: Corwin.

Yosso, T. (2002). Toward a critical race curriculum. *Equity and Excellence in Education. 35*(2), 93–107.

Young, M.D. (2003). Troubling policy discourse: Gender, constructions, and the leadership crisis. In M.D. Young & L. Skrla (Eds.), *Reconsidering feminist research in educational leadership* (pp. 265–298). Albany, NY: State University of New York Press.

Young, M.D., & Skrla, L. (Eds.). (2003). *Reconsidering feminist research in educational leadership.* Albany, NY: State University of New York Press.

Contributors

(from left to right) Annice H. Williams, Amy L. Anderson, Susan Walters, Catherine Marshall, Gloria H. Jones, Wanda Legrand

Catherine Marshall is Professor in the Department of Educational Leadership at the University of North Carolina at Chapel Hill. She writes about the politics of education, qualitative methodology, and women's access to education careers. Marshall is author or editor of numerous books, including: *Rethinking Educational Politics; Leadership for Social Justice: Making Revolutions in Education; Leadership for Social Justice; The Assistant Principal; Designing Qualitative Research;* and *Feminist Critical Policy Analysis* (2 vols.). AERA bestowed the Willystine Goodsell Award on Dr. Marshall in 2003 for her career of scholarship and activism on behalf of women and girls. She started "Leadership for Social Justice," a grassroots group pushing to put equity research into action. Her next projects will look at the work/family stresses of entry level administrators, and another project will focus on state legislatures' policymaking affecting sexuality and gender in education.

Amy L. Anderson is an Evaluation Specialist with Evaluation, Assessment, and Policy Connections (EvAP) in the School of Education at the University of North Carolina at Chapel Hill. She completed her PhD at the School of Education at UNC—Chapel Hill in Culture, Curriculum, and Change. Amy's scholarship works to ensure that teachers' experiences and expertise are part of the public discourses of education. Her dissertation work: *Language Matters: A Study of Teachers' Uses of Language for Understanding Their Work* (2006) looks at how teachers are positioned in languages of education that sentimentalize their rich and complex understandings of children and schools, excluded from both the discourses of theory and policy. She has made numerous presentations at AERA and AESA.

Annice Hood Williams is an Elementary School Principal who has previously served as a teacher, central office specialist, and assistant principal. She earned her EdD in Educational Leadership at the University of North Carolina at Chapel Hill, where she was awarded the Patrick W. and Janet R. Carlson Dissertation Award in 2003 during the completion of her dissertation, *Impact of Involvement in Race-Related Activism on the Careers of Black Educators.*

Susan Walters is currently an Elementary Principal and has been an assistant principal, school counselor, and teacher during her more that 25 years in education. She was selected as a Reynolds Scholar in the School of Education at the University of North Carolina at Chapel Hill where she received her EdD in Educational Leadership in December 2003. Her dissertation topic was *Quiet Activists: Women in Educational Leadership.*

Gloria Hines Jones, EdD, is currently a Middle School Assistant Principal. She has also worked as a special education teacher, mentor to assistant principals, and served in numerous leadership capacities during her 20-year tenure in K-12 education. Gloria was honored as the 2006 assistant principal of the year in one of the largest school systems in North Carolina. She received her doctorate in Educational Leadership from the University of North Carolina at Chapel Hill. The title of her dissertation published in 2005 is *Site-Based Voices: Dilemmas of Educators Who Engage in Activism Against Student-to-Student Sexual Harassment.*

Wanda Legrand is an Instruction Manager for American Express who has previously served as a teacher, assistant principal, principal, and central office executive director. She earned her EdD in Educational Leadership at the University of North Carolina at Chapel Hill. Her 2005 dissertation was entitled: *Activism for LGBT Rights: How Participation Affects the Lives of Activist Educators.*

Index

* successes: gender, AR, LGBT - from Clause 28 to now in Ofsted criteria.
5. What inhibits activism? Informal prof. rules; Evasion of real roots;
9. Ts are pol. actors.
17 Identity theory